ADVANCE PRAISE

"*On Becoming a Racially Sensitive Therapist* by Dr. Hardy and his colleagues offers a profound exploration of how whiteness shapes our identities, cultures, and society. Through case presentations, compelling stories, and reflections, the authors guide therapists toward cultural authenticity and healing. This book challenges readers to confront systemic oppression, embrace their true selves, and reclaim their cultural voices in transformative work both inside and outside the therapy room."
—**Larry G. Tucker, LMFT**, owner of Kente Circle and president/executive director of Kente Circle Training Institute, Minneapolis, MN

"It is rare to encounter both a deeply practical and beautifully written edited volume on the topic of therapist training. Kenneth V. Hardy, along with a highly experienced set of contributors, has done just that. This work serves both as a call to action and as a point-by-point roadmap for exploration of the therapist's racialized Self through the imposing terrain of internalized whiteness. Instructive and truly soul healing!"
—**Antoinette U. Rodriguez, LMSW**, marriage and family therapist practicing in New York, NY

"Dr. Hardy has once again orchestrated an exemplar of powerful self-explorations that cultivate compassion, courage, curiosity, and connection. While mainstream textbooks are saturated with whiteness, and focus on teaching techniques, this book offers a blueprint of how to deconstruct the experience of race to foster meaningful conversations in therapy. If therapists are vehicles for change, this book is a must-read manual of operations!"
—**Liang-Ying Chou, PhD, LMFT**, therapist in private practice, trainer, and educator of marriage and family therapy at Iona University

"Wow! As someone on a journey to become a more racially responsible therapist, this book is the exact blueprint I have been craving! Dr. Hardy and colleagues have boiled down the daunting and complex process of becoming a racially sensitive therapist into concrete competencies using language and examples that make the process accessible and attainable. This is an absolute must-read for every healing practitioner and training institution that cares about serving *all* people (not just a subset of people)."

—**Bukky Kolawole, PsyD**, couples therapist, executive coach, and founder of Relationship HQ

ON BECOMING A
RACIALLY
SENSITIVE
THERAPIST

ON BECOMING A RACIALLY SENSITIVE THERAPIST

Race and Clinical Practice

KENNETH V. HARDY PHD, EDITOR

Norton Professional Books
An Imprint of W. W. Norton & Company
Independent Publishers Since 1923

This book is intended as a general information resource for professionals practicing in the field of psychotherapy and mental health. It is not a substitute for appropriate training or clinical supervision. Standards of clinical practice and protocol vary in different practice settings and change over time. No technique or recommendation is guaranteed to be safe or effective in all circumstances, and neither the publisher nor the author can guarantee the complete accuracy, efficacy, or appropriateness of any particular recommendation in every respect or in all settings or circumstances.

Names and identifying details of patients described in this book have been changed. Some patients described, and the session transcripts, are composites. Any URLs displayed in this book link or refer to websites that existed as of press time. The publisher is not responsible for, and should not be deemed to endorse or recommend, any website other than its own or any content that it did not create. The author, also, is not responsible for any third-party material.

Chapter 11: From: Transforming Careers in Mental Health for BIPOC edited by Doris F. Chang and Linda Lausell Bryant, © 2024 by Routledge. Reproduced by permission of Taylor & Francis Group.

Copyright © 2025 by Kenneth V. Hardy
Contribution copyright © 2025 by Vanessa Bing
Contribution copyright © 2025 by Toby Bobes
Contribution copyright © 2025 by Bonnie Cushing
Contribution copyright © 2025 by Elana Katz
Contribution copyright © 2025 by Niketa Kumar
Contribution copyright © 2025 by Sharon RC Lee
Contribution copyright © 2025 by Gloria Lopez-Henriquez
Contribution copyright © 2025 by Yasmeen Rubidge and Lane Arye
Contribution copyright © 2025 by Virginia Seewaldt

Soul Work: A Pathway to Help Communities of Color by Kenneth V. Hardy in Transforming BIPOC Careers in Mental Health edited by Doris F. Chang and Linda Lausell Bryant, © 2024 by Routledge. Reproduced by permission of Taylor & Francis Group.

All rights reserved
Printed in the United States of America
First Edition

For information about permission to reproduce selections from this book, write to Permissions, W. W. Norton & Company, Inc., 500 Fifth Avenue, New York, NY 10110

For information about special discounts for bulk purchases, please contact
W. W. Norton Special Sales at specialsales@wwnorton.com or 800-233-4830

Manufacturing by Sheridan
Production manager: Ramona Wilkes and Gwen Cullen

ISBN: 978-1-324-08249-1 (pbk)

W. W. Norton & Company, Inc., 500 Fifth Avenue, New York, NY 10110
www.wwnorton.com

W. W. Norton & Company Ltd., 15 Carlisle Street, London W1D 3BS

1 2 3 4 5 6 7 8 9 0

. . . To the Manufacturers of Hope who work tirelessly to promote hope in all the places where it has been depleted, assaulted, and long since ceased to exist.

Contents

Acknowledgments — xiii

About the Contributors — xv

Preface — xxi

I. THE PROCESS OF BECOMING

1. Seeing, Being, Doing: A Critical Epistemological Process — 5
   KENNETH V. HARDY

2. The Process of Becoming: Principles, Preparation, and Practice — 21
   KENNETH V. HARDY

3. A Primer for Practicing Racially Sensitive Supervision: A Practical Guide for Supervisors — 39
   KENNETH V. HARDY AND TOBY BOBES

4. Moving Toward Racially Sensitive, Equity-Focused Training: Confessions of a Recovering White-Centered Trainer — 58
   SHARON RC LEE

II. RACIAL STORIES AND THE SELF OF THE THERAPIST

5. Racial and Cultural Storytelling: A Clinical Tool for Promoting Racial Sensitivity   77
   KENNETH V. HARDY

6. Wandering and Wondering in the Wilderness: On Being White and Jewish in the United States   99
   BONNIE BERMAN CUSHING

7. From Shame to Pride: MY Mother/your mammy and the Making of a Racially Sensitive Psychologist   113
   VANESSA M. BING

8. Unpacking My Invisible Racial Luggage: The One I Brought From Colombia and Failed to Unpack   134
   GLORIA LOPEZ-HENRIQUEZ

9. At the Intersection of Whiteness, Trauma, and Relationship   147
   SHARON RC LEE

10. Notes From a Diary: Does Jewish Identity Cloud or Clarify an Understanding of Race?   158
    ELANA KATZ

III. THERAPEUTIC ISSUES AND APPROACHES

11. Soul Work: A Pathway to Help Heal Communities of Color   171
    KENNETH V. HARDY

12. Names: An Effective Approach to Enhancing the Therapeutic Alliance and Addressing Racial Trauma   182
    NIKETA KUMAR

13. Racial Harm in Helping Relationships and an Uncommon Journey Toward Repair   198
    YASMEEN RUBIDGE AND LANE ARYE

14. Getting to the Heart of the Matter: White Therapists Working With White Clients Around Race   226
    VIRGINIA SEEWALDT

15. Race and the Need for Racial Reckoning in Clinical and 246
Educational Training
VANESSA M. BING

Notes 265

References 266

Index 280

Acknowledgments

I want to thank all my *families* for their dedicated support throughout this process. You, individually and collectively, have constituted my village, without which the completion of this project would not have been possible.

First I wish to thank my Norton family for your steady guidance, support, and willingness to provide me with a platform to write about topics that have been historically marginalized and in many cases ignored within the psychotherapy field. I would like to express my gratitude to Mariah Eppes, Olivia Guarnieri, Sara McBride Tuohy, McKenna Tanner, Jamie Vincent, and the entire Norton team for your guidance and support. I would especially like to thank Deborah Malmud, vice president of Norton, for her vision, support, collaborative spirit, and willingness to be a thought partner throughout our work together. I look forward to our continued work together.

I would also like to thank my Eikenberg Institute for Relationships family for always serving as an incubator for new ideas. Thank you for taking the time to review drafts and provide invaluable feedback and critical questions along the way. A very special thanks to Dhara Mehta-Desai for attending so keenly and meticulously to all the finer tasks, details, and editing that transformed a rough draft into a polished finished product.

Fifi Klein, thank you for your contributions that helped usher this project across the finish line during the final hours.

Of course, there would not be a finished product to celebrate if not for the thoughtful and heart-rendering contributions of my colleagues and former trainees of the Eikenberg Academy for Social Justice *Race and Racial Equity Train-the-Trainer Residency*. My heartfelt gratitude to each of you for the time, commitment, and expertise you devoted to this project.

To my ancestral family, to whom I am eternally indebted and whose broad shoulders I stand, sometimes with strength and conviction and at other times wobbly and unsure. As always, thank you for the divine inspiration. You live in me and in the souls of my beloved family as well.

And to my beloved Hardy family, as always thank you for your unconditional love, support, generosity, and for being such a stabilizing force in my life. It would be impossible to complete a project of this magnitude without the patience, understanding, and inspiration that each of you, and all of you, selflessly extend and grant to me unconditionally. In all of life, there is no greater gift!

About the Contributors

Lane Arye, PhD, is a white senior trainer of Process Work (developed by Arnold Mindell), is a founding faculty member of the Process Work Institute in Portland, Oregon, and works in private practice. He has facilitated conflicts between Aboriginal Australians and European Australians, and between Dalits (so-called untouchables) and high-caste Hindus in India. In Oakland, CA, Lane facilitated and helped resolve a long-standing conflict between then mayor (later governor) Jerry Brown and an African American cultural arts center. He co-led a six-year UN-funded project in the Balkans that brought together Serbs, Croats, and Muslims after the war to work on ethnic tension, building sustainable community, and postwar trauma. Author of *Unintentional Music: Releasing Your Deepest Creativity* and "The Vicious Cycle of White Centrality" in Dr. Kenneth V. Hardy's *The Enduring, Invisible, and Ubiquitous Centrality of Whiteness*, Lane is a facilitator and trainer for the Racial Justice Collaborative.

Vanessa M. Bing, PhD, is a licensed clinical psychologist, educator, trainer, and community activist who has worked for more than 25 years providing educational, therapeutic, and consulting services to a range of populations. She has been responsible for developing health and wellness initiatives and programs in educational and clinical settings and has provided organizational training and consultation on the topic of diversity, equity, and inclusion in corporate and educational settings. Dr. Bing has published several articles addressing the experiences of minoritized populations and gendered issues in psychology. She has also lectured extensively on the topic of trauma and intimate partner and family violence. Dr. Bing holds certificates in mediation and dispute resolution and couples therapy; has trained in EMDR, Crisis Management, Sensorimotor Psychotherapy, Aboriginal Focusing Oriented Therapy (AFOT), Imago and EFT therapy; and utilizes a variety of mindfulness-based practices in her work to support the health and wellness of clients. Dr. Bing is committed to achieving equity and social justice in educational, professional, and community-based settings. She works tirelessly mentoring and supervising undergraduate and graduate students in psychology to ensure that the next generation of scholars and practitioners are not only culturally competent but partners in broader efforts to achieve equity and social justice in the antiracist practice of psychology. She holds a faculty position at the City University of New York, is a consultant at Manhattan School of Music, and has a private practice in New York City.

Toby Bobes, PhD, is a licensed marriage and family therapist with experience teaching graduate-level courses at Antioch University and Pacifica Graduate Institute. Toby's career includes 28 years in private practice. She has worked at various agencies as a clinical supervisor and has taught many supervision courses. Toby is coauthor of two books: *Doing Couple Therapy: Integrating Theory with Practice* and *The Couple Is Telling You What You Need to Know: Couple-Directed Therapy in a Multicultural Context*. She is also coeditor of two books: *Culturally Sensitive Supervision and Training: Diverse Perspectives and Practical Applications* and *Promoting Cultural Sensitivity in Supervision: A Manual for Practitioners*.

Bonnie Berman Cushing, LCSW, is an antiracist organizer and educator. She has worked in the mental health field for over 34 years as a systems therapist serving individuals, couples, and families. For the past 30 years, she has also been devoted to the movement for racial and social justice and to infusing both her own and others' clinical practices with an analysis of the dynamics of power, privilege, and oppression. Bonnie is a core trainer with the People's Institute for Survival and Beyond, a senior consultant with the Human Solidarity Project, and a facilitator with the Center for Racial Justice in Education, the Eikenberg Academy for Social Justice, and the Center for the Study of White American Culture. She is a cofounder of the North Jersey Chapter of the AntiRacist Alliance and an affiliate of the Antiracist Mental Health Alliance of NJ. She also sits as a trustee on the boards of the Center for the Study of White American Culture and the Human Solidarity Project. Bonnie has authored various articles about race and clinical practice, as well as a chapter in the book *The Enduring, Invisible and Ubiquitous Centrality of Whiteness*, published by W. W. Norton & Company in 2022. Previously, she was the lead editor of the multiauthored books *Accountability and White Antiracist Organizing: Stories from Our Work* and *Living in the Tension: The Quest for a Spiritualized Racial Justice*, both released by Crandall, Dostie & Douglass Books.

Kenneth V. Hardy, PhD (editor), is a clinical and organizational consultant at the Eikenberg Institute for Relationships, where he also serves as director. He is a former professor of family therapy at both Drexel University in Philadelphia and Syracuse University in New York, and has also served as the director of the Center for Children, Families, and Trauma at the Ackerman Institute for the Family in New York. He maintains a practice in New York City.

Elana Katz, LCSW, LMFT, is a trainer and supervisor in emotionally-focused therapy and a senior faculty member at the Ackerman Institute for the Family, where she teaches couples therapy and directed the Family Mediation Program for 20 years. She has also completed a Train-the-Trainer Residency in Racial Equity with Dr. Kenneth V. Hardy at the Eikenberg Institute in New York City. In addition to her role as therapist and trainer, Elana has applied her knowledge of attachment and relationships to help mediation and collaborative law clients and their professional teams intercept the recurring patterns that shape high-conflict negotiations. Elana has published a number of articles and book chapters, and she's been quoted by *The New York Times*, the Associated Press, and other media outlets. She teaches nationally and internationally, most often in the Midwest and Israel, and her private practice is in Manhattan.

Niketa Kumar, PhD, is a clinical psychologist in private practice based in San Francisco, CA. She was born in India and immigrated to the United States with her family when she was five years old. Her practice focuses primarily on the experiences and needs of People of Color and immigrants. She is licensed in both California and New York. She received her doctorate in clinical psychology at St. John's University.

Sharon RC Lee, PsyD, is a white, female-identifying, cisgender psychologist in private practice since 2003 in Portland, Oregon. Sharon has been training and supervising therapists for the last 10 years in emotionally-focused therapy for couples. In the last few years, Sharon has been developing approaches to training and supervising attachment-focused, relational therapy that centers race and equity.

Gloria Lopez-Henriquez, DSW, LCSW, is a light-skinned mestiza, bicultural, and bilingual psychotherapist, supervisor, and consultant with extensive experience working with individuals, families, and communities with diverse racial and ethnic backgrounds. She is a clinician at CONCERN EAP at Atlantic Behavioral Health System, an adjunct faculty member at the School of Social Work, Rutgers University, and an Ackerman Institute for the Family faculty member. Also, she maintains a private practice in Morristown and Princeton, NJ. For the last several years, she has been involved in writing extreme hardship and asylum immigration evaluations. In addition, she is a board member of the Latino Action Network Foundation, a grassroots organization committed to engagement in collective action at the local, state, and national levels for the advancement of Latino communities in the United States.

Yasmeen Rubidge, MA, is founding director of Leadership Pathways and facilitator at Atlantic Fellows for Racial Equity. Her work is elemental, arising at the nexus where the fire of justice meets the spiritual truth of our equality, the waters of our healing, and the ground of all our belonging to the earth and each other. Yasmeen has over two decades of experience supporting organizations and groups with systems and conflict transformation, racial and gender justice, dismantling anti-Black racism, and creating inclusive and equitable cultures. Based in South Africa, she works with leaders in United Nations agencies, in the private sector, and with grassroots activists, artists, and organizers, locally and globally. Facilitator, coach, witness, and midwife, she makes brave spaces for people to dialogue, reauthor themselves, and see each other anew, lead courageously, heal gently, and create new futures together. Of all the ways she is called, "mama" is her best loved and hardest earned. She is learning to live into Báyò Akómoláfé's words: "We need a politics of tenderness now more than ever."

Virginia Seewaldt, PhD, is a psychologist in private practice in New York for over 15 years with training in multiple trauma modalities. She is part of the Racial Literacy Group collective, where she participates in ongoing racial literacy development and cofacilitates whiteness process and learning groups. Virginia has a particular interest in using the Internal Family Systems and Somatic Experiencing models of healing to address racial trauma. Virginia views antiracism work as collective liberation, working with an understanding that each and every one of us is harmed by living in a system that functions by way of violent oppression.

Preface

The centrality of whiteness is a critical organizing principle that is pervasive throughout society. As an ideology, whiteness is deeply and craftily integrated into the core of what it means to be an "American." It is based on an adherence to Eurocentrism and all the major tenets associated with it, such as exceptionalism, Anglocentrism, dualism, and stoicism, just to cite a few examples (Hardy, 2022). Some, such as proponents of the Black Lives Matter movement, for example, would argue that whiteness even defines what, how, and who is considered human. While such a claim often immediately evokes a strong visceral reaction and defensiveness among some whites, how else might one make sense of the bevy of societal practices that elevate and protect the sanctity of white life while simultaneously marginalizing the lives of People of Color? For example, there are differential policies and practices regarding immigration and who is welcomed into the country with empathy and compassion, and who is rejected and returned to poverty-stricken countries often ravaged by crime, tyranny, and oppression. All these actions and inactions advance powerful narratives regarding who and what hue are deserving of human embrace, care, and understanding. The presumption of guilt and demonization of Black and Brown life has contributed to the unwarranted police-involved murders of countless numbers of innocent, unarmed Black and Brown people who are too numerous to respectfully acknowledge in this book, let alone this preface. It all serves as a stark and grief-stricken reminder of the lack of humanness that is accorded to the lives of People of Color, and most notably Black people. Unfortunately, this is not a current or recent occurrence but rather one that is deeply etched in the soul, psyche, and historical practices of what it means to be a non-white, that is, an American* and human* with an asterisk (which is necessary to denote the distinction from those who are fully franchised in these roles).

It would be considered barbaric and inhumane to place human beings in bondage and shackles, or to systematically infringe on and restrict their pursuit of life, liberty, and happiness through well-manicured systemic practices, if those subjected to such unspeakable and unimaginable brazen acts of brutality were in fact white. The common everyday assaults against Black people participating in common everyday activities (e.g., driving, shopping in supermarkets) are contemporary examples of the long history of racially fueled hatred directed at Black people and other People of Color. There are always constant reminders that the rules of human compassion and engagement are different for People of Color, and especially for those who happen to be Black.

Whiteness ensures and reinforces the notion that "what is white is right," and as I learned as a child, "if you are Black, step back" and "if you are Brown, you can stick around." This "innocent" childhood jingle, and many others like it, that have been passed down through the generations of People of Color is hardly innocent or void of damage to the mental health of People of Color, our relationship to whites, theirs to us, and ultimately what we think and feel about ourselves as a people. It can be debated whether these types of lethal, self-destructive, self-esteem-puncturing messages are promulgated as overtly today as they once were during my childhood. However, even if the content of the message is different, the perpetuation of the underlying ideology of white supremacy has not abated and remains delicately threaded throughout all sectors of society. The world in which we live is one where white people are imbued with the privilege to be the rule makers, rule interpreters, and rule enforcers. Thus, what is often considered normal, acceptable, best practice, standard, or even professional, and so on, is largely, if not exclusively, defined by whiteness.

It is difficult to imagine that the United States or any of its institutions can ever live up to the lofty ideals that theoretically constitute the bedrock of who, how, and what we aspire and claim to be as a nation without interrogating and deconstructing the centrality of whiteness. Neither the individual nor the structural dimensions of racism can be effectively addressed, dismantled, or circumvented without an intentional commitment to understand and interrogate whiteness as a homeostatic ideological principle that ensures and protects the racial status quo.

Unfortunately, the clinical field historically has not been shielded from the pervasive influences of whiteness. Guthrie (1997), in his classic publication *Even the Rat Was White*, provided an insightful overview and exposé examining the racial bias implicit in psychology. Hardy (1989), in the article "The Theoretical Myth of Sameness: A Critical Issue in Family Therapy Training and Treatment," discussed how the field promoted the notion that all families were essentially the same while perpetuating a "neglect of context" that "licensed" the practice of ignoring the significant impact that sociocultural forces such as race, gender, class, and sexual orientation, to cite a few, had on overall personality development and family functioning.

Fortunately, race and other contextual variables have been gradually integrated into clinical literature and to a lesser degree into clinical practice. Several practitioners, including Boyd-Franklin (2003), McGoldrick et al. (2005), DeGruy (2005), Nealy (2017), McGoldrick and Hardy (2019), and Menakem (2017), among others, have offered sociocultural critiques and recommendations regarding how the field can be more attentive to a range of cultural issues and address the influences of whiteness in clinical theory, practice, and training.

It is critical to examine and interrogate the centrality of whiteness in and outside of psychotherapy, because it is a dominant ideology that shapes not only clinical practice but the world at large as well. Whiteness, as an ideology, does not just infect and affect white people; instead, it permeates the hearts, minds, and souls of all of us (Hardy, 2022). Metaphorically, we all drink our water from the same well of whiteness. Thus, being a Person of Color does not preclude one from being an adherent to whiteness as a governing ideology. Because we all are prone to subscribing to the ideology of whiteness, it is essential that each of us commits to understanding in a deep way how our lives are impacted by it. While such a task is crucial for all of us, it is infinitely more crucial and dire for whites, and especially white clinicians. People of Color, as a racially stigmatized and dehumanized group, who essentially live under white occupation (Hardy, 2022), must know, understand, and recognize even the most subtle of subtleties regarding whiteness as a precondition for survival. Therefore, many People of Color are significantly more knowledgeable about the parameters of whiteness than are their white counterparts, many of whom live their lives as white people, void of conscious recognition.

Since our field strives to provide culturally competent care to diverse clinical populations regardless of identity, it is vital for therapists to abandon therapeutic approaches that fail to consider the life experiences of those who are perceived as beyond the bounds of the mainstream; that is, those who are not wealthy, neither white nor presumably heterosexual. Therapeutic approaches that heavily rely on principles of universality (e.g., theoretical myth of sameness), objectivity (with the therapist defining what this is and isn't), and/or color blindness, tend to reinforce the prevailing ideology of whiteness that shapes the field. Historically, the therapy field, like much of society, has advanced the misguided, naive, and dangerous notion of color blindness. This heartwarming assertion perpetuated the belief that therapy, and those who sought and performed it, was essentially color-blind, and matters of race were inconsequential to the process. This recurring belief was detrimental to both therapists and clients. It provided white clinicians with a shield and deflection from seeing and attending to the wide array of racial biases that were and remain so deeply embedded in the practice of psychotherapy. It coerced Therapists of Color, like me, to become white-like as a precondition for being considered competent and legitimate. Psychologically based diagnostic nosology historically has reflected the interpretations and analyses of white social scientists, researchers, and clinical diagnosticians demonstrating little need or regard for racial inclusion or racial relativity. For example, Youth of Color were diagnosed as "oppositional and defiant" without regard for the ways in which they lived and had to adjust to living in a world that was often experienced by them as anti–Youth of Color. Not to mention that often white youth exhibiting similar behaviors were diagnosed with "Adjustment Reactions." The myth of color blindness that permeates the field and therapeutic practice make it convenient to ignore the ugliness and inequities of race within and outside of the field. Therapists committed to working effectively with Clients

PREFACE   xxv

of Color, and even doing so more conscientiously with white clients, would be well served to devote time, effort, and energy to becoming racially sensitive practitioners. This book is designed to provide experienced therapists, as well as those in training, with a comprehensive guide to the principles, practices, and developmental processes necessary for becoming a racially sensitive practitioner.

The book is composed of three sections: (I) "The Process of Becoming" (a racially sensitive therapist); (II) "Racial Stories and the Self of the Therapist"; and (III) "Therapeutic Issues and Approaches." These sections, and the chapters contained within them, are organized to highlight and parallel "seeing, being, doing," which, as noted in Chapter 1, is a process that facilitates the development of racial sensitivity and is essential to becoming a racially sensitive therapist.

The chapters contained in Part I provide a detailed discussion of what it means to be a racially sensitive practitioner, and what is required to become one, whether a clinician, supervisor, or postgraduate degree trainer. Hardy (Chapters 1 and 2) and Lee (Chapter 4) both maintain that the process of becoming a racially sensitive therapist involves more than simply acquiring new clinical skills. It requires knowing oneself, especially as a racial being, and demonstrating the willingness and ability to bring one's whole self to the therapy process. Thus, racially sensitive therapy is not solely based on what you do, or what you know, but also centers around who and how you are as well. Demonstrating racial sensitivity is of paramount significance, and it is not just based on what is said verbally but also what is conveyed nonverbally and relationally. Consequently, the task of preparing and producing racially sensitive therapists requires a paradigm shift from the traditional ways in which therapists have been trained and therapy is conceptualized. Due to the pervasiveness of racial bias throughout all spheres of life, and the blind spots that often accompany it, a greater emphasis on Self of the Therapist work is a must for those who aspire to provide racially sensitive treatment. Efforts to train and prepare racially sensitive therapists must also rely on experientially based teaching, learning, and supervisory strategies as well. The second part of the book delves into what some of these practices and tools might look like.

Part II consists of six chapters, written by a diverse group of clinicians who provide potent examples of how to use racial and cultural storytelling as an effective Self of the Therapist tool to help uncover unknown parts of oneself and to demonstrate what it means to engage in processes of self-examination, self-interrogation, and self-reflection. In Chapter 7, Vanessa Bing, using racial and cultural storytelling, provides a powerful and vulnerable story of how she was able to transform her life from one of deeply rooted and intense shame to becoming a racially sensitive clinician. All the chapters contained in this section are emblematic of what Hardy (Chapter 1) describes as the process of being. That is, they accentuate the fact that the process of becoming a racially sensitive therapist requires internal examination, interrogation, and reflection, and that who we are and what we see (or fail to see) are inextricably connected to what we do as therapists.

The third and final section contains five chapters that transport the reader from the processes of seeing and being to doing. Kumar (Chapter 12) provides an insightful overview of how exploring the essence and origins of names can be a powerful tool for fostering conversations about race and culture, as well as providing an antidote to racialized trauma and psychological homelessness. Seewaldt (Chapter 14) also focuses on the use of racially informed intervention methods that support racially sensitive work with clients. She provides tips and strategies for how white therapists can work more effectively with white clients regarding race, a phenomenon that is rarely discussed in the field. This chapter challenges the popular notion that focusing on race in therapy is a "People of Color issue" that is irrelevant when both the therapist and client are white. Like Seewaldt, Rubidge and Arye (Chapter 13) also discuss a phenomenon that is rarely discussed overtly despite being a common occurrence. Rubidge and Arye invite the reader into their interracial world composed of a white, Jewish, American male trainer (Arye) and a Black, Muslim, South African woman trainee (Rubidge) and their difficult and painful journey to repair a race-related rupture that destroyed their relationship for a period. Since racial ruptures and harm are frequent occurrences, especially in cross-racial relationships, possessing the commitment and skills to engage in racially based repair work is integral to the role and function of a racially sensitive therapist.

The 15 chapters contained in this book are written by a widely diverse group of experienced clinicians who have been on long-term journeys to unlearn what they learned about race and therapy, both prior to becoming therapists and during the process of their therapy training. Since we all have been trained in models that are saturated in whiteness and reify it as not only a dominant ideology but the only viable one, we all are in desperate need of a process of unlearning and relearning. This book is intended to offer a huge step in a course-correct direction for the process of therapy and for those of us who are privileged enough to provide it.

ON BECOMING A
RACIALLY SENSITIVE THERAPIST

PART I

THE PROCESS OF BECOMING

CHAPTER 1

Seeing, Being, Doing: A Critical Epistemological Process

KENNETH V. HARDY, PhD

During the past several years, there seems to have been a slow and gradual uptick in the gravity of attention devoted to the exploration of racial issues in clinical practice. Despite this nascent trend, there is still much room for continued growth and development. Efforts to effectively address race-related issues in therapy continue to be a major challenge for many clinicians of all racial backgrounds. The difficulties associated with adequately addressing race and racial issues in therapy are a microcosm of how it is dealt with in the broader society. In society, as in therapy, efforts to fully engage in substantive conversations about race, for example, are often characterized by avoidance, gingerly walking on metaphorical eggshells, or by denial, defensiveness, and occasional explosiveness. These predictable responses often stifle most attempts to engage in meaningful conversations about race, regardless of the situation or circumstance, in or outside of therapy. Second, the persistent denial of the significance of race within the clinical field, coupled with the invisible, enduring, and ubiquitous centrality of whiteness (Hardy, 2022) in all sectors of society, has fostered and significantly contributed to a widespread epidemic of racially based clinical ineptitude throughout the field. This assertion is not an attribution to all areas of the entire clinical field, only to the current situation pursuant to working effectively with race. Hence, the consequences of the abject failure to acknowledge race and adequately prepare clinicians to address it reverberate throughout the field, often in ways that are unrecognizable.

The historical inattention devoted to race and clinicians' lack of preparation to address it have had a profound and significant impact on the field in several critical ways: (1) It has contributed to a condition that inadvertently relegates the clinical treatment of many Clients of Color to the status of on-the-job training. This is particularly the case when treatment is provided by clinicians who lack a thorough understanding of the sophisticated and multitudinous ways in which race significantly affects the everyday lives of clients, and especially those from economically oppressed backgrounds. As such, many Clients of Color, regardless of other sociocultural factors, are burdened with either having to teach their therapists about the rudiments of race and its clinical implications or to be patient and accepting of their expert's lack of racial expertise. (2) It ensures that the racially based trauma experienced by many Clients of Color is misguidedly entrusted to the metaphorical hands of many practitioners who lack sufficient knowledge of the condition, its major symptoms, or how to effectively treat and/or manage it when it manifests clinically. (3) Finally, Clients of Color must blindly trust and be amenable to entering the intimate process of therapy with practitioners, many of whom have not been trained to consider how their respective racial backgrounds and experiences might taint, enrich, or otherwise impact every potential stage of the clinical treatment process.

Unfortunately, the systemic neglect of attention to race within the field, coupled with the concomitant significant role that it occupies in all facets of society, contributes to significant clinical and conceptual gaps in therapy practice. These apertures that often exist in the core of our clinical work are neither easy to overcome nor ameliorate.

Many of the clinically based questions that are often raised regarding the intersections of race and therapy are indicative of the tension that exists between the significant role that race plays in society and the relative inattention it receives in clinical education, training, and ultimately practice. Despite conventional wisdom, acquiring the ability and skill set to address racial issues in therapy thoughtfully, sensitively, and effectively requires more than cursory attention. The tasks at hand involve much more than watching a video or deconstructing a clinical tape, taking racially targeted trainings, or receiving intensive case-based, client-centered clinical supervision. Hence, the rebooting process of transitioning from an effective practitioner to becoming an effective racially sensitive therapist requires Self of the Therapist (SOT) work centered around self-examination, self-interrogation, and self-reflection (Hardy, 2023). In addition to the acquisition of new skills, which is crucial, the heart of the work must also focus on deep existential inquiry and soul work (see Chapter 11). It requires a three-step process of seeing, being, doing.

Seeing, Being, Doing

Seeing, being, doing is a process. It is also, in many respects, an epistemology predicated on the assumption that racial sensitivity, which is a prerequisite for becoming a racially sensitive therapist, requires immersion into experiences of seeing, followed by and intermixed with being, that ultimately crystallizes doing. The seeing, being, doing process is critically needed since therapy training and practice are frequently based on mechanistic approaches that aim to master the doing (i.e., overfocus on strategies and techniques), without first devoting proper and appropriate time to the preceding steps of seeing and being. The doing dimension of the overall process refers to the demonstrated ability to work effectively and sensitively with issues of race in therapy.

To help further explicate what the seeing, being, doing process is, it is important to also clarify what it is not:

- A theory of therapy, supervision, or change
- A theoretical orientation to therapy or supervision
- A therapy model or protocol
- A therapeutic training model

It is an epistemology that contributes to the development of a mindset that is more focused on the evolution of one's being and how it is ultimately connected with what we do—specifically with regard to race and trauma. It serves as a reminder that seeing, being, doing is intricately entangled, and is often fluid, subjective, relational, and multidirectional. This assertion will be explained in greater detail in the ensuing sections of this chapter.

Seeing

Seeing is a process that not only refers to that which is visual but to that which is also conceptual. Thus, it is as much about establishing a deep understanding of what is seen as it is about seeing what is seen. It is ultimately concerned with how we (re)train our eyes to see what they may have been trained not to see. Winawer (2022), in a powerfully written personal narrative about her formative years of growing up white and Jewish, coined the term "unseeing" to refer to the subtle and deliberate ways in which the eyes of white children are trained not to see their whiteness or themselves as racial beings. It is the process of seeing that enables us to see and understand the phenomenon of race in more nuanced ways. Through this process, we learn to change what we look for, in order to change what we might see. For example, the therapist whose eyes are trained to see, and ultimately look for, a client's strengths is very likely to see them. The reverse is also often true; thus the search for pathology often makes it seeable. Similarly, when our eyes are trained to see and appreciate the intricacies of race and our relationship to it, we de facto develop a heightened level of visual acuity that makes components of the unseeable seeable. The process of seeing is multidirectional and not only equips the therapist to see the dynamics of race as they pertain to other, but to the Self as well.

It is in this regard that the process of seeing also facilitates the development of a *racial lens* and a *racial sense of self*, both of which are discussed in greater detail in Chapter 2. The development of a racial lens enhances the ability for one who sees to see all the myriad ways in which race is intricately and at times complexly interwoven within the fabric of all areas of our existence. This development is vital for everyone to have since each of us has a racial identity through which we ostensibly perceive the world around us, whether we realize it or not. Technically, the real task here is not solely to develop a racial lens, but also to develop a consciousness and awareness of the fact that we have it. In fact, it is the willingness and capacity to embrace a racial lens that facilitates developing a keen racial sense of self.

Developing a racial sense of self is a by-product of developing a racial lens, which in turn is greatly enhanced and facilitated by possessing a racial sense of self. As noted earlier, these processes are richly dynamic, fluid, and multidirectional. Successfully developing a racial sense of self enables one to begin to see, imagine, interrogate, and explore oneself as a racialized being. It invites each of us to begin to think critically about what it means to be who we are racially; how it has shaped or contributed to who, what, and how we are. It is the racial sense of self that paves the way for us to have more racially ethical, compassionate, and sensitive relationships. It promotes and helps to fortify a self-in-relationship-to-other mindset, which is the nexus for empathy, and especially racial empathy.

Whereas seeing prepares one to begin to see and conceptualize race from slightly afar in a quasi-abstract, detached, and disembodied manner, the process of being, on the other hand, shifts one's focus to seeing and thinking about race in a much more personal, embodied, and granular way. It is during this progressive process that issues of race become exceedingly more personal.

Being

Being ultimately involves establishing a sense of existential clarity about who one is racially. It represents the stage of development where racial (self) inquiry becomes personal. Hence, it refers to the inevitable phase of the seeing, being, doing process where one develops a heightened sense of one's self as a racial being. It is during this phase that race ceases to be an issue that only refers to an "other" completely segregated from considerations of (one's) self. It is the engagement in the process of being and the intensive self-examination, interrogation, and reflection it requires that enables one to think about oneself through a lens of race. It is during this phase that one engages in a critical self-critique of significant issues, such as one's exposure to race and racial diversity, how one has been racially socialized, and an examination of racial messages and implicit biases that have been internalized or never seriously considered or questioned, and so on. The being phase provides an impetus for one to ask of oneself, "Now that I see what I see and know what I know about race and myself as a racial being, what are my responsibilities for action?" Other relevant questions: "What action(s) am I willing to take on behalf of self and others?" "What are the competencies and skills that I need in order to effectively carry out the plan of action I have assigned to myself?" This is the critical point when one begins to perceive and metabolize race as a social justice, humanitarian issue. The actions that one takes are less informed by politics, political correctness, or being performative and are instead driven more by what is considered just, moral, and responsive to a broader ethical imperative. This heightened level of seeing and being ultimately culminates in increasing one's capacity "to see" the interconnectedness of all suffering that is a by-product of oppression, domination, and social inequities. Hence, doing nothing becomes increasingly hard.

When time, effort, and energy have been devoted to the "being" dimension of the seeing, being, doing process, racial defensiveness, reactivity, and racially inspired emotional cutoff become less frequent occurrences both in and outside of therapy, and infinitely more manageable when they do occur. When one establishes a clear and firm sense of racial being, it becomes far easier to distinguish between what is "me and not me," "when I am the aggressor/perpetrator and when I am the victim," and so forth. This level of internal clarity can free one to speak up, take proactive racial actions, and be unencumbered by the stifling fear of saying the wrong thing or internally debating what to do.

Through this important developmental process one not only becomes more acutely aware of what it means to be a racialized being, but equally aware of the parts of one's being that are privileged, subjugated, racist, antiracist, and so forth. Establishing this level of seeing and being and personal resolve regarding "who I am, what I am, and how I wish to be," especially in relationship to race, provides the foundation for doing in ways that exude racial awareness, sensitivity, confidence, and integrity.

Doing

The term "doing," as it is used throughout this chapter, refers to therapeutic actions, including the application of strategies and techniques that a therapist might invoke to affect a desirable outcome with a client. It is the part of the therapeutic process ostensibly designed to address or ameliorate a presenting problem and/or to enhance the overall dynamics of the process. Efforts by the therapist to effectively address race in therapy that commence with a sharp focus on the doing, without prior initial immersion into the seeing and being process, are often fraught with therapeutic missteps, setbacks, and clinical impasses. Alternatively, when the therapist's preparatory process and SOT work have guided them through the seeing, being, doing process, the doing becomes less arduous and is more efficiently, effectively, and in many cases sensitively executed.

Doing is the culmination of the seeing, being, doing process. It reflects the therapist's ability to execute timely, racially well-informed, sensitive, and thoughtful actions on behalf of clients. It is the ascendance to being that enables and empowers the therapist to be fully emotionally, psychologically, and humanly present with clients in ways that help to facilitate the joining process and fortify the therapeutic relationship. It is during this process that the therapist not only embraces but exudes the transformational and healing position that "being is doing," and when working with those who have been marginalized, traumatized, and oppressed, having the capacity to *be* just may be one of the most potent forms of doing that one can do.

The seeing, being, doing process positions the therapist to address racial issues in therapy with a sense of poise, confidence, and clarity. This, of course, is true when the therapist has invested in participating and completing the necessary SOT work that the process invariably requires. There is an array of experiences that therapists can engage in that will facilitate movement through the seeing, being, doing process.

Seeing, Being, Doing, and Self of the Therapist Strategies

Intensive Dyadic Self of the Therapist Work

As has been intimated throughout this chapter, SOT work provides a wonderful context for hosting the seeing, being, doing process. Historically, the hallmark of SOT work has been to encourage critical self-interrogation and reflection regarding how the personality constitution and unique family of origin dynamics, as well as other life circumstances, potentially contribute to, and/or influence, the molding of who and how one is as a therapist. The internal analysis that SOT work requires makes it a reliable and durable vehicle for engaging in the seeing, being, doing process. However, not unlike other areas of the field, many of the traditional approaches to SOT work have been relatively silent and remiss in uplifting race and other sociocultural factors as critical points of therapeutic inquiry. This oversight has not been insignificant, particularly given the role that race plays in all our lives, whether it is overtly acknowledged or not. A very strong similar argument could be made regarding lack of attention devoted to gender, sexual orientation, and other salient sociocultural factors as well. The bottom line is that each of us is so much more complex than a focus on any singular dimension of who we are would otherwise suggest. Thus, the examination of our early childhood experiences and traumas, relationship, or the lack thereof, with a significant parenting object, and so on, are all irrefutably important historical data points to consider in the context of our evolution as therapists, and it is not enough. It is far too simplistic and myopic to assume a minimalist position when considering the relationship between identity, beliefs, and behavior, especially given the complexity of the human spirit. Consequently, a more expansive, racially informed, sociocultural blueprint is needed as a conceptual framework for guiding culturally informed SOT work that is intended to facilitate racial sensitivity and the process of becoming a racially sensitive therapist. Hardy (2016) identifies the Multicultural Relational Perspective (MRP) as such a framework.

According to Hardy (2016), the MRP "forges a paradigm shift that highlights the significance of 'self' work, culture, attention to the dynamics of power, powerlessness, privilege, and oppression, and a worldview that values the incessant examination of 'Self' in relationship to other" (p. 10). This approach proposes the adoption of a metaphorical wide-angle lens that encourages clinicians to look for (and see) not just the impact and influences of personality development issues, family of origin experiences, and exposure to trauma, but to be equally vigilant in exploring the plethora of culturally based issues that help define and constitute who they are as well.

Experiential Group-Based Self of the Therapist Approaches

In addition to applying the MRP to the more traditional individual or dyadic SOT approach to supervision, it can also be embedded in a host of experientially group-based SOT practices as well. As noted previously, the seeing, being, doing process is achieved most effectively by actively engaging in relational processes that simultaneously encourage, require, and support self-examination, self-interrogation, and critical self-reflection. This can be obtained through clinical education programs and supervision approaches that advocate experiential learning. Relationally focused supervision and consultation approaches that center experientially based learning are invaluable in promoting the seeing, being, doing process. Regardless of the format or strategy used, experiential approaches to training and supervision unfailingly imbue the clinician with a deepened degree of racial sensitivity that is a foundation for becoming a racially sensitive therapist. Laszloffy and Habekost (2010) argue that

> the capacity for sensitivity hinges to a large degree on talking with and interacting with others whom one is different from and struggling to relate across and through differences. Inevitably, during interactions with people from other groups, mistakes are made. We say things that the other perceives as a slight, or we may look foolish for not understanding the meaning of a certain thing. It is these strained and awkward moments that promote sensitivity-based learning and growth. (p. 335)

The value and benefit of experiential approaches to SOT work is that they provide participants with spontaneous unscripted opportunities to learn by doing, which is a centerpiece of the process of being. Other ancillary benefits are that they offer unlimited opportunities to struggle with and embrace complexity, understand one's reaction to a variety of emotions, and to attend to critical relationship dynamics. There are numerous approaches to training and supervision that offer clinicians rich opportunities to participate in experiential group-based SOT work. The following are a few brief examples of experiential group-based SOT strategies that support the seeing, being, doing process.

Genograms

The Cultural Genogram (Hardy & Laszloffy, 1995), the Racial Genogram (Hardy, 2023), racial and cultural storytelling (see Chapter 5), and the Racial Awareness Sensitivity Exercise (RASE) (Hardy & Bobes, 2017) are but a few examples of experiential, relationally based, SOT supervisory and training resources that help facilitate seeing and being with a critical eye toward doing. The Cultural and Racial Genogram processes often provide such a wealth of culturally elucidating and valuable information that it is often possible to extract other experientially based SOT work that can be highlighted as separate but related training experiences. As a spinoff of the Cultural and Racial Genogram process or as a stand-alone exercise, exploring the cultural-racial significance of names is a very powerful experiential training exercise that facilitates the seeing, being, doing process.

Exploring the Cultural–Racial Significance of Names

Asking therapists in training and supervision to explore the origins, anatomy, and stories associated with their names (see Chapter 12), a seemingly benign activity, can also be a powerful tool for promoting seeing and being as well. It is virtually impossible to participate in a group-oriented substantive conversation about names without also implicating and referencing a variety of other sociocultural factors ranging from religion and gender to race and ethnicity, as well as a host of many others. Names, who is assigned what name, when, how, and by whom, as well as a bevy of other related factors, are all complexly entangled in race and culture. The naming exercise derives its transformational potency from the high-quality and open-ended sharing it engenders, the deep listening it requires, and the reflective processes that it inevitably creates. This simple but powerful exercise provokes a sense of curiosity not only about others' names but about one's own name(s) as well. It also builds a strong sense of community within the group that teaches and reinforces lessons about the power of relationships. This is a common artery that flows through all the experiential, group-based SOT work, and the intensive racial sensitivity groups probably offer the most in-depth work out of all the approaches.

Intensive Racial Sensitivity Groups

The intensive racial sensitivity groups, like all the other experiential group-based SOT approaches, are specifically designed to foster the seeing, being, doing process. Like its counterparts, it is another effective SOT approach that inevitably provokes self-examination, self-interrogation, and self-reflection. These groups are offered in a variety of contexts and over a wide-ranging period. Whether offered as a free-standing training or in conjunction with clinical supervision, the groups work best when structured to meet over a protracted period, with a controlled number of racially heterogenous participants (when possible), to ensure community, continuity, depth, and intensity.

Over the course of the intensive group experience process, participants are encouraged to participate in a range of open-ended but focused, semistructured exercises and tasks designed to enhance seeing and being, as a precursor to reviewing intervention techniques and strategies (i.e., doing). The following questions represent a sample of the standard starter questions that participants are required to explore with members of their respective supervision or consultation group:

1. Please introduce and discuss how you identify racially and how the way you identify racially shapes how you see yourself, others who identify similarly, those who identify differently, and how you believe you are seen by each of the aforementioned.

2. In the family you grew up in, who was the racial group that was demonized, villainized, or pathologized? What did you hear, experience, and/or observe within your family that exposed you to this form of "othering"? How did it influence decisions and actions you have taken in your life? How does it impact you now? Your relationship with members of that group (or groups)? Which of those old beliefs have you held onto?

3. What is an unwelcomed, disavowed, or troubling internalized racial belief that you consciously reject but have difficulty completely rejecting unconsciously?

4. What is the biggest and perhaps most dangerous racial blind spot you believe whites possess?

5. What is the biggest and perhaps most dangerous blind spot you believe People of Color (name Black, Asian, Latinx) possess?

6. Please discuss at least one issue of pride and one issue of shame that is associated with how you identify racially. In other words, what is one characteristic, trait, or attribute connected to who you are racially that is a source of pride for you? Source of shame?

7. What is a critical defining, potentially life-altering moment that you have had related to race, your racial identity, or racism? If you have not had one, please share what hypotheses you have related to the fact that you have not had one.

8. What or who is the racial group, excluding the one you belong to, that you (embarrassingly) feel a low-grade, nagging angst toward because of a particular behavior, trait, ideology, and so on? And what is the angst-inducing behavior, trait, and so on? How does this dynamic affect how you interact with members of the group?

9. Who is the racial group that you experience the most anxiety interacting with? The most fear? Why?

10. Have you ever been on the receiving end of race-related harm or injury? If no, what is your theory about why that is? If so, how would you describe your process of recovery?

These starter questions are designed to be racially engaging and to provoke authentic emotions, thoughts, and critical reflection. The range of what will be verbalized, felt, and addressed, both within a given supervision or consultation group as well as between them, will vary quite substantially since every experience is unique. Intense conflict is often unavoidable and inescapable, and it is an integral aspect of the work! Obviously, the knowledge, racial sensitivity, acumen, and experience of those in the facilitator role is of paramount importance (see Chapter 3). In fact, it is another reminder of just how important the process of seeing, being, doing and SOT work are to the process of becoming a racially sensitive therapist (and by extension, a culturally competent, socially just practitioner).

Regardless of the particular method employed, SOT work from a Multicultural Relational Perspective is vital to the seeing, being, doing process and ultimately to becoming a racially sensitive therapist. The quest to become a racially sensitive practitioner is severely compromised when the important prerequisite and foundational steps of seeing, being, doing are circumvented.

Seeing, Being, Doing, and Clinical Competencies

Subsequent to engaging in intensive SOT work, which incorporates the seeing, being, doing process, the therapist is better equipped to demonstrate improved mastery over some of the salient competencies that are integral to racially sensitive therapy. Some of these competencies may include, but are not limited to, the following:

1. **Use direct and indirect strategies to catalyze conversations about race and other sociocultural factors.** This competency is germane not only to the early stages of treatment to help facilitate joining and engagement, but throughout the middle and later stages as well. It is here that the therapist demonstrates the ability to initiate relevant race-related conversations directly, as well as to frame questions and assign tasks that are likely to generate conversations about race. The therapist is also poised and prepared to address any impediments that might appear unexpectedly.

2. **Engage in respectful, authentic, nonperformative racially based self-disclosure and location of self.** This competency, prima facie, seems simple and relatively easy to execute. However, if the therapist is awkward in delivery or lacks the proper temperament and decorum when either locating themselves or self-disclosing, this can be a major setback to establishing trust and engaging effectively with a client. Again, this is not a matter of the actual words that are used or that shouldn't be used by the therapist, although words and tone are exceedingly important. Instead, the effectiveness of the therapist's location of self and therapeutic self-disclosure is ultimately based on the level of comfort, humility, and authenticity expressed and demonstrated. This competency is predicated on the therapist's ability to identify themselves racially in a way that is clearly

stated, purposeful, matter of fact, and appears neither gratuitous nor performative.

3. **Effectively respond to client-generated racial slights, aggressions, and microaggressions.** Unfortunately, expressions of microaggression, racial slights, and the use of racial epithets occur far more frequently in therapy than some of us would want to believe. Interestingly, too often racially bigoted, ignorant, harmful comments are either considered by some therapists to be too benign to warrant addressing in session or too egregious to address without disrupting the therapeutic alliance. These situations are even more challenging for Therapists of Color who are often either direct or indirect targets of racially unsavory comments made in therapy. These difficult matters require will (the intestinal fortitude to act) and skill (access to the tools and tactics needed to effectively address the circumstance). Fortunately, the seeing, being, doing process equips the therapist with a fortified will, racially based emotional–psychological stamina, and the requisite skills necessary for addressing racial microaggressions, slights, and harm. Remember, the task at hand is not just a matter of possessing high-level skills but also about one's ability to navigate the slippery and treacherous slopes of race and relationships.

4. **Conscientiously and seamlessly integrate racial issues, analyses, and interpretations into the therapeutic process and/or the presenting problem, whenever and wherever necessary.** One of the multitudinous benefits and therapeutic payoffs of developing a racial lens and racial sense of self is the facility with which one sees race and has a newfound fluency in speaking about it. This competency enables and empowers the therapist to not only initiate conversations about race but to also integrate them seamlessly as a natural and fundamental dimension of the therapeutic process as needed and when appropriate. The racially sensitive therapist treats the topic of race as a natural and normal dimension of therapy, so that it can become a natural and normal dimension.

5. **Be proactive in initiating a repair process for addressing racial ruptures.** Race is such a complicated, volatile, value-laden, and polarizing topic that it is virtually impossible to authentically address it, in any context, free of conflict and rupture. Thus, racial conflict is predictable, inevitable, unavoidable, and to be expected, particularly when there is a concerted effort to address it in lieu of avoiding it. Thus, having the ability to initiate a process of repair constructively and proactively is an essential skill for racially sensitive practitioners to possess. As noted previously, this important, delicate process requires the therapist to be able to do, that is, to have the skill set and the knowledge to apply it to advance a process from hurt to heal. Similarly, it is equally important for the therapist to be, which requires consistently demonstrating the ability to remain racially centered, aware of one's racial triggers, and free from the grips of emotional reactivity in all possible forms in which it might manifest.

These crucial competencies are an outgrowth of the seeing, being, doing process and are embedded within the critical tasks that therapists must negotiate to become racially sensitive practitioners. Chapter 2 provides a detailed discussion of these tasks and how they intersect with the seeing, being, doing process and the development of the clinical competencies necessary to conduct racially sensitive therapy.

Active and wholehearted engagement in the seeing, being, doing process not only prepares one to actually do therapy, but also to see and, importantly, to be a racially sensitive therapist. It ensures that clients, and especially Clients of Color, can look forward to working intimately with those who will bring to the work a sense of mastery, relational ethics, racial sensitivity, and integrity.

Summary

Seeing, being, doing is a process. It is an epistemology predicated on principles of holistic thinking. It asserts that racial sensitivity, as an attribute and process necessary for becoming a racially sensitive therapist, cannot be achieved by singularly focusing on skill acquisition. Instead, the complex interplay of the trivariant process of what our eyes are trained to look for and see; who, what, and how we are racially and the essence of our (racial) being; and the acquisition and enhancement of clinical skills is what is ultimately needed. The seeing, being, doing process is vital to becoming a racially sensitive therapist by helping to inform and shape racially attuned clinical competencies, strategies for addressing challenging racially based clinical issues, and by preparing racially adroit practitioners.

CHAPTER 2

The Process of Becoming: Principles, Preparation, and Practice

KENNETH V. HARDY, PhD

Becoming a racially sensitive therapist is an ongoing process that is neither simple nor expedient. It requires considerable personally focused work that can, at first glance, appear to be far beyond the parameters of what the process of becoming a therapist typically entails. Becoming a racially sensitive therapist requires so much more than solely focusing on the specific strategies a therapist employs; ultimately it is about a process of becoming. It is not the sum of what skills, techniques, and tactics the therapist has amassed to deploy with this or that type of client, although these are important considerations. Instead, it is strongly driven by who and how one wishes to be. It is a process that marries "who I am, who and how I wish to be," with "what I do." It cannot be achieved simply and solely by an acute focus on skill acquisition in the strictest sense of the term or what should be done with this type or that type of client or presenting problem. Becoming a racially sensitive therapist requires the clinician to engage in intensive, racially focused Self of the Therapist work. Ideally, the core focus of this intense work enables the therapist to explore and come to terms with eight critical factors associated with becoming a racially sensitive therapist.

To strive toward becoming a racially sensitive therapist, one must effectively negotiate the following tasks that emanate from the seeing, being, doing process discussed in Chapter 1: (1) Challenge the notion of color blindness and the theoretical myth of sameness; (2) develop a racial sense of self; (3) develop a racial lens; (4) develop relational muscles and racial fluency; (5) develop the necessary skills to function as broker of permission; (6) develop a skill set for repairing race-related relational ruptures; (7) develop skills to effectively address racial microaggressions; and (8) develop a racially sensitive trauma-informed lens. While these tasks are presented and discussed individually, it is the complex interplay between and among them that significantly enhances one's efficacy as a racially sensitive therapist.

Challenging the Theoretical Myth of Sameness

The theoretical myth of sameness (Hardy, 1989) is a worldview that espouses, both explicitly and implicitly, that all people, and by extension all families, are essentially the same. This view is partially reflected in the feel-good notion that "there is more that unites us than divides us." While this sentiment has considerable merit and is laudable and uplifting, it should not dissuade us from also acknowledging how we are also (too) divided. It is a universalist approach to the human condition that helps to support notions of racial oblivion and color blindness. After all, why attend to, or highlight race, when we are all the same? As a clinical supervisor once cautioned me early in my career, "I think you will be much more effective as a clinician if you spend less time focusing on issues like race and devote more attention to understanding the rudiments and intricacies of complex family functioning. If you learn and master this, then you can work with any family, anywhere, and of any race." Unfortunately, learning about race and the rudiments of complex family processes were treated as if they were mutually exclusive, with the issue of race relegated to a position of insignificance. The theoretical myth of sameness has been a major force in perpetuating, as well as justifying, an inattention to race and its impact on clients, therapists, and the entire therapeutic process.

The process of becoming a racially sensitive therapist requires developing a comprehensive and nuanced understanding of the similarities and differences that exist not only between families, but among them as well. It means embracing the notion that Families of Color and their white counterparts are both the same and different. It is incumbent upon the therapist to use this framework as a foundation for assessment and treatment. This also means that the therapist must be adept at discerning the critical distinctions that might exist not only between white families and Families of Color, but those that may well exist within those groups as well. This is the essence and outcome of seeing.

Developing a Racial Sense of Self

As noted in Chapter 1, this step highlights the significance of the clinician becoming intimately acquainted with themselves as a racial being. Developing a racial sense of self means that one has spent time developing an understanding of the intricacies and complexities of one's racial identity, what it means, and how it contributes to how one is perceived racially. For white clinicians, this means coming to terms with what it means to be white—to themselves and others. This process of intensive racial (self) interrogation is critical for white clinicians. Since many white people rarely think of themselves racially in comprehensive and nuanced ways, it is essential for white clinicians to engage in an intensive process of racial self-interrogation. Developing a racial sense of self can help whites imagine, expand, and conceptualize their identities beyond simply thinking of themselves (only) as American, human, or in terms of their ethnicity or religion. Failure to do so increases the probability of white therapists unknowingly and innocently contributing to a range of racially harmful actions, missteps, and microaggressions. Unfortunately, these transgressions are seldom acknowledged or overtly and proactively addressed in a reparative fashion.

For many Therapists of Color in the United States, seeing oneself racially is often integral to what it means to be a Person of Color. The visibility of race is virtually always on full display and subjects many People of Color to widespread societal surveillance. Thus, many People of Color lack the privilege of seeing or thinking of themselves nonracially, especially in white-dominated places. Being perpetually cognizant of who one is racially often means sorting out and through the entanglements of who one really is racially from how one is racially defined and perceived by the white society. Developing a racial sense of self is critical to becoming a racially sensitive therapist and is a crucial developmental step for therapists of all races. The process also enables People of Color to analyze and metabolize what it means to have a single dimension of their identity being as visible and sometimes emotionally charged as their race can be. On the other hand, it invites whites to think critically about what it means to be white in a world that values whiteness. One of the most significant benefits of developing a racial sense of self is that it makes the theoretical myth of sameness nearly impossible to adhere to as an organizing framework for conceptualizing individual and family functioning. Moreover, the more one begins to see and appreciate oneself as a racialized being, the easier it is to begin to see others similarly. Many of the experiential training strategies discussed in Chapter 1, including racial and cultural storytelling (see Chapter 5), are tools that can be helpful in promoting a deeper exploration of the racial sense of self process. The increasing ability to see and recognize the significance of race for oneself and others is a pivotal fundamental step to developing a racial lens.

Developing a Racial Lens

Since the relevancy of race is often downplayed and/or denied throughout most facets of society, it is often so nuanced that it can be difficult to recognize. The development of a racial lens means that our eyes are (re)trained to see racial issues and dynamics with impeccable clarity regardless of how subtle or nuanced they might be. When clinicians employ a racial lens, it enhances their ability to see and consider how the intricacies of race may be connected to the presenting problem, the therapeutic process, the therapeutic relationship, or one's preferred approaches to healing. When the therapist can see, it compels them to want to do, and address issues of race in a thoughtful and engaging manner. Unfortunately, developing the ability to see race does not de facto equip one with the necessary fortitude and skill set to address issues of race effectively—however, it does help. Developing the necessary relational muscles and racial fluency to effectively address race is a critical dimension of the preparation process for becoming a racially sensitive therapist.

Developing Relational Muscles

Hardy (2022) describes six relational muscles that require attention and development as a prerequisite to addressing and discussing race. He identifies the six muscles as: *intensity* (the ability to tolerate discomfort); *intimacy* (willingness and ability to be vulnerable); *authenticity* (ability to say want you mean and mean what you say); *congruency* (alignment between what one is thinking and expressing verbally and nonverbally); *transparency* (the ability and willingness to show one's self and to be seen); and *complexity* (the ability to tolerate or hold two disparate, opposing thoughts, feelings, or positions). The interplay of these relational muscles is essential to being able to successfully navigate important, tense, and difficult conversations about race, especially since the efforts to do so are often marred by conflict, discomfort, and/or awkwardness. As these muscles get stronger, so does the therapist's willingness, ability, and confidence in leaning into more substantive conversations about race. There is a relative ease and heightened comfort level with which therapists can engage in conversations about race without it feeling forced, performative, awkward, or trite. Thus, the development of these muscles can imbue the therapist with the sense of courage, confidence, and tenacity to lean into, rather than avoid, conversations about race. Furthermore, the development of these important relational muscles is central to the therapist being able to exercise one of the most critical roles for the racially sensitive practitioner to execute, that is, serving as the *broker of permission*.

The Broker of Permission

Too often, too much of what could be addressed relative to race in and outside of the treatment room dies from a type of loud silence. Even therapists who are committed to addressing race in therapy often fail to do so because they are often trapped in an internal self-constructed prison of endless questions about what is appropriate, how it should be introduced, and by whom. Questions such as, What if I say the wrong thing? or What if I offend someone? are important, sensitive queries to ponder, and they require resolution and action. The development of the six relational muscles should assist the therapist in addressing some of the uncertainty about talking about race and doing so with some modicum of decorum and efficacy. Some mastery of these relational muscles is central to becoming *racialingual* and developing fluency in talking about race. It is important for the therapist, as the person with the greatest power and privilege in the room, to initiate conversations about race, which means to serve and function as the broker of permission (Hardy & Bobes, 2016). There is a commonly understood, widespread, unspoken, and rigidly followed "rule of engagement" throughout society regarding race talk. Quite simply, the rule is that talking about race openly, candidly, and especially in cross-racial spaces should be avoided to prevent conflict, harm, and/or misunderstanding. This rule is widely followed throughout all of society, and the therapy room is no exception. Therefore, it is rare for race to enter into the therapeutic conversation in a substantive way, even if/when it is connected to the presenting problem, the therapeutic process, or the therapist-client relationship. The color-blind notion that it is not an issue, and if/when it is, the client will raise it, is naive, deeply flawed thinking, and lacks a comprehensive understanding of the dynamics of race, racial oppression, and trauma. Conversely, it is important for the therapist to benignly acknowledge race. This acknowledgment is most effective when it is a routine part of the therapeutic process and does not have to be triggered by or in response to a racist act, racial microaggression, or anything else harmful or diabolical. The following short vignette provides a poignant illustration of how the issue of race gets erased from the process of therapy when the therapist fails to function as a broker of permission.

The Case of: "I See You"

In a recent live supervision session, Adrianna, a skilled couples therapist working with a Black–white interracial couple, empathetically said to the husband, Malik, "It is clear to me that your experiences as a man and husband have shaped you profoundly and that it is important for your wife to see this."

Brief Case Analysis

It was curious to me, as the supervisor, as well as to the remainder of the supervisory team, why Adrianna neglected to say "as a man, husband,

and Black person" or "as a Black man and husband . . . " It seemed odd in the moment that the racial element of his identity was unacknowledged even though it was obvious to all of us that he was the only Black person in the room. This was particularly important since some of the concerns he raised in therapy seemed deeply connected to race and his efforts to navigate these issues within the context of his interracial marriage. It is worth noting here that it would have been just as important to name a white male's whiteness under a similar set of circumstances.

If Adrianna, the therapist, had executed her Broker of Permission role, it would have conveyed to Malik, as well as his wife, Tammi, that "this is a place where we can and will discuss race and it is perfectly okay and normal to do so." In the absence of "granting permission," the topic of race will likely continue to be the very awkward and uncomfortable topic it often is, both in and outside of therapy. Adrianna attributed her reticence to name Malik's racial identity to a worry that he might have been offended by her raising the issue of race when in fact he had elected not to do so. Interestingly, she later acknowledged that he had not mentioned being a man either, yet it didn't deter her from overtly naming gender. When the therapist has a solid sense of herself as a racial being, has developed a racial lens, and has developed the relational muscles that are critical to having conversations about race, many of the thoughtful race-related therapeutic dilemmas and uncertainties that often arise tend to become a little easier to navigate.

Becoming a racially sensitive therapist also means that one is often willing to actively engage in relational risk-taking with the understanding that doing so may culminate in an elevated sense of intensity, misunderstanding, or conflict. Thus, learning and knowing how to adequately address and repair race-related ruptures are of paramount importance to the process of *becoming* (a racially sensitive therapist).

Repairing Race-Related Ruptures and Missteps

Given the volatility, discomfort, and awkwardness often associated with talking about race regardless of venue or circumstance, the fear of offending or saying the wrong thing is ever present. The fear of doing so is often exacerbated by the uncertainty regarding the next plausible step one should take once a misstep or rupture occurs. It is virtually impossible to have fully engaged, authentic conversations about race void of discomfort and possible missteps. Misunderstandings, missteps, and quite possibly racial microaggressions are often inevitable, especially since it is rare that many of us engage in honest, candid, and transparent conversations about race. Considering this inevitability, understanding and demonstrating the ability to repair race-related relational ruptures, microaggressions, and missteps are essential clinical skills that the racially sensitive therapist must possess.

Understanding and demonstrating both the willingness and ability to proactively initiate and engage in a process of relational repair eases the burden and potential anxiety of saying the wrong thing. To be clear, the willingness to repair should not be construed as a license to be cavalier, insensitive, or racially reckless in one's approach to engaging in racial conversations. Instead, it means that the therapist keenly understands and assumes full responsibility for effectively addressing any racial microaggressions, missteps, or slights that may be remotely harmful to a client. By assuming this stance and understanding, it serves as a poignant reminder to the therapist that if and when the "wrong thing" is said, repair is necessary, which requires further engagement, not a shame-based, self-indulgent, self-protective retreat to silence or disengagement.

The process for repairing race-related ruptures involves five steps that the therapist must be able to execute, utilizing all six previously referenced relational muscles that are vital for effective conversations about race. The stages of race-related relational repair are (1) acknowledgment, (2) affirmation, (3) action, (4) apology, and (5) asking for forgiveness. These steps must be initiated and executed by the therapist in a proactive and authentic manner. There is no set timetable or rigid rule stipulating how long each step takes, or whether it is possible or under what circumstances it is possible to move smoothly and expeditiously from one step to the next. Much of this is dictated by the nature and gravity of the offense, as well as the client's needs. Regardless of these factors, it is incumbent upon the therapist to proactively initiate the process with immediacy, authenticity, and clarity of purpose. Acknowledgment is always the first critical step.

Through the process and act of acknowledgment, the therapist essentially conveys to the client through words and deed, "I want you to know that I *know* that what I said/did was harmful to you." This step can be as simple as the aforementioned statement, or it can require more detail, specificity, and nuance depending on a variety of factors (relationship status, nature and gravity of the offense, legal/liability issues, etc.). Following the successful and effective execution of this step, it is important for the therapist to express another level of acknowledgment, which is affirmation. During this phase of the repair process, the therapist authentically assures the client, "The way you see it, say it, expressed it, and experienced it, is the way it is and how I am receiving it (and ultimately accept it)." During this phase of the process, there is absolutely no effort to talk the client out of their experience or issue caveats or explanations about therapeutic intentions or the client's misinterpretations. Affirmation is unconditional. When appropriate, the therapist then advances the conversation to the third stage of the process, which is the action phase. It is during this important step that the therapist reassures the client of specific actions the former pledges to implement, practice, demonstrate, and so on to effectively address the issue at hand and to ensure that the offending behavior will not be replicated. It is only after the first three steps have been effectively executed that the therapist offers an apology, which is the fourth stage of the repair process. The rationale for issuing an apology so late in the process is twofold: First, it allows the therapist to center the client's thoughts, feelings, and behaviors, rather than their own, which is essentially what an early apology does; and second, it affords the therapist the opportunity to develop a deeper understanding of the offense and thus strengthen the weight of the apology. Once a sincere, authentic, and substantive apology has been offered, it paves the way for the therapist to cautiously implement the final stage of the repair process, which is to ask for forgiveness. This is the most difficult and delicate phase of the repair process because of the power imbalance in the therapist-client relationship. Consequently, it is crucial for the therapist to work assiduously to ensure the client that: (1) the request for forgiveness does not entitle one to it; (2) it is the aggrieved or harmed (the client) who determines if, when, and under what circumstances forgiveness may eventually be extended, if ever; and (3) while forgiveness is requested and genuinely desired, it is not a requirement for continuing the work, if the client feels comfortable doing so.

Regardless of whether forgiveness is ever granted, the pursuit and engagement of the racial rupture repair process is necessary for the racially sensitive therapist to effectively execute. It helps to enhance the therapist's ability to deal with the complexities inherent in having race-related conversations, and especially those that are fraught with misunderstanding, miscalculations, and microaggressions. The process, even when it doesn't culminate in immediate expressions of forgiveness, has a way of deepening the therapeutic relationship and helps to create a context of healing and transformation. And finally, it also models the steps of relational repair in the event it might someday be helpful to the client.

Addressing Racial Microaggressions

When there is a willingness and commitment to have open, honest, and earnest conversations about race, racial microaggressions—intentional, unintentional, benign, or egregious—are, unfortunately, common occurrences. The racially sensitive therapist functions with an acute awareness of racial microaggressions and possesses the skills necessary to effectively address such infractions when they occur, both those that are therapist-generated and those that might be potentially committed by a client.

It is practically inevitable that a therapist may use a racially based word, phrase, or reference point that might be experienced as a microaggression by a client. Since some clients may not feel the necessary comfort or safety to confront or overtly address the microaggression, it is crucial that the therapist remains highly attentive to their own words and deeds as well as the client's nonverbal communication. This is another benefit of the therapist developing a racial sense of self and a sharply attuned racial lens through which to see the process of therapy and the therapeutic relationship. When the therapist is confronted about the perpetration of a racial microaggression, it is imperative that the therapist responds openly and nondefensively while resisting the temptation to overexplain, clarify intentions, or highlight misunderstandings or misinterpretations. In fact, it is vital that the therapist employs the relational rupture repair model to effectively address and resolve the matter.

Since there are instances where a client may not feel the freedom or comfort to confront or name a microaggression, it is crucial for the therapist to constantly check in regarding the use of certain terms, phrases, or anything that could be potentially awkward, offensive, or uncomfortable for a client. Asking questions such as, "How did that word land for you?" or "Is that a term that you would have used?" is a prudent measure for a therapist to take as a potential safeguard against microaggression, particularly regarding circumstances where the client may not feel empowered to confront the therapist.

Since clients can and often do perpetrate racial microaggressions, it is equally important for the therapist to constructively engage them around their microaggressions. Due to the stark power differential between therapist and client, the strategies and decorum used by the therapist during these incidents are of paramount significance. Rather than confronting or issuing dictums and mandates regarding what words, for example, are permissible or not to use in therapy, it is important for the therapist to engage the client in what can be an informative, transformative, and therapeutic conversation. One way in which the therapist might accomplish this feat is by employing the microaggression mini-model.

The microaggression mini-model is a strategy designed to effectively engage with clients who use racially insensitive terms in therapy and who are the perpetrators of microaggressions. Too often the therapist's silence or failure to address microaggressions in therapy becomes an act of complicity, whether intentionally or unintentionally, and in my view, antithetical to conducting racially sensitive therapy. The mini-model is an accountability measure and is not predicated on confrontation in the purest sense of the term. It paves the way for the therapist to address the microaggression in a manner that invites personal reflection, self-exploration, and personal accountability, while protecting the sanctity of the therapeutic relationship.

The microaggression mini-model centers around the therapist's pursuit of meaning, method, and/or motivation in responding to a microaggression. The pursuit of *meaning* is designed to uncover and ascertain what a client means by a given term, description, action, or assertion. *Method*, on the other hand, explores the actual tool or approach that a client uses to express themselves that relies on racial bias or stereotyping. At times, method and motivation can overlap. The pursuit of *motivation* is an attempt to understand the reasoning behind what is said or done and/or the impetus for saying it, especially now. The pursuit of motivation is often designed to uncover the "why this, why now" that undergirds a certain statement or behavior.

The efficacious use of the mini-model requires the therapist to adhere to two core principles: (1) a commitment to the effective use of self-disclosure, and (2) a willingness to engage with clients through authentic curiosity-based inquiry. A breach of these two principles diminishes the effective execution of the model. The following brief vignettes highlight examples of the microaggression mini-model.

The Case of: "We Ain't Prejudiced"

Larry and Connie, a white couple in therapy, are distraught about their 17-year-old daughter Amanda dating a Black teenager, Justin. The following is an excerpt from our conversation.

> *Larry:* To be honest, we are petrified that this thing is getting out of hand and going too far. Connie and I know that they are sexually active and neither of us can sleep because of constant thoughts about where this nightmare can end up.
>
> *Connie:* She is too young to be so wrapped up into one person.
>
> *KVH:* Does it also concern you that Justin is Black?
>
> *Larry:* Well . . . hell yeah, it does. We ain't prejudiced but Connie and I have asked ourselves a million times where did we go wrong? Out of all the decent young men out there, why has Amanda chosen to align herself with a nigger?
>
> *Connie [looking slightly embarrassed]:* Honestly, we are not prejudiced. We just don't think that he is good for our daughter. It is not just because he is Black. He is just not a good fit.
>
> *KVH [using meaning]:* I couldn't help but notice that you referred to Justin as a "nigger" and, to be quite honest, I have a construction about what that word means. However, I am curious about what it means to you when you use it and what does it mean when you refer to him using that particular term.

Brief Case Analysis

I could easily have issued a cease-and-desist order to Larry and Connie about the inappropriateness of such a racially charged, derogatory, and dehumanizing term as the one they used. Perhaps doing so would have shut down the conversation and discouraged any further use of the term. Instead, I pursued meaning as a mechanism to invite a much deeper conversation about their underlying prejudices and biases. I could easily have pursued motivation by asking them to share with me what was the motivation behind using such a derogatory term to refer to Justin, or was there some motivation to using such a racially insensitive term to refer to Justin while in therapy with their Black therapist? Embedded in each of these approaches is the underlying goal of leaning into and fostering a deeper, more critical and substantive conversation about race.

The pursuit of method is also another viable approach to engaging clients around microaggressions. The following case provides a brief illustration of this approach.

The Case of: "Those Damn Mexicans!"

Paul was frantic when he arrived 15 minutes late for his 5 p.m. therapy session. As he entered the office, harried, frustrated, and flustered, he stated, "Doc, I am so sorry to be late. I should have been in here 20 minutes ago. I got behind a damn Mexican, who instead of pulling over in a parking space, decided to block all traffic while he is double-parked and blasting loud-ass Mexican music like no one else has anywhere to go. Those damn Mexicans are notorious for doing shit like this."

I replied, "No worries about being late. I assumed something unusual had occurred, since you are never late. As I listened to you describing the driver that was blocking traffic, I was so intrigued that you knew they were Mexican. I am never sure whether someone identifies as Latinx Hispanic, and when I am, I am never sure what ethnic group within the broader Latinx culture they identify with. I was impressed that you had such clarity. I am curious about what method you used to determine that they were Mexican and not a member of another Latinx group."

Brief Case Analysis

Once again, the goal is to create a pathway for a deeper conversation that will allow the client to explore deeply ingrained biases, rather than reactively shutting down possibilities for deeper reflection, self-interrogation, and examination. Pursuing method also allowed me to pursue with Paul whether he would have had a similarly strong reaction if the perpetrator was a white male like himself, or whether he would have been as apt to describe the driver by his race. Would he have implicated all white people based on the actions of a single person, as he did in this case? What did he think it meant that he was willing and able to make such broad, sweeping negative generalizations about the driver with so little information? From my perspective, this would be a much more potentially fruitful and transformative conversation to have than it would be if the interaction culminated in simply reprimanding Paul and subsequently shutting down the conversation

The microaggression mini-model is designed to create emotional, psychological, and relational space to deconstruct microaggressions in a way that hopefully brings about substantive change. It requires the therapist to be racially attuned, nonreactive, and fully engaged in and committed to constructive engagement with clients, even and especially during their most racist moments.

Addressing and confronting microaggressions in therapy usually present two fundamentally different challenges for white therapists and Therapists of Color and is an infinitely more difficult proposition for the latter. For many Therapists of Color, the perpetration of racial microaggressions in therapy, particularly by self-proclaimed, well-intentioned white clients, are not only commonplace, but they assault the core of one's sense of personhood. They trigger a racial trauma response that often requires the Therapist of Color to be highly, skillfully trained and personally evolved in order to stay focused on the therapeutic process and to execute the microaggression mini-model. It becomes critical, albeit often easier to say than do, for the Therapist of Color to have readily accessible internalized self-soothing, self-regulatory strategies and techniques that they can embrace to help counteract the jarring impact of a racial microaggression. For Therapists of Color, this, unfortunately, is an integral component of the preparation necessary for becoming an effective racially sensitive therapist.

For many white therapists, the challenges associated with addressing racial microaggressions are not nearly as intimately personal and assaultive as they often are for many Therapists of Color, although there could be exceptions in some rare cases. Most white therapists grapple with what to say, how to respond, if it's appropriate to respond, and the like. Unlike their Therapist of Color counterparts, it is rare that the perpetration of microaggressions in therapy leaves the white therapist wrestling with how to bounce back from having the core of their personhood summarily punctured or pathologized.

The final step that is crucial to becoming a racially sensitive therapist centers around adopting a racially focused trauma-informed approach to clinical treatment. While the impact of psychological trauma on human functioning and how it can best be treated therapeutically has been well documented in the literature thanks to the groundbreaking contributions of trauma-informed clinicians and theoreticians such as Herman (1997), van der Kolk (2014), Levine (2015), Menakem (2017), Fisher (2021), and others, unfortunately, only scant attention has been devoted to the impact of racial trauma on the lives of People of Color. Fortunately, a few contemporary clinicians and theoreticians, such as DeGruy (2005), Hardy (2013, 2023), Menakem (2017), and Wise Rowe (2020), have highlighted the salient role that racialized trauma plays in the everyday experiences of those who are and have been racially oppressed. Although they all approach this work from slightly different theoretical perspectives, they all nevertheless reinforce the notion that simply being trauma-informed is not enough to meet the complex racially based needs of People of Color; instead, to do so, one must also be race informed. The racially sensitive therapist must have a thorough understanding of the dynamics of race, racial oppression, racial trauma, and the resultant invisible wounds that emanate from these experiences as the nexus of suffering experienced by many People of Color. Thus, the therapeutic approaches employed by therapists must be equipped to address the intersection of these issues.

Although the *Diagnostic and Statistical Manual of Mental Disorders* (American Psychiatric Association, 2022) does not acknowledge the existence of racial trauma, and there is currently no widely acclaimed clinical nosology for it, therapists should nevertheless be positioned, poised, and prepared to assess, diagnose, and treat it. This can be achieved by developing a racially sensitive trauma-informed lens, which is a way of (re)conceptualizing human suffering. The therapist must demonstrate a keen understanding of trauma through the dynamics of race, as well as see race through the lens of trauma. In this regard, it would become increasingly difficult to think about trauma without considering race, or to think about race without being curious about trauma. Hardy (2023) maintains that there are seven critical invisible wounds of racialized trauma that clinicians working with Clients of Color must be prepared to acknowledge and treat. These wounds are often equally invisible to both the victims and the perpetrators. According to Hardy (2023), the invisible wounds are (1) internalized devaluation, (2) assaulted sense of self, (3) loss and collective grief, (4) voicelessness, (5) orientation toward survival, (6) psychological homelessness, and (7) rage. Hence, possessing a comprehensive knowledge of racial trauma is central to understanding the inner worlds of both Clients and Therapists of Color, who share the near-universal experience of being People of Color.

Develop a Racially Sensitive Trauma-Informed Lens

The process of developing a racially sensitive trauma-informed lens requires therapists to understand the intricacies of racial oppression, individual and systemic racism, and how these powerful life forces shape the everyday existence of People of Color regardless of gender, social class, sexual identity, or religion. It also means that the therapist develops a thorough understanding of the ways in which these experiences are not just random, isolated, benign events, but instead are life-altering, systemic, and traumatizing forces. This level of understanding compels therapists to continuously ask themselves as well as their Clients of Color: "How might this particular presenting problem be shaped, maintained, and/or exacerbated by the impact of race, racial oppression, and/or racism?" It is also imperative for the therapist to consider how well-established and predictable trauma-based emotional reactions such as hypervigilance, fight or flight responses, and emotional dysregulation, for example, might be expressed and perceived differently when they are racialized. Would it shift how we potentially perceived and responded to the notion of angry Black people or unarmed Black men who continuously run away from police officers, or resist and fail to comply if considered through a racially sensitive trauma informed lens? Unfortunately, it doesn't always appear that People of Color often receive the benefit of having their suffering viewed through the proverbial "what happened to you" trauma-informed prism before being plagued with racially based accusations about "what is wrong with you." The consequences of this oversight and failure, both in and outside of therapy, are dire in that the suffering of People of Color is often responded to by some form of punishment and/or control rather than treatment and healing.

The development of a racially sensitive trauma lens is key to becoming a racially sensitive therapist. It ultimately means that the therapist is thinking critically, not only about how the intersection of race and trauma affects the client's life, presenting problem, and so on, but its potential impact on the therapeutic process as well. This perspective invites the therapist to be more circumspect about therapeutic pacing, specific words, phrases, or terms that might be used, or shouldn't be used, as well as a host of other issues that could be conceivably normal and benign for white clients and yet retraumatizing for Clients of Color suffering from racial trauma. While these dynamics can be particularly delicate, awkward, and uncomfortable for white therapists working cross-racially, Therapists of Color are not immune from these issues simply because they are Therapists of Color. Unfortunately, virtually all therapists, regardless of racial background, theoretical orientation, or academic background and training, have been trained and professionally socialized in ways that have been significantly influenced by the centrality of whiteness. Hence, we are all, to some extent, victims of the white-centric, whitewashed approach to therapy that has historically permeated our field. Thus, we must be intentional in our ongoing efforts to challenge widely held misrepresentations promoting the myth of sameness, the insignificance of race, and false claims of color blindness. Our efforts as therapists to meet the ever-changing and emerging demands of our complex society and its reckoning with race, both within and outside of therapy, require each of us to understand, deconstruct, and dismantle the centrality of whiteness and the varied ways in which it pervades and invades our lives. For those of us aspiring to be effective healers, we must strive to become racially sensitive therapists fervently committed to dismantling the centrality of whiteness. Doing so must be considered a moral and ethical imperative as well as a much-needed antidote to counteract the centrality of whiteness that not only affects the practice of our profession but that threatens to attack our souls and humanity as well.

CHAPTER 3

A Primer for Practicing Racially Sensitive Supervision: A Practical Guide for Supervisors

KENNETH V. HARDY, PhD, AND TOBY BOBES, PhD

The process of becoming a racially sensitive therapist, as discussed in Chapter 1, is not a solitary, independent-study, self-taught phenomenon. Instead, it develops and is refined in relationships, and there is no relationship that is as critical to the therapist's process of becoming a racially sensitive therapist as the supervisory relationship. Supervisors can help expedite and consummate the racial sensitivity preparatory process for clinicians if they themselves have refined their ability to provide racially sensitive supervision. Many of the tasks for therapists, discussed in Chapter 1, to some degree, rely on racially sensitive supervisors to help navigate these processes. This chapter outlines the important tasks that supervisors must accomplish to be in the optimal strategic position to make an impact with supervisees in their journey to become racially sensitive therapists.

Racial Awareness

While promoting racial sensitivity in supervision is the central focus of this chapter, we would like to start with a brief discussion of racial awareness to help distinguish the two interrelated concepts. It is also useful for supervisors and supervisees to distinguish between the two concepts as well. It is commonplace for supervisors, as well as many clinicians, to confuse and conflate racial awareness and racial sensitivity. The former refers to a state of intellectual understanding regarding race and diversity. It is often achieved through didactic and intellectual endeavors, such as reading books, watching videos, and attending workshops. These are all educationally rich, growth-producing activities that we highly recommend; and we believe they can be simultaneously elucidating and limited in scope. Awareness-oriented experiences may rarely involve a holistic approach to personal interrogation. There may be some intellectually based self-directed queries about one's beliefs, often conducted in ways that are totally divorced from any accompanying underlying emotional connections that might also exist.

Racial and cultural sensitivity, on the other hand, refers to "a state of attunement to, resonance with, and meaningful responsiveness to the needs and feelings of others" (Laszloffy & Habekost, 2010, p. 334). The pursuit of racial sensitivity, in addition to requiring a cognitive and intellectual understanding of race, also demands a personal exploration and interrogation of one's relationship to race, as well as an in-depth self-analysis of oneself as a racial being. Thus, one can achieve racial awareness void of racial sensitivity; however, racial sensitivity always encompasses racial awareness. Ultimately, we believe that it ideally should be the goal of every supervisor to enhance both racial awareness and sensitivity on the journey to becoming a racially sensitive supervisor, which is a way of thinking and being that significantly informs what a supervisor does.

Racial Sensitivity

Racial sensitivity is the process of becoming emotionally resonant with the needs and feelings of others' lived experiences. It is an affective and intuitive sense of another person's experience. With this intuitive sense, the listener is better able to anticipate and imagine the emotional experience of their conversational partner. Using oneself and one's intuitive sense to promote connections is enhanced with acknowledgment of what has been heard and especially understood (Hardy & Bobes, 2016). Racial sensitivity also involves actively using oneself to challenge interactions that reinforce racial injustices (Hardy & Laszloffy, 2008). The active use of self means that you may actually "choose which parts of your true self you want to bring forward" (Sung, 2022, p. 221).

As noted in Chapter 1, racial sensitivity is a process that is fluid. It is not a static, measurable, concrete phenomenon with a definable endpoint. Hence, as described in Chapter 2, it is a process of becoming that is ongoing, developmental, and boundless. In this regard, what it means clinically is that one does not essentially become a racially sensitive therapist and de facto become a racially sensitive supervisor, in the same way that being a clinician does not de facto make one uniquely qualified to be a supervisor. There is a heightened level of personal and professional responsibility, preparation, skill acquisition, and Self of the Supervisor work that must be accomplished to embrace the journey of becoming a racially sensitive supervisor. The critical task of the supervisor is not only to have and model racial sensitivity, but also to concomitantly help contribute to the therapist's quest to have it as well. This is no small task for even the most experienced supervisors.

In addition to developing some degree of mastery with the eight tasks discussed in Chapter 2, the aspirant racially sensitive supervisor must also master a set of relevant tasks and supervisory-level core competencies.

Supervisory Core Competency Tasks

Core competency tasks are the specialized skills that are central to the process of becoming a racially sensitive supervisor. The beliefs and values that underpin the competency tasks will be highlighted. These core competency tasks consist of a mixture of conceptual skills (thinking) and executive skills (doing), thus connecting what we think with what we do. As supervisors integrate the process of thinking and doing, they become more deliberate, intentional, and focused in their supervision practices. The five core competency tasks necessary for supervisors to master for providing racially sensitive supervision are: (1) articulate a personal philosophy and model of supervision (PPMOS); (2) demonstrate, understand, and promote the phenomenology of race, power, and privilege; (3) treat race as an artery, not an appendage; (4) engage in ongoing racial self-interrogation; and (5) function as broker of permission.

Task 1: Articulate a Personal Philosophy and Model of Supervision

Articulation of one's PPMOS is a critical first step supervisors must take toward developing a conceptual framework for promoting racial and cultural sensitivity to the core of their work. This task is a strategy that provides a road map akin to a global positioning system (GPS) (Alford, 2022). When taking a literal or metaphorical journey for the first time, operating without a GPS can contribute to ambiguity and confusion. Hence, when well-grounded and clear in one's conceptual framework, moving deliberately and decisively to an effective plan for implementation becomes an easier feat to accomplish. This road map not only informs how supervision is implemented, but it also dares to make explicit many of the implicit elements of the process and the accompanying contract. It is through this procedure that supervisors clarify expectations and rules of engagement that underpin the supervision process.

It is imperative that the PPMOSS statement explicitly addresses how race, racial issues, and other sociocultural factors will be addressed in supervision. This approach not only makes the modus operandi of the supervisor and the ensuing supervision process transparent, but it also normalizes issues of race and other sociocultural factors as integral components of the process. Finally, naming and incorporating race in the PPMOSS also prevents race and other sociocultural factors from becoming siloed, or treated as an appendage to be addressed situationally, only when People of Color are involved in the process as supervisees, clients, or supervisor. When introduced explicitly and transparently as a component of the PPMOSS, race and other contextual variables become mainstreamed into the heart of supervision. To do this effectively requires the supervisor to have given critical thought to these issues as well as to have completed critical Self of the Therapist work.

Task 2: Develop a Keen Understanding of the Phenomenology of Race, Power, and Privilege

It is imperative for supervisors to develop a comprehensive understanding of the dynamics of race and demonstrate the ability and willingness to conscientiously integrate this awareness into all areas of supervision, including but not limited to the PPMOSS. During this critical process, supervisors possess and demonstrate the ability to see, name, and critique all the infinite ways in which race is intricately entangled in virtually all aspects of society. Supervisors must also be willing and able to capably deconstruct the ways in which various models of therapy, for example, may contain or be shaped by unacknowledged racial dynamics, influences, and in some cases, biases. Supervisees at the behest of their supervisors should be routinely questioned and encouraged to consider what race-based assumptions or implicit and unintended bias may be embedded in their theoretical orientation of choice and evolving theory of change.

As supervisors increase their proficiency in understanding the intricacies of the phenomenology of race, it becomes impossible to ignore the saliency of power and privilege and its entanglement with race. Hence it is incumbent upon the aspiring racially sensitive supervisor not only to develop a deep conceptual understanding of the intertwinement of race, power, and privilege, but to have a well-conceived mechanism for addressing these dynamics in supervision. There are 10 core principles of power and privilege that must be incorporated into any meta framework that supervisors use to guide their supervisory work. These organizing principles are as follows:

1. Power is an omnipresent critical intervening variable in all human relationships.

2. Power is never equally distributed; thus inequities in power are inevitable.

3. Inequitably distributed power inevitably defines the dynamics of the relationship where this exists.

4. Egalitarian relationships predicated on rigid, fixed, equally distributed power sharing are virtually nonexistent and unattainable.

5. There is a symbiotic-type relationship between power (the ability and resources to influence others) and privilege (special rights, goods, and accommodations provided to a select few); thus, those

with greater power tend to have greater access to privilege and those with greater privilege tend to have greater access to power.

6. Power is fluid and contextual; thus power can shift as a context shifts.

7. Those who have greater power must assume and be assigned greater responsibility in relationships defined by power inequities.

8. Power and privilege are not feelings; thus, one does not have to feel privileged or powerful to possess either.

9. Race, power, and privilege are complexly and inextricably intertwined.

10. Whiteness, whether socially constructed or not, is assigned universal power and privilege over all other racial hues in society.

Supervisors' increasing understanding of the phenomenology of race, as well as the principles of power and privilege, inevitably promote a greater understanding of the ideology of whiteness, the subtleties and potency of white privilege, and the centrality of whiteness embedded in clinical practice. It also helps supervisors to deeply understand the pervasive impact of racial oppression on the lives of Clients of Color, as well as an increased ability to detect the hidden wounds of racial trauma. It is the supervisors' sophisticated and robust understanding of these issues that empowers them to assist clinicians with the critical process of developing a power-informed racial lens. Perhaps the biggest benefit of supervisors investing considerable time, effort, and energy into developing a greater understanding of the phenomenon of race, power, and privilege is that it highlights the uncompromising importance of addressing the significance and relevance of race in all domains of clinical practice.

Task 3: Embrace and Promote Race as an Artery and Not an Appendage

This task requires thinking critically about race and developing a strategy for mainstreaming it. When supervisors have a firm and expansive understanding of the phenomenology of race, it profoundly shapes their evolving race-related worldview. Rather than ignoring the significance of race altogether, or merely perceiving it as a clinical focus to be intermittently and/or arbitrarily considered when convenient or needed as a performative act, supervisors recognize that it must be thoughtfully integrated throughout the entirety of the supervisory process. In this regard, supervisors recognize and treat the phenomenon of race as a major metaphorical artery that runs through the body of supervision, rather than an appendage to be attached when and where it might be convenient to do so. Consequently, race becomes an integral component of the supervisory process, regardless of the racial identity of the supervisor or supervisee, whether in individual or group supervision, or without regard to the specific issues presented for review and discussion. Supervisors demonstrate due diligence in considering the potentiality of race as a critical intervening variable and clinically socialize their supervisees to do likewise. The significance and centrality attached to the phenomenon of race compels supervisors to carefully consider how their own racial identity and background might provide a prism through which supervision is conceptualized and executed. This of course includes being intentionally curious about the possible connections that might exist between supervisors' racial background, identity, and lived experiences and their supervisory conceptual frameworks.

Task 4: Develop the Skills to Engage in Ongoing Racial Self-Interrogation

When assuming the responsibility of training racially sensitive therapists, it is of paramount importance for supervisors to assist supervisees in developing a racial sense of self. This can be extremely challenging work for both supervisees and supervisors, and it often requires engaging in a perpetual process of racially focused self-interrogation. It is difficult, if not virtually impossible, for supervisors to spearhead this work effectively and thoroughly if they have not engaged in a parallel process en route to becoming racially sensitive supervisors. It is crucial for supervisors to have participated in intensive and comprehensive racially focused self-interrogation work, ideally prior to commencing their supervisory work.

While this core competency task is critical for supervisors of all racial backgrounds, it is vitally necessary for white supervisors, many of whom have spent little time thinking critically about their whiteness, what it means to be white, or what the clinical implications of this unattended work might be.

For example, I (TB), as a white person, lived most of my life without exploring or even acknowledging my sense of self as a racialized being. I continually reflect upon how it could be that I lived a life with a visceral understanding of suffering yet free from serious contemplation of my whiteness until recent years. I grew up in the segregated South entrenched in the values of the centrality and superiority of whiteness. Racial divisiveness was blatantly expressed in my young world all around me, and yet whiteness remained unnamed. I was complicit in perpetuating the toxicity of whiteness. The alleged inherent superiority of whiteness prevailed, and white supremacy was continually reinforced then, as it is today. It was reinforced by a continuing and reflexive return to my emotional comfort as a white person through retreat and escape into white equilibrium. Utilizing this escape route was not just relied upon by me, but it is what I now recognize to be a widely held practice for us whites to avoid facing the pain of our own discomfort.

Surprisingly, or perhaps not, none of this ever deterred me from conducting therapy or supervision, while never ever once thinking about how my experiences with race, or the absence thereof, were impacting my work with clients and supervisees. I operated naively and happily in this context without critical self-interrogation. It wasn't until I attended a racial sensitivity group a few years ago that a pivotal event occurred that transformed my experience of myself as a white person. In the group, I told a story about my "other mother," Ruby, an African American woman my family had hired as a housekeeper. Ruby was very dear and special to me. Her warmth and emotional presence provided love and comfort to me as a young girl. My disclosures to the group triggered painful memories and experiences for some African American participants, who resonated deeply and identified with my story. They were the symbolic daughters of Ruby who were reminded of their mothers who had left them alone to provide for families like mine. I experienced in that moment their deeply seated, nameless, and unrecognized pain rooted in the trauma of racial subjugation and oppression. I experienced their suffering and anguish, which was inextricably connected to my privilege, benefit, and entitlement. I came to recognize more deeply and viscerally the racial suffering of People of Color. My lifelong veil of racial oblivion lifted a bit as I began to develop an affective understanding of racial oppression, the racial suffering of others, and the racial privilege that I possess and had long ignored.

My contributions to this chapter reflect the evolution of my worldview as a white person, clinician, and supervisor. As an octogenarian, I recognize that from the beginning of my career, I was oblivious to my whiteness. However, recently, through participation in racial sensitivity trainings, teaching, and writing, I have sought out opportunities to name my white racialized self, examine what it means to be white, and venture outside of my comfort zone. This is an ever-evolving work in progress. I was trained and professionally socialized in predominantly white educational and training institutions that were complicit in perpetuating myths of color blindness and false claims of sameness. Thus, my worldview had been informed and limited by the centrality, invisibility, and superiority of whiteness.

As a clinician, educator, and supervisor, I (KVH) realized that my efforts to address race and diversity in the classroom and in supervision were greatly hampered without engaging in an intensive process of self-interrogation, as well as challenging the centrality of whiteness as a dominant ideology and influence within clinical practice.

> The centrality of whiteness and its philosophical underpinnings do not require one to be phenotypically white in order to subscribe to the prevailing worldview. People of Color can and do often become major purveyors of the centrality of whiteness. In fact, the acquiescence of People of Color to the centrality of whiteness is a mandated precursor for surviving in the white world. It is as lethal as it is invisible. It infects the souls of each of us. (Hardy, 2022, p. 11)

Given that whiteness does affect us all, it is important for all supervisors to engage in an intensive process of racially focused self-interrogation. It is important for Supervisors of Color to engage in a self-interrogation process as well, even though many of us are born and socialized into a world where being aware of race and our difference is inescapable. Unlike Toby, there has probably never been a time or point in my life where I (KVH) had the luxury or benefit of being oblivious to my race. In therapy and supervision alike, my race was virtually always a dynamic in the room, even when it wasn't overtly stated. My socialization in the world, unlike Toby's, has been not only to see race, but to be painfully and perpetually reminded that I am perceived racially first and foremost above all and any other way—not therapist, not supervisor, not doctor . . . not even human in some cases. The hypervisibility of race in the lives of People of Color, coupled with whites' insistence on not seeing race, have left me and many other People of Color with deeply rooted scars, trauma wounds, and intense emotions that range from despair to rage. These emotions and experiences don't simply disappear because one becomes credentialed as a supervisor. The racially focused self-interrogatory work for Therapists and Supervisors of Color is critical. The supervisor, regardless of racial background or identity, who avoids or has been denied such valuable work is often at a huge disadvantage at providing the same to therapists in supervision. When supervisors have engaged in an ongoing intensive process of racially focused self-interrogation, the task of helping supervisees develop a racial sense of self and a racial lens increases exponentially. Moreover, it is the confluence of understanding the phenomenology of race, mainstreaming the consideration of race in one's world, and intensively engaging in a process of racially focused self-interrogation that empowers supervisors to participate in delicate conversations confidently and competently about race. It is the supervisor's facility and frequency in participating in relatively stumble-free conversations about race that ultimately prepares one to both assist supervisees in becoming racialingual and function as a broker of permission.

Task 5: Be a Broker of Permission

Hardy (2023) posits that in most of our cross-racial relationships, whether personal or professional, there is a tendency to treat talking about race as if we were operating under stringent rules of a gag order. Direct, open, and honest conversations about race are either avoided completely or approached with considerable trepidation, often while speaking in code. This gag order is often implicitly demanded and reinforced in clinical work as well. Even against a backdrop of widespread societal racial turmoil, it is rare that race is comprehensively discussed in therapy or supervision. Abandoning the implicit invocation of the gag order requires something extreme to happen (for example, rampant police use of unjustifiable deadly force in Communities of Color) or someone to grant permission for race to be overtly named and discussed. The broker of permission "grants permission" for conversations about race to take place, not necessarily by dictate or mandate, but rather by their deeds and actions. It is not a role that is executed by a supervisor, for example, simply verbally reassuring supervisees that "It's okay to talk about race here," while failing to do so substantively themselves. Instead, the supervisor models the broker of permission role by initiating and engaging in meaningful, self-revelatory disclosures and conversation about race that extend well beyond that which is usually cursory and performative.

Supervisors and therapists, in their respective roles as persons with the greatest power and privilege in their supervisory and therapeutic relationships, respectively, become brokers of permission when they deliberately initiate conversations about race. They grant permission to speak the unspeakable and give voice to previously silenced topics.

There are several ways, in addition to the PPMOSS, that supervisors can effectively execute the broker of permission role: (1) disclosing location of self, (2) idiosyncratic acknowledgments and discussions about race, and (3) executing acts of racial accountability.

Disclosing Location of Self

Supervisors who name their racial location, prior to requesting the same from their supervisees, are modeling how to be brokers of permission. For example, prefacing comments with acknowledging whiteness such as "As a white person . . . " is a way of raising the issue of race in supervision and thus ultimately increases the potential for racial sensitivity. Modeling and self-disclosure promote a climate of safety and risk-taking in conversations with supervisees. Supervisors should invite supervisees to name their racial and cultural selves as a routine part of the supervision process. Supervisors should take great latitude in creating a context whereby supervisees begin to dialogue early on about their key identities and how these intersecting identities influence supervision and therapy. The following sample disclosure by a supervisor would be an example of how this process might work in supervision:

> *Supervisor:* As a white woman and white supervisor, I have been on a personal journey for the last several years to be more thoughtful about race, and more specifically, about my whiteness, than I have ever been. In my role as a supervisor and therapist, this has meant that I am more conscientious and deliberate in my efforts to center race, and especially whiteness, and how it has shaped our profession and this process. As we meet as a group, get to know each other, and work together, I will be working tirelessly to make sure that the work we will be doing together will always be attentive to the intersections of race, other sociocultural factors, and the clinical process. I will hold myself accountable, hold you accountable, and invite you to also hold me accountable when my years of white socialization fail me.

Here the supervisor not only grants permission for race and other sociocultural factors to be attended to in supervision, but she does so by locating herself within the conversation. Notably, her disclosure does not culminate in a request for the supervisees to share in kind, although she clearly conveys the message that it would be permissible and welcomed if they wished to do so.

Idiosyncratic Acknowledgments, Discussions, and Disclosures About Race

It is an unfortunate and commonly held belief that when race is introduced in clinical practice, it must be designed to correct, challenge, or address some form of racial transgression. Admittedly, issues such as these do occur in therapy and supervision and should be effectively addressed when they do. There are, however, numerous other ways for a supervisor to introduce (and invite) discussions about race that are not precipitated by a mini-crisis or the need to address a racial insult, microaggression, or discriminatory act. For example, supervisors can and should offer disclosures (as noted earlier) that serve the purpose of making race a natural conversation so that it can be an integral component of the supervisory process. The key factor is that it is important that the conversation is initiated by the supervisor and not by asking the supervisee to self-disclose before the supervisor has. Here are some examples:

Example 1

Supervisor: As a supervisor, it has become increasingly important for me over the years to start addressing the issue of race in my therapy and supervision work. This was something that I neglected to do earlier in my career, and I think that it diminished my effectiveness as a clinician and supervisor. The conversations that I initiate and lean into now are the same ones I used to avoid for fear of saying the wrong thing or that the conversation would spiral out of control. I now realize that some of the most powerful and life-changing supervision sessions that I have been a part of have been those where we took risks and had difficult conversations about race that ultimately helped all of us become better practitioners. Thus, my goal here is to create a space where we can have open and direct conversations about race and other matters that really matter. I accept that it is my role and goal to do the necessary work to get us there.

Brief Analysis

The supervisor not only initiates the conversation about race but is also transparent about sharing why it's important. Moreover, the supervisor also demonstrates vulnerability and transparency by acknowledging past missteps and failures in supervision, which can be permission-giving to supervisees. And finally, the supervisor executes another important step by refraining from asking the supervisees to similarly share at this juncture of the supervision. In this regard, the supervisor is granting permission for conversations about race to take place without placing any immediate burden on the supervisee to do likewise.

Example 2

As a matter of standard practice, Jusef, a supervisor who identifies racially as Indigenous, starts each supervision session with a check-in. During this process, each supervisee provides a description of that which constitutes a metaphorical headline for them as they enter the supervision session. Supervisees are free to share whatever feels relevant for them at the time, whether it is work or school related, family of origin, or a comment about a favorite movie or sporting event. After each supervisee has shared, Jusef offers his share and states the following: "Wow! Thank all of you for the depth of your sharing and your willingness to bring your outside life in and connect it to the world of our supervision. I am bringing into our space today many thoughts and feelings I have been having about the world around us and how it seems to be getting more challenging for People of Color. It is hard for me to ignore all the ways in which we seem to be becoming more racially polarized as a country. I have been thinking a great deal about how I can use my platform as a therapist and supervisor to promote greater opportunities for healing and togetherness. Thanks for listening—that is my share for today. Who would like to present the first case?"

Brief Analysis

In this case, Jusef does not initiate the sharing in the session, but does however initiate a conversation about race. He also, like the supervisor in Example 1, demonstrates transparency, vulnerability, and risk-taking while also granting permission for the group to talk about race. As is the case with the broker of permission role, while he remained open to reactions and feedback regarding his disclosure at any point throughout the process, he did not compel, subtly pressure, or express any expectation that the supervisees needed to respond.

In these examples, the supervisor relies upon idiosyncratic acknowledgments, discussions, and/or disclosures about race as a pathway to executing the broker of permission role. Regardless of the technique employed, the two crucial goals are to (1) grant permission for race-related conversations to occur; and (2) to help ensure that if and when we normally talk about race, conversations about race can become normal conversations. In addition to brokering permission via self-location or idiosyncratic acknowledgments, discussions, and disclosures about race, supervisors may also rely on executing acts of racial accountability as another mechanism to function as the broker of permission.

Executing Acts of Racial Accountability

It is our belief that striving toward becoming a racially sensitive supervisor requires one to relinquish all existing goals and expectations of being or remaining clinically neutral. Thus, it is important for supervisors to be prepared and willing to execute acts of racial accountability, which is difficult to do from a stance of neutrality. This responsibility often requires supervisors to be a broker of permission by proactively addressing racial hurts, microaggressions, and/or discriminatory practices or interactions that may occur during either therapy or supervision. In real time, executing acts of racial accountability means that supervisors demonstrate the willingness and commitment to proactively introduce, name, address, or highlight race-related issues regardless of size, scope, or the perceived severity of the offense. It is often through the execution of these deeds that supervisors function as brokers of permission and grant permission for issues of race to be attended to overtly and with a modicum of depth. Effectively executing these processes is not only essential to becoming a racially sensitive supervisor, but also equips and prepares supervisors to train racially sensitive therapists. Supervisors' mastery of the broker of permission role and the strategies that are employed to execute it play an instrumental role in preparing one to assist therapists in their process of becoming racially sensitive through the acquisition and refinement of several key competencies. Racially sensitive supervisors, through their mastery of the broker of permission function, will inevitably be better equipped to assist their supervisees in (1) increasing their racial visual acuity—which refers to the ability to see race in places where it might otherwise appear invisible and to hear it when it isn't spoken overtly; (2) becoming more racialingual—which is the ability to name and talk about race; (3) proactively address racial slights, hurts, missteps, and microaggressions without compromising relational connectedness; and (4) demonstrate racial accountability. The following case example provides a snapshot of these principles captured during a group supervision session.

"I Didn't Wanna Talk About This"

Ayanna, a supervisee who self-identifies as Black, is presenting a case of a poor, Black family in which a single, depressed mother of four young children is overwhelmed, feeling isolated in the community, without social supports, and struggling with the tasks of parenting. Ayanna raises the question in supervision of whether the depressed mother, Janae, has the capacity to mother her young children. As the supervisor, I (TB) inquire about the family's racial background as I routinely do, since it is always an important piece of contextual information in therapy. I also notice that Ayanna hasn't identified the family's race in her presentation. In response to my query, Ayanna responds, "The family I'm working with is Black." After a brief pause and some guardedness, she decides to provide a bit more detail. "I am uncomfortable presenting this case to begin with. I was dreading supervision today." Almost immediately Ayanna begins to become teary, with her voice breaking. She states, "I identify so much with Janae. I grew up in a poor Black family, and I wonder how you, as a white person, can even understand how hard it is to grow up poor and Black. You sit here perched in your place of privilege as a white person and as a supervisor. I didn't even want to bring this up here. I am also wondering about the other supervisees in the room here and what they think about Black people growing up poor." Ayanna's voice gets louder as tears continue to steadily stream down her face more forcefully. Her external emotional expression, which is a complex combination of deep sadness and anger, very likely mirrors the very complexity she is experiencing internally within herself and in our supervision group as she sits surrounded by a group of white people.

As the supervisor, and especially one who is white, I am deeply moved by Ayanna's courage to share and give voice to her experience as a racial being in our supervisory context so poignantly. I respond, "Ayanna, I am so moved by your courageous sharing with me and the group, as well as the amount of agony that presenting this case here today to us, as a group of white people, caused you. You named the underlying racial issues connected to the case and how they resonated personally with you in such an authentic way. You also named my whiteness and my privilege with the very valid question about how my whiteness will impact my understanding of you and your client's circumstances. I appreciate your invitation to me to be accountable, and I hope each of you here will do so as well. I will address your question. I will also invite other supervisees in our group to respond once I have had the opportunity to do so. This is an opportunity for us all to talk about our experiences of race, how we identify as racial beings, and our experiences of race in the clinical context."

Ayanna stays engaged in our conversation and maintains eye contact with me. The group listens attentively. I continue, "You are right on to question how my whiteness and privilege will impact my understanding of you as you work with this family. As a white person, I will never really know what it feels like to walk in your shoes as a Black person. I am slightly ashamed to admit to you and the group that I have gone through much of my life and practiced much of my career without ever thinking critically about race, especially in the insightful way that you just demonstrated here. However, despite my slow start, I use my 'not knowing' as a powerful reminder of my ongoing need for new learning and giving up my superior knowing about how others should be in their lives. Indeed, as a white supervisor, I have the greatest power and privilege in the room, and I bear the responsibility for attending to discomforts when they arise, especially in conversations like the one we're having now."

I choose a moment to check in with Ayanna about how our conversation is going for her: "Ayanna, I'm just wondering what you're experiencing now. Would you share your thoughts?"

She says, "I feel relieved that I brought up what I've been holding since I saw my client and her children a few days ago. Maybe it is even what I have been feeling here even before my client. These feelings have been weighing on me until now." I respond, "I appreciate your staying with the intensity of your emotions and your honesty and transparency. Most of all, I appreciate your willingness to have this difficult conversation with me about race and being white. I will continue to think about these issues as we all work together here. I'd also like to invite others in our group to speak and process their thoughts and feelings."

Brief Analysis

The supervisor executing the broker of permission function in this exchange, as well as in prior sessions, paved the way for Ayanna to honestly and authentically risk sharing what her experience was like as the only Black supervisee in an all-white supervision group. The supervisor's initial, seemingly benign question, "What is the racial background of the family?" conveyed a willingness to see, consider, and talk about race. This was further demonstrated by the supervisor's willingness to lean into the conversation rather than quickly end it due to guilt, fear of saying the wrong thing, or some other manifestation of personal discomfort. The permission giving to talk about race in a meaningful, substantive, and self-exploratory fashion was extended to all the white supervisees as well. In fact, the supervisor's willingness to share and be transparent about her evolving struggles with her white identity gave permission to the white supervisees to do likewise. It conveyed to them that the expectation was for them to talk about their whiteness and its impact on the supervision group, rather than to share platitudes with Ayanna about how courageous she was.

Summary

In many ways, becoming a racially sensitive supervisor is a career-long, lifelong endeavor. It evolves as we evolve and is often difficult to divorce from who we are and how we live our lives. Becoming a racially sensitive practitioner is not like pursuing a terminal degree marked by a definable beginning and end. It is not a clinical credential, but instead a life skill, one that endows and inspires those who aspire to be healers, working with the human spirit, to do as many of us theoretically have been trained to do, that is, to truly meet those we serve where they are and, more importantly, need to be met. It is a way of being that requires that something else that extends well beyond skill acquisition.

Becoming a racially sensitive supervisor requires supervisors to continue evolving beyond their role as therapists. Just as being a therapist provides valuable wisdom and insights for becoming a supervisor, the latter still involves additional work, whether it is expanding one's theoretical foundation or simply understanding some of the critical points of difference between the two processes. The same case can be made for transitioning from a racially sensitive therapist to becoming a racially sensitive supervisor.

There are five core competency tasks that supervisors must grapple with and ultimately master while on a pathway to becoming a racially sensitive supervisor. While we have listed and discussed these as separate, singular, unrelated tasks, they are very much intertwined in ways that are inextricable in practice. In fact, it is the totality and synergy of these tasks operating harmoniously together that ultimately defines and constitutes the essence of becoming a racially sensitive supervisor.

CHAPTER 4

Moving Toward Racially Sensitive, Equity-Focused Training: Confessions of a Recovering White-Centered Trainer

SHARON RC LEE, PsyD

As a caring profession, mental health should, it would seem to me, be finely attuned to the most vulnerable in our society. Yet our theories come largely from white, cisgender, heterosexual men working in a vacuum of their uninterrogated own identity and privilege far removed from the experiences of the most marginalized people; we are a profession steeped in whiteness (Hardy, 2022). Often, therapists are serving communities that are global majority culture, but they have not been equipped to serve these populations. Black- and Indigenous-identified people have many strong historical reasons to mistrust health professionals. The history of harm that medical and mental health professions has done to People of Color (Washington, 2007) is too long to explore here, but nonetheless is an important part of this conversation. There is a desperate need for highly skilled, well-trained, racially sensitive therapists to reshape the field and provide more well-rounded services to marginalized communities (Hardy, 2018b).

In Chapter 2 of this book, Kenneth V. Hardy elucidates the process and foundation that develops racial sensitivity in professional therapists in a culture that has been profoundly shaped by the ideology of whiteness. He calls the process "becoming" because the depth and breadth of unlearning internalized whiteness is a lifelong effort for all of us, not a destination to be sought. Hardy defines the becoming of a racially sensitive therapist in this way:

> To strive toward becoming a racially sensitive therapist, one must effectively negotiate the following tasks . . . (1) Challenge the notion of color blindness and the theoretical myth of sameness; (2) develop a racial sense of self; (3) develop a racial lens; (4) develop relational muscles and racial fluency; (5) develop the necessary skills to function as broker of permission; (6) develop a skill set for repairing race-related relational ruptures; (7) develop skills to effectively address racial microaggressions; and (8) develop a racially sensitive trauma-informed lens. While these tasks are presented and discussed individually, it is the complex interplay between and among them that significantly enhances one's efficacy as a racially sensitive therapist. (pp. 21–22)

As a trainer, teacher, and supervisor, and as an individual who is engaged in becoming racially sensitive as Hardy has defined the term, the question for me in recent years is, "How can my trainings, which have been focused on emotion, attachment, and relational healing in psychotherapy, also be trainings that move therapists toward racial sensitivity?" This question seems applicable also to graduate programs, internships, and really any setting where people are coming together to learn. Often explorations of issues of race and marginalization are relegated in our field to "special topics" apart from our professional training. This separation keeps us in a cycle of not owning the whiteness at the core of our profession. Without addressing whiteness directly and integrating racial sensitivity, our trainings will perpetuate the harm that whiteness does to us personally and professionally. This is true across modalities and approaches. While the trainings may offer different approaches, what they all have in common is that we live in a culture that is founded in white supremacy, which infects all of our systems.

The problem of how white supremacy culture impacts and shapes our professional trainings is multilayered. In this chapter, I will explore the layers that need to be addressed to move our trainings forward toward racial sensitivity. I will discuss leadership, group culture, training method, training content, and systemic issues that need to be addressed to move toward racial sensitivity. I hope to establish a beginning point for further exploration of the question of how we can move toward an integration of racial sensitivity into any modality of psychotherapy or training program.

Background

For the last few years, I have been training therapists in emotionally-focused therapy (EFT), a modality of couple therapy (Johnson, 2019) that is based in attachment theory. I began studying EFT in 2006 and started supervising in 2011, and training people in 2018. I became invested and focused in climbing the ladder of EFT. This is in itself a characteristic of white culture, that there is greater value and reward for those at the top of the ladder (Okun, 2022). I became a trainer with the intention of seeing if I could use my power and influence as a trainer for the betterment of the community. The first community issue that I wanted to address was the fact that my local therapist community was mostly composed of white, middle-aged, cisgender and heterosexual women, despite our intention to provide a warm and welcoming professional home for everyone. From the outset of this endeavor, I was white and naive, with substantial privilege and blind spots. I began my efforts by offering "diversity scholarships" for people from marginalized backgrounds to attend the trainings at a lower fee. I didn't understand why more People of Color weren't participating in our trainings or engaging in the therapist community, but I hoped that making the trainings more financially accessible would make them feel valued and reduce financial barriers where they existed. I began to see, however, that our helpers, community members that support the learning and continue their own growth, were not equipped to support trainees from marginalized communities. There was a lack of racial understanding and sensitivity, which led to microaggressions and missteps. Unfortunately, we weren't equipped to deal with those mistakes, either. It's no wonder why many of the diversity scholars didn't want to continue to be involved in the community. We were hurting people, and often we didn't know it or understand it. I started to see the need for myself as the trainer, and indeed the whole community, to engage in deeper antiracist work. I started to wonder what we needed to do to become a community that People of Color would want to be a part of.

In 2020, after the murder of George Floyd, I was called to a deeper examination of my own internalized white supremacy. This exploration placed my professional efforts in a new light. I started forming whole groups of training cohorts (fellows) that consisted entirely of people from marginalized backgrounds in terms of race or sexuality or gender identity, all being trained at low or no fees. As I worked with these groups, I noticed that they were much more vocal than my earlier scholarship recipients had been about what it was like for them to be in white-dominated professional trainings. Instead of one or two People of Color in a training cohort, the group was majority People of Color. I heard more stories and experiences of isolation and devaluation than I had ever heard before or had previously been aware of, and it slowly opened my eyes. I began to understand how inhospitable most mainstream trainings are for People of Color, especially Black and African American trainees. These groups of trainees taught me a lot about the kind of trainer I should aspire to be.

Some of the early scholarship recipients I worked with remarked that the trainings I was providing were "so white." I admit, I didn't understand this comment, and it left me confused and a little hurt. It didn't occur to me until much later that while I had always thought I had a solid graduate education, there was no exploration of racial issues or identity in grad school. Later when I learned EFT, once again, there was no exploration of race or identity. It took time for me to see that in fact my education had been white centered and so of course the trainings I was providing were also white centered. That was not my intention; I wanted to create welcoming trainings for everyone, but it was true because my own whiteness, the whiteness in the profession and what I was teaching, was invisible to me at that point. I was teaching in a way that harmed, excluded, and misunderstood people I wanted to bring into the community, and I couldn't see any of it. In retrospect it is so clear that my intention was meaningless without self-reflection and the education and enlightenment that many of my trainees later gave me with their sharing and vulnerability.

In this chapter, I outline some of the lessons that I have learned through these experiences in hopes that others may benefit. There is a lot of work that needs to be done to make professional trainings more racially accessible, more welcoming, and applicable to more people. Since 2020, many professional training organizations have made efforts in this direction, hiring consultants and working to change the makeup of leadership. Some modalities seem to be making more advances in this work than others, but for the most part, from what I can tell, most People of Color are still likely not to feel welcome or understood in these trainings, and white trainees are not being challenged to see themselves as racial beings. I did not start out with much expertise, experience, or support to draw on to make my trainings more equitable and inclusive. The ideas I share in this chapter are the product of exploration and trial and error. This process for me as a white trainer is ongoing, and I expect it to go on for the remainder of my career and my lifetime. Certainly, what I am offering here is a starting point, and my ideas may be more relevant for white trainers and leaders. I will use the terms trainee, training, and trainer, because this has been my experience and the language I have used for many years. But for the purposes of this discussion, these terms are interchangeable with teacher, professor, mentor, academic, TA or student, helper, or participant. The issues are universal because the underlying issues of white supremacy impacting our culture are also universal.

Training Leadership

As trainers, sometimes in our rush to convey our ideas, we can lose sight of the fact that in the end we are a group of humans coming together and impacting one another. How the trainer, supervisor, or helper makes the trainees feel is probably what will have the biggest impact in the long run. People will forget our slides and our clinical demonstrations, but they will remember if they felt alone or connected, if they felt respected and honored for their individual experiences or marginalized and othered. How do we create a culture of training that can be a place of challenge, growth, and sometimes conflict, while also being a place people feel connected in the experience of the training? How do we create a training environment where white trainees can grow in their racial identity and racial sensitivity? In a field that is overwhelmingly white, where leadership is often white, how do we make trainings a place where People of Color and other marginalized groups feel included?

Currently, if a Therapist of Color wants to learn one or more of the dominant and/or popular therapeutic modalities, they have to risk entering an environment where their perspective very likely will not be included in the training, and some form of racially based harm seems virtually inevitable in some way. Repeatedly, Participants of Color have told me that after they learn the model, they then have to figure out on their own how to adapt the model for it to meet the needs of the clients they work with.

There are a number of steps that a racially sensitive trainer could take that would improve this situation for Trainees of Color. The trainer needs to set the tone for trainings by demonstrating a facility with talking about their own racial identity and others' identities. For example, a trainer could include in their introduction a discussion of earned and unearned privileges specifically related to their racial identity that helped to pave the way for them to become a trainer (Hardy, 2018b). In doing so, the trainer is sending a clear message that power differentials, race, and identity are going to be a part of the discussion. Likewise, setting up introductions that include location of self (Watts-Jones, 2010) will set a tone of acknowledging and talking about identity.

There will always be content that needs to be covered. However, when we make room for people to bring their lived experiences into the training, especially when those lived experiences contradict or expand the material that is being taught, then more people will feel invited to bring their whole selves into the training environment. Encouraging people to question and contradict the trainer will bring more voices and more complexity into the discussion. Their lived experiences should be considered valuable and welcome contributions to the conversation rather than a distraction from the teaching. I have learned that the fellows have at least as much to teach me as I have to teach them. If I value their perspective and allow my views to be influenced by them, we can build a collaborative and less hierarchical training structure.

Conversations about identity, self-location, framework, and lived experiences require additional time. If we only allocate enough time to focus on just getting through the material, we will not be attuned to our trainees. There is always a delicate balance to strike between offering content and engaging the trainees, but when we engage in topics about race and identity, we need to make more time and take the pressure off. Flexibility, then, becomes a key element to building an equitable training environment.

One of the most important qualities a racially sensitive trainer can bring to the professional space is a willingness to be wrong, to be challenged, and to be corrected. In our culture shaped by white supremacy, the trainer-as-leader is supposed to be the all-knowing expert, to be right, and to be at the top of the hierarchy. This approach disempowers trainees, especially People of Color, who are used to being devalued in professional environments; this kind of hierarchy and perfectionism will silence their perspectives. As I worked with the fellows, I began to see how I could be a healing presence in their lives by acknowledging and accepting when I was wrong, by being corrected, or by having my blind spots exposed. I learned to show deference and to prioritize their perspectives when they were introduced into the group conversation. I learned to let our relationship and interactions be more important than the material I had planned to teach or the model I was trained in. Being in charge and being graceful and humble when challenged can be difficult. Unfortunately, there were times I felt defensive when I couldn't see what I had missed. However, over time it became clearer to me that being challenged by my fellows was a gift where I had the opportunity to build relationship with them. I just needed to slow down, listen, and be humble. There is a slow building of trust that these moments foster over time that is essential to building a training culture of inclusion and connection where slow healing becomes possible.

Representation within the leadership of the training is also important in setting up a training culture that supports diverse voices. In the long term, trainers and leadership in all modalities need to be a more diverse and representative group. But how can the training team move in the direction of being more representative when it has been historically mostly white? Sometimes it is a matter of taking the time to invest in the People of Color who are already interested in what you are teaching, to support them in developing a level of expertise where they could assume leadership and training. The first and probably most important investment we can make is to develop relationships with the people we are training where they feel seen, heard, and valued.

Supervisors and helpers can provide mentoring, modeling, and support; they should be as diverse a group as possible.[1] In my trainings, when people who are marginalized, such as Black and African American trainees, saw people in leadership who were also Black, they expressed to me how this made them feel more at ease and in some cases it made it possible for them to actually participate more fully and be more engaged in their learning. With each training group, an assessment should be made about what the particular needs of this group are, and how best to meet them. One could provide mentorship or supervision (Hardy & Bobes, 2016) that is tailored to the specific identities of the group. For example, when I had a large number of fellows who were Spanish speaking, I hired a Spanish-speaking supervisor to fill in for me and to assist at trainings. Over the last couple of years, I collaborated with a supervisor who was a Black woman and arranged to pay her for her time mentoring the fellows.[2] The mentorship from this supervisor was key for many of the fellows and helped them to feel safer and more comfortable in their cohort. The collaboration between her and me set a tone for the interactions of the group as well.

In sum, the way we get to the learning matters as much, if not more than, the learning itself. Part of undoing white supremacy in our teaching and learning environments is prioritizing our humanity and relatedness over our lessons and agendas. There is rich experiential learning that we can provide by focusing on our connection and presence with our trainees, regardless of anything else we strive to teach.

Training Group Culture

Developing a training group culture that embraces multiple perspectives, encourages vulnerability, and allows for connection as well as tension within the group is not an easy process. Trainees are all coming from different backgrounds with different levels of awareness. In my experience, therapists in training tend to bring significant trauma histories with them. The community that forms in a training group has a life of its own. This is the part of the process that the trainer can guide and influence, but not control. If the trainer does nothing to address race and simply focuses on the content, the default culture that will develop will be one where white trainees feel comfortable and People of Color will feel marginalized, perpetuating the painful cultural inheritance of white supremacy. Instead, the trainer can foster a tone of community building where everyone is giving and accepting support. If we want the group culture to support the growth and process of everyone involved, we have to be tuned in to the experience of our trainees and noticing their dynamics as they get expressed in the group. One of the challenges of this for me as a white trainer is that even though I consider myself very skilled in attunement, I am more likely to be misattuned to my Trainees of Color. I found it was helpful to spend extra one-on-one time with them, inviting them to give me feedback about their experience on a regular basis throughout the training. I also provided an anonymous form for them to be sure that trainees could provide feedback without fear of receiving a negative or punitive response from me.

Every training group is different and requires different support and containment from the trainer. In the early part of the experience there should be a discussion and exploration of how the group will deal with differences of perspective and opinion. The culture of the training group will emerge over time, but it will also be shaped by the trainer, especially in the beginning. If we take the time to talk about how we will navigate through difficult moments in the training and engage participants in the setting of group norms, this can help set up a collaborative structure of engagement that will set the tone for future rocky moments.

Part of building a training community that is inclusive and moving toward racial sensitivity is encouraging helpers and supervisors to do their own self-examination of their respective identities, learning ways of dealing with microaggressions and calling in (Brown, 2020) other trainees who may have a conflict with each other. When I began my training with the fellows, my therapist community that was supporting the trainings simply didn't have the diversity we needed to support the trainees in this way. For our community, we started with an antiracist training in which all helpers had to participate. Every year, we train our helpers who support that year's trainings, and we keep looking for ways to better train them to meet the needs of our Trainees of Color and other marginalized communities. For example, before 2020, our helper training consisted mostly of how to support trainees in role-plays and building relationships with each other. Since then, we have expanded our helper training to include an exploration of the helpers' location of self, a discussion of handling microaggressions, and working with identity in role-plays. Our goal is that our community would be, on the whole, racially sensitive and able to address missteps. This is a lofty goal and will likely be an ongoing work in progress for us.

Training Method

Separating out matters of racial identity ensures that race will be seen as a side issue only relevant or important to some, that is, People of Color. In this way, People of Color continue to carry the burden of the awareness of the impact of race in our culture and in our profession. Professional mental health trainings should instead include a space to recognize that we are racial beings and that this is always impacting us as clinicians, trainers, trainees, and community members. Therefore, racial awareness must shape both the content and process of our training programs. If all mental health trainings included an embedded racial lens, we would be facilitating healing and growth throughout our communities for all members.

As a new trainer, I was taught that discussions of race, identity, and marginalization would distract or detract from our goals of training therapists in a modality. In fact, Trainees of Color are already distracted by misattunement of many therapy models to their lived experience. Moreover, as I have pursued the goal of being a more racially sensitive trainer, I have found that beginning a training with an exploration of identity, race, gender, and culture can be a rich and vulnerable conversation that brings a training group together. How do we create the conditions in our trainings and classes in which our students and trainees will grow in their racial sensitivity and racial identity? What are the structures and practices that create the environment in which trainees can be open enough that this growth and development will occur? This exploration is much more likely to happen when the container for the conversation is strong enough, and parameters of good-enough engagement have been articulated and practiced. This is an important conversation for a new training group. How will we address conflicts and hurts? How can we create a professional environment that also makes room for our personal contributions to be honored? The racially sensitive trainer can welcome rich engagement, which will include conflict at times and hold the space for people to engage and dialogue.

In general, because race has been a side topic in our field, people sometimes feel blindsided by the discussion of race when they are expecting to learn skills. White people who have not explored their own racial identity can get reactive because they are not prepared for the feelings that the conversation stirs. People of Color can also react negatively to a conversation about race that they didn't expect in a training. Many People of Color have been harmed in these discussions and have come to expect that they will not be understood or be safe enough to say how they truly feel. From the beginning, it is helpful to be clear and explicit in the advertising and in the preparatory materials to be distributed that race will be a topic of discussion in the training. Letting people know that this is a part of the training approach sets the expectation that race will be a part of the conversation. Setting the frame for engagement will support the group to have better engagement.

It can be helpful to have a racial affinity space and/or small-group experience as part of any training that includes a discussion about race. Having an affinity space creates safer space for the exploration of racial identity and the development of community. These discussions are best supported by multiple teachers or trainings from multiple identities, sharing their process and opening discussion. It is important to have group parameters about how we will engage with each other when we are inevitably activated by discussions of race. For white trainees, it can be a place where they can learn to show up, be honest and vulnerable about their experience of race (or lack thereof), and learn from others in the training. It can also be important to explicitly ask white trainees to notice their activation and invite them to bring that to the affinity space for exploration.

Sometimes in my experience with the fellows, we would encounter situations where people with differing marginalized identities would have conflict or tension. For example, we emphasize the use of pronouns that align with people's identities in our work and in our role-plays. When people are learning about using self-identified pronouns for the first time, they usually need a lot of practice and reminding and correcting to form those new habits. For anyone who is learning this new way of relating, there can be shame or discomfort in the learning process. Sometimes there has been tension between Black participants who identify as cisgender with white or multiracial participants who identify as nonbinary or gender queer, which was precipitated by being corrected in their use of pronouns. Even if you only have People of Color in a training group, there will still be other aspects of identity, such as gender or ability, that can create these moments of tension or harm. In these situations, I have found the model of the multidimensional self (Hardy, 2016) to provide a helpful framework for engagement. In this model, we all have privileged and subjugated selves in many facets of our identity, such as race, class, gender, or ability. When we are in conversations about identity, most of us are drawn to lead with our subjugated identities regardless of the focus of the conversation. This is one way that conversations about race get disrupted, because white people want to be seen in their subjugated identities (for example, Jewish, woman, queer). It is uncomfortable and goes against our impulses to stay connected to our privileged identities when we are in moments of conflict or tension. This is a practice that takes education, intention, and repetition to develop. For example, as a white, cisgender, heterosexual woman, if I am in a conversation about race, I need to stay focused on my identity as a white person and the privilege that comes with that, rather than distracting or defending myself with my subjugated identities. We learned it was helpful to work with trainees to identify everyone's subjugated and privileged selves and to establish a group norm of "staying in the lane" of one identity category at a time in these complicated moments. We try to start with race and complete those conversations before we move on to other identity lanes, such as sexuality, gender, or ability. This makes room for people to engage with each other and be recognized as multidimensional beings who all have the capacity to harm or to be harmed. When we have been able to have these conversations thoroughly and vulnerably, they have been transformational and bonding for the group.

If we want our trainings to be an undoing of white supremacy culture, then we must ask ourselves how racial identity and sensitivity are a part of any therapeutic model or approach. One of the impacts of white supremacy is that white people tend to begin their racial identity development in racial oblivion (K. V. Hardy, personal communication, December 15, 2022), while People of Color can feel their lives are racialized and that they are constantly struggling with the negative consequences of our racialized culture. We know that racial identity is an ongoing process that has developmental stages for white-identified people, People of Color, and multiracial people. If professional trainings include time and space to explore racial identity for all trainees, we are helping people continue their process from racial oblivion to racial sensitivity. Over time, these efforts could have a profound impact on our self-concept, our professional culture, our ability to adequately serve marginalized populations, and ultimately toward the healing of the deep foundations of white supremacy in our culture and profession.

Training Content

Many of the current approaches of therapy have been developed by white clinicians with no intrinsic lens on race. Therefore, the content of what is being taught is often out of step with the experience of People of Color, as well as people from other marginalized groups. To be a racially sensitive training, there must be an interrogation of the whiteness of the model and the training itself. Who is represented by this model of therapy? Who does the model serve? Are there limits to the model or adaptations that need to be made for groups of people? If the model has a body of research, what are the limits to the research? These are questions that People of Color are more likely to grapple with while white people usually don't have this awareness. If we begin with the assumption that the model is built with whiteness integrated into it, then we can be curious about the ways that whiteness shows up.

There are a number of ways that white supremacy culture shapes our training environments. One of the most prominent ways is the idea that there is a right way to practice psychotherapy or the model we are teaching, and the people in charge know what that is. This kind of thinking and culture oversimplifies issues and creates a hierarchy where some people know and others do not. It limits creative thinking because the trainees are looking to be told how to do it right rather than exploring within themselves how the ideas of an approach apply or do not apply. It also discourages trainees from finding their own embodied way to work with what they are learning. When one studies a model of therapy and is then tasked with training others in it, it can be tempting to fall into the right-way thinking that says we know the way this model works and we are here to teach others. But if we know that most of our models are white centered, then we know that they are incomplete and biased. We know they have white supremacy embedded in them. If we make room for voices from the margins to show us where the ideas break down, don't apply, or need adjustments, then we can reconceptualize our understanding of what helps people heal together as a community. For trainees to feel valued, the trainer must create an environment that is nonhierarchical where the trainees feel comfortable saying when the ideas that are being explored don't make sense in their context.

One way to disrupt right-way thinking is to teach concepts in terms of tension between opposing or balancing forces. For example, as an attachment model, I learned that coregulation is always a way through relational difficulty. Over time I began to understand that this cannot always be true because relationships are so complex. If an attachment theory concept such as coregulation were taught as tension between our needs for autonomy and connection, then there would be more room to explore the many ways our attachment systems function in relationship. Complexity is a valued construct associated with antiracist teaching and systems. By embracing complexity and using dialectics in trainings, trainers encourage people to find their way as professionals rather than to make themselves fit into any specific model. Ideological flexibility and adaptability are key ingredients in a racially sensitive training program.

Representation within the training content is also important in a training that aims to be racially sensitive (Hardy, 2023). Whether we are using recorded clinical material, other videos, or slides with images of people on them, it is important to strive for a wide range of identities to be represented in the materials so that trainees from various backgrounds can see themselves in training material. This can be a challenge to achieve without tokenizing people's identities. I use live consultations to teach from in my trainings, as many others do. I have had to work over the years to get a library of training clips I could teach from that would represent many different identities and backgrounds. At the same time, I did not want to tokenize the participants who volunteer to do demonstration sessions. To me this means that identity needs to be one of many factors in selecting demonstration participants, and those choices need to be carefully thought out, including questioning the trainer's level of expertise and exposure to working with issues of race as well as racial trauma.

Systemic Issues

Finally, there is a systemic aspect to creating a training that is racially sensitive and equity focused (Hardy, 2018a). Organizational consultation on matters of equity, inclusion, and diversity is an expansive and important topic that is beyond the scope of this discussion or the expertise of this author. For the purposes of the questions posed here about how trainers and professors in mental health can aid in the development of racial sensitivity of trainees, some attention must be paid to the context in which trainings are developed and conducted. Our profession is splintered into hundreds of approaches and trainings, all competing in a capitalist society for training money and for dominance in the field. There are often a few people at the top who are benefiting the most from the success of more specialized models and the popularity they enjoy in the marketplace. There is limited collaboration or cross-pollination in our field because of competitiveness and the drive for self-promotion. These dynamics limit collaboration and mutual influence in our field and enhance the expert or one-right-way thinking that already pervades our profession.

For training programs to become supportive of racially sensitive trainings, they must interrogate their adherence to a white supremacy ideology as a guiding principle that underpins its approach to pedagogy and training. This usually requires the perspective of outside consultation in conjunction with consulting the marginalized voices within the training program. Since 2020, many training programs have made efforts toward becoming racially inclusive, but there is a wide range of how far these efforts have gone. Indeed, one consultation experience or diversity statement will not be adequate to address the pervasive roots of white supremacy in our bodies, minds, theories, and organizations. There needs to be an ongoing conversation and a commitment to exploration and a culture of related interrogation where we continue to ask the question about how whiteness shows up in us. We need to care more about who we serve and what is being healed than we do about our value in the marketplace.

If we want our training programs to be a place where more People of Color feel welcome and included, we need to explore more equitable structures and practices in our training organizations. Systemically, people at all levels of the training program will be impacted by the culture of the program itself. The systemic analysis that must be explored is about how the training program is structured, who has power, how conflicts get addressed within the organization, whose voices are included in decision-making, and whose needs are being centered, to name a few. The training program has the responsibility and power of setting a tone of respectful related interrogation of white supremacy that could trickle down to trainings, trainees, and eventually therapy rooms.

Summary

This chapter has highlighted a series of starting points that are critical for addressing and expanding teaching approaches so that we are increasing racial sensitivity in our clinical training programs regardless of the modality we teach. There is much work to be done to expand the steps I have laid out here. At the heart of most mental health professions and most modalities is a desire to improve the world and bring about healing. But without bringing a racial and equity lens to our programs and the material we teach, we are ignoring such a foundational aspect of our cultural conditioning. How can we hope to bring deep healing into our communities without considering the very foundation of our culture and how it shapes our work and humanity? As James Baldwin (1962) said, "Not everything that is faced can be changed. But nothing can be changed until it is faced" (p. 11).

PART II

RACIAL STORIES AND THE SELF OF THE THERAPIST

CHAPTER 5

Racial and Cultural Storytelling: A Clinical Tool for Promoting Racial Sensitivity

KENNETH V. HARDY, PhD

Stories, Storytelling, and Culture

Stories are inevitably embedded in culture and throughout many cultural traditions. They can help explain, translate, or deconstruct certain patterns and dynamics of a group, as well as socialize members into one's culture by promoting shared meaning and sense of connection. Stories can also serve as instruments of healing and liberation by highlighting the traditions, strengths, resiliencies, and pride issues of an individual or group. In many cultures, it is through stories that the cultural mores, values, and folklore are transmitted intergenerationally. Similarly, they also can serve as a vessel to record, transmit, honor, and acknowledge an individual's or group's hardships and setbacks as well as their resiliencies.

Just as stories play a crucial role in many of our lives, storytelling also plays a very prominent role in the lives of virtually all cultures and is a universal phenomenon that is promulgated through a variety of mediums. The written and spoken word, song, photography, especially more recently in digital forms, as well as chants, religious scriptures, and gestures, are all forms and components of storytelling depending on the cultural tradition and storyteller.

Storytelling, historically, has been a powerful mechanism for passing on family and cultural legacies, myths, mythologies, and values, as well as constituting a major form of entertainment. In fact, some cultural groups rely heavily on a variety of spoken word mediums and/or oral history telling as a form of storytelling that is considered preferable to the written word.

Stories, regardless of how they are told, or who is telling them, are usually not necessarily heralded for, or judged based on, their accuracy, objectivity, or even truthfulness. There is often an implicit understanding that the very nature of the storytelling process may involve some degree of harmless distortion, embellishment, and/or subjectivity. The telling of and listening to a story, in many instances, is as potent and significant as the story itself. For this reason, many racial, ethnic, and religiously oppressed groups often place a premium value on some form of oral storytelling, especially racial and cultural storytelling.

In one sense, almost all stories are cultural stories because culture is deeply and inextricably embedded in virtually all stories. Culture is also often entangled with the medium that is used for storytelling, as well as the methodology employed by the storyteller. The point here is that even in stories that are not deemed cultural stories, there are elements of culture incorporated into both the story and the storytelling process that are inextricable. This chapter focuses on racial and cultural stories as two separate but interrelated processes. Cultural storytelling refers to stories that explicitly address issues of culture, which is defined by Hardy and Laszloffy (1995) as a broad-based multidimensional concept that includes, but is not limited to, race, class, gender, religion, sexual orientation, and a host of other contextual variables. Cultural storytelling typically features stories that highlight one or more dimensions of culture, which includes race. However, since it is possible to engage in cultural storytelling and not specifically address race, for the purposes of this chapter, the latter is singled out and highlighted given the focus of this book, even though race is obviously a dimension of culture. While a focus on race does address and implicate culture, the reverse may not always necessarily be explicitly evident. For example, one could ostensibly engage in cultural storytelling that addresses issues of class, gender, sexual orientation, or religion, and never explicitly reference race. In fact, this phenomenon is more commonly practiced than is often noted. For example, the Hollywood movie industry for decades often told a wide range of stories examining virtually all aspects of our lived experiences and often did so without ever recognizing race unless the story was specifically about race. Even though race was never explicitly named or considered, many of these stories nevertheless contained powerful messages and substories about it, while egregiously failing to acknowledge it. Movies that featured Black people, for example, were often labeled "Black movies," while the voluminous body of cinematic productions that featured all white cast members were never labeled as "white movies." While cultural storytelling is a valuable enterprise for us all to engage in, racial storytelling is particularly poignant and essential for all of us to embrace given the widespread effects of race and racial bias on our everyday lives.

For many racially oppressed groups, racial storytelling serves a multitude of important functions that are well beyond the purview of those typically ascribed to storytelling. For example, there are stories that honor and celebrate acts of defiance and sociopolitical resistance that provide alternative stories to those chronicled by those who oppress; while yet other stories offer emotional catharsis and healing, recognition of heroism and the counteracting of devaluation. Stories can also empower those who have been stripped of their voices, commissioned, and coerced into learned voicelessness. Stories, and the process of storytelling, provide a pathway for the voiceless to rediscover and reclaim the power of their voices. Stories and culturally rich, sophisticated approaches to storytelling often grant freedom to the racially oppressed to verbalize and discuss issues that they were often forbidden to say out loud, or directly say at all.

Racial storytelling can also be a very powerful instrument for white people to use as a vehicle for exploring white identity development, racial bias, and the myriad subtle and overt, intentional and unintentional, experiences with the intergenerational transmission of racial harm, as well as engagement of racial activism, where relevant. It is common for many whites to engage in cultural storytelling that highlights ethnicity, religion, immigration history, or some other aspect of their cultural identity, with minimal to no attention devoted to their stories as racial beings.

Therapy, Stories, and Storytelling

Historically, stories and storytelling, in the strictest sense of the phenomena, were not commonly recognized as viable and legitimate therapeutic tools. While it was common for clients to share parts of their story, this process was often particularly limited to those aspects that the therapist deemed germane to the presenting problem and/or the therapeutic process. In the rare instances where storytelling was incorporated into the therapeutic process, it was often done with brevity and usually void of any acute attention to race. Unfortunately, having the overall space to discuss extensive and intricate racially focused stories in therapy was not routinely considered a viable dimension of mainstream psychotherapy. For example, Milton Erickson, psychiatrist and internationally acclaimed hypnotist, was one of the first clinicians to recognize stories and storytelling as a component of his clinical hypnosis work (Rosen, 1991). This work, although highly regarded within the psychotherapy community both historically and contemporarily, did not center sociocultural issues, and especially not race.

Creating space for the meaningful incorporation of racial storytelling into the process of therapy is of paramount significance. In fact, one of the critical tasks associated with striving toward becoming a racially sensitive therapist ultimately involves rethinking the process of therapy and the tools, tactics, and techniques that we have historically relied upon to effectively engage and treat Clients of Color. There are various vehicles of racial storytelling that therapists can utilize to help foster racial conversations in treatment as well as augment clients' ability to seamlessly introduce and address race without it appearing forced, disjointed, or awkward.

Narrative Means to Stories

White and Epston (1990), in their groundbreaking book *Narrative Means to Therapeutic Ends*, introduced the notion of stories as a potent dimension of clients' lives and the therapeutic process. Their theory and treatment approach were predicated on the premise that we all live lives ensconced in stories (narratives), many of which are shaped by dominant stories promulgated by the broader culture. Clinicians influenced by White and Epston's work often expanded their therapeutic approaches beyond the parameters of narrowly focused, traditional talk therapy. They often did so by their reliance on the power of story and by encouraging their clients to write letters, poems, essays, and stories to themselves as well as to their loved ones and many others. Stories, in narrative therapy (White & Epston, 1990), serve a multitude of roles, including personal transformation and healing, as well as serving as a powerful vehicle for emotional catharsis and acknowledging the potency of subjugated stories. In narrative's storytelling approach to therapy, the client's suffering and problems are treated as internalized stories that must ultimately be externalized if healing is to be actualized. In fact, this is a major goal of the treatment that paves the way for the client to "re-story" (i.e., reauthor or retell) their story, which promotes self-liberation, healing, and new ways of conceptualizing one's problem.

Songs as Stories

Raheim (2019) asserts that

> narrative theory provides useful analytical tools to examine how songs serve to support people who are experiencing oppression and its effects. Because many songs are stories set to music, a narrative perspective is ideal for understanding how songs may operate in people's lives, because it emphasizes the principle that multiple realities exist and are socially constructed through our narratives. (p. 552)

Songs as stories can be major instruments for promoting hope by assisting clients in revealing the inner contours of their souls and finding sources of inspiration. As Duffy (2007) confirms, "the music we carry within us also influences the dreams we create for ourselves" (p. 18).

Hardy and Laszloffy (2006) used "songs as stories" as a major conduit and therapeutic staple in their work with angry and aggressive youth in therapy, and especially with those who refused to talk or were struggling with dehumanizing loss. Hardy and Laszloffy (2006) noted,

We have yet to meet an adolescent who doesn't love some type of music, whether it's rap, country, gospel, rock, blues, reggae, or even classical. Whatever an adolescent's musical taste might be, we have found that music facilitates an instant pathway to an individual's nerve center. For this reason, we often invite adolescents to share their favorite songs or musical pieces, and we ask them to explain why this song or piece of music is meaningful to them. Some of the most passionate, introspective, and vulnerable disclosures from adolescents occurred in response to the question "What song would you pick to say something about your life, and why?" (p. 232)

Movies and Video Clips as Stories

As is the case with songs, movies are visual stories that can be a powerful therapeutic tool. The use of movies and video clips as vehicles of storytelling can facilitate connecting with a client, as well as promoting self-reflection and self-exploration via metaphor and symbolism. While utilizing and relying on movies in individual therapy can be quite challenging due to the time constraints associated with the 50–60-minute clinical hour, they do make for excellent homework assignments that then can be explored during therapy. Carefully edited clips from movies can also be a very potent therapeutic tool in instances where it may not be feasible to effectively utilize a full-length movie. On the other hand, I have used movies as a pathway to storytelling extensively in group therapy and with adolescents in individual and family treatment. Hardy and Laszloffy (2006) warn that it is important to have a series of structured questions available as prompts to help frame the storytelling experience. Five standard questions that are frequently employed with adolescents in therapy are as follows:

1. What was the basic story about?

2. What messages about life did this movie teach?

3. Which character did you identify with the most and why?

4. Which character did you identify least with and why?

5. What scene in the movie affected you most powerfully and why? (Hardy & Laszloffy, 2006, pp. 230–231)

The purpose of the questions is to help facilitate the telling of the client's story. The precise answers, whether they are true, false, real or imagined, authentic or fabricated, are irrelevant. In fact, very little energy, if any, is ever expended attempting to ascertain which elements of the story are in fact accurate or not. There is a therapeutic value in the actual telling of the story, whatever it might be, for both the client and the clinician.

For many Clients of Color, who are often the recipients of an endless stream of a lifelong bombardment of devaluation, shame, and embarrassment, mistrust can often be a powerful impediment to fully participating in therapy in an open and transparent way, at least during the early stages of the process. Storytelling can be a potent and effective tool for mitigating the impact of racial trauma wounds on the therapeutic process. Using music, poetry, videos, or other mediums, the clients' stories can be told (and exposed) metaphorically, symbolically, and indirectly. During the formative stages of the therapeutic process especially, racial storytelling can afford clients the benefit of being seen, heard, and understood without the burden of being or feeling prematurely exposed. The efficacy of this approach is highly dependent on the therapist's ability and willingness both to create space for storytelling and to be amenable to adjusting the pace of the process in a way that the story can be told in accordance with the needs of the client. Too often, the rules of engagement that undergird traditional approaches to therapy do not leave adequate space for the type of pacing and clinical modifications that are needed to provide more innovative, racially sensitive approaches to treatment.

Impediments to Integrating Racial and Cultural Storytelling in Therapy

For many clients experiencing marginalization, and especially the racially traumatized, racial storytelling is a very powerful and liberating therapeutic tool. Given the deeply rooted experiences that Clients of Color have with racialized trauma, and especially internalized devaluation (Hardy, 2023), many aspects of traditional Eurocentric approaches to psychotherapy present some formidable challenges for some clients, even when therapy is sought and desired. Traditional white-centered, Eurocentric approaches to therapy with the therapist as the professionally distant, non-self-disclosing, aloof, emotionally detached, objective observer and interpreter are problematic in two major ways. First, this therapeutic stance organizes the therapy in a way that what the therapist ultimately gets and discovers is often dictated by what is pursued. Unless the therapy is some psychoanalytically oriented form, there is often very little space for clients to talk frankly and uninhibitedly without the therapist framing and rigidly structuring the session. Second, and perhaps more importantly, the aforementioned approach and structuring of the session, for many Clients of Color, as noted earlier, can activate internalized devaluation, which in turn can heighten worry, suspicion, or guardedness about certain questions they are asked and whether their responses are "being (negatively) analyzed." These issues are often exacerbated by factors such as these: (1) the therapist's need to demonstrate fidelity to a particular manualized model of treatment; (2) the therapy must be conducted and completed within a predetermined number of sessions; or (3) if or when there is a hyperfocus on product over process. All these factors tend to restrict the degrees of freedom that the therapist may exercise to improvise the process or to make other seamless clinical adjustments necessary to sensitively respond to extenuating race-related circumstances that may emerge. Given the racial history of the United States and the racial context of the broader society that is always a backdrop to therapy, these issues are even more pressing in cross-racial therapy, with a white therapist working with Clients of Color.

Integration and creation of therapeutic space for racial storytelling are often critical dimensions associated with providing racially sensitive therapy. Unfortunately, however, utilizing racial storytelling as a therapeutic strategy is hardly considered mainstream. It is not codified in a way that would be easily billable as a legitimate approach to treatment. As an approach to therapy, it is often questioned, if not discredited, by claims that it is not empirically based, or lacks outcome data, and other claims rooted in the centrality of whiteness. Furthermore, it is time-consuming, and it requires the therapist to have patience and exquisite tracking skills utilizing a racial lens. While many clinicians are imbued with the former, the latter is often an ongoing challenge.

Over the course of my career, I have supervised numerous clinicians who have never discussed or mentioned the issue of race in therapy. In the rare instances where it was addressed, it was often done in a perfunctory or cursory manner often lacking in depth and substance. Even when collecting elaborate family and psychosocial histories, as well as using genograms as a centerpiece of the clinical process, critical family of origin issues were routinely discussed in a deracialized way, void of any attention devoted to sociocultural issues. When working with racially traumatized and other oppressed populations, as noted by White and Epston (1990), storytelling can be a powerful therapeutic tool. Hardy (2023) has identified three types of stories that are critical to explore when addressing the invisible wounds of racial trauma. These stories are important to pursue whether they are connected to or constitute the presenting issue or not. The pursuit of stories of suffering, stories of struggle, and stories of survival, according to Hardy (2023), provides a framework that grants the client permission and an extensive metaphorical runway to engage (and indulge) in racial storytelling. In our lived experiences, these three stories are not nearly as clearly and distinctively delineated as they will appear in the discussion that follows. In fact, they are so complexly intertwined that conceptualizing and placing them in discrete categories is daunting. Yet, despite this challenge, it is imperative for the therapist to attempt to disaggregate them during the treatment process, at least initially, to help facilitate the client's understanding of how each story-theme shapes their life. Highlighting each story unto itself also invites the client to think critically and comprehensively about each specific one in a much more focused way. Hence, part of the therapist's role is to then take the fragments of each story and help the client develop a more integrated story that honors their re-storied past, recognition of the impact of trauma and oppression, their strengths, and the consummation of a reconstituted sense of self.

Stories of Suffering, Struggle, and Survival as Therapeutic Strategies

Stories of Suffering

Stories of suffering refers to the myriad painful life-shaping, life-altering, and life-defining experiences that are somewhat universal dimensions of what it means to be human. In short, these are the stories connected to the core of our hurt and pain. They are boundary-less in terms of age, life cycle, gender, race, and all other sociocultural variables. While the term "suffering" can be construed as a synonym for pain, hardships, or setbacks, its preferred use throughout this chapter is intended to convey the lifelong and enduring nature of the experience. It is used to acknowledge what Cassell (2004) describes as the "threat against the intactness of a person" (p. 131). Racism, sexism, homophobia, and other oppressive forces are perpetual lifelong threats against the intactness of one's essence and personhood. For this reason, the term "suffering" seems appropriate.

Most clients' early experiences with trauma, regardless of racial background, are usually contained within their stories of suffering. A story of suffering is rarely a single story but rather a complex amalgam of sociocultural oppression, developmental, and family of origin issues. With gentle infusions of curiosity and probing questions by the therapist, many clients begin to see how their personal problems and ultimately their (psycho-emotional) suffering are inextricably entangled with race and other sociocultural forces. Moreover, these experiences are often enmeshed with a host of complicated emotions ranging from anger and rage to shame. In fact, it is virtually impossible for clients to tell their stories of suffering without also painfully rubbing against deeply buried feelings of shame and devaluation. Yet it is often liberating, especially for Clients of Color and other oppressed clients, to have opportunities to tell their story, uninterruptedly, and without question, censure, or judgment. To be afforded this opportunity in therapy is a gift because unfortunately, it is far beyond difficult to do in everyday civilian life, where many white people believe and behave as if it is their inalienable right to deny, negate, (re)define, and/or rewrite the experiences of People of Color as a matter of routine.

Supporting Clients of Color and creating emotional, psychological, physical, and spiritual safety for the telling of their stories of suffering is a therapeutically transformative experience. It facilitates the seamless integration of race into the clinical process while also ensuring that the therapist executes the broker of permission role in the most efficacious way. Thus, race is not treated as a separate independent issue severed from all other dimensions of the client's life. Instead, it is prominently woven into and connected to other facets of the(ir) story. The verbal prompts that are used to invite stories of suffering are usually short, concise, and open-ended. The following sample prompts are instrumental in promoting the telling of stories of suffering:

1. Can you tell me a story about when [how, where] you experienced being slighted, harmed, or discriminated against based on your race (color of your skin or some other variable/physical characteristic)?

2. Can you tell me a story about a time when you were confronted with a major race-related life obstacle that you had to overcome but doubted that you could/would? What part of your doubt was attributable to race?

3. What is the story about you and race that you will always remember? What is the story about you, your family, and race that you will always remember?

4. What is a story about you, your family, and race that you have a hard time telling [forgetting, remembering], and so on?

5. Can you tell me about a time [story] that highlighted the painful impact of race in your [or your family's] life?

All questions connected to stories of suffering should ideally be designed to encourage clients, regardless of their racial background, to think critically about and consider the ways in which their suffering occurs within a broader sociocultural context. Regardless of the racial background of the client or therapist, this premise is an important one to remember because it paves the way to develop a more comprehensive understanding of the connections between classical manifestations of trauma and racial and sociocultural trauma. As noted earlier, stories of suffering are predictably and invariably interspersed with stories of struggle in a way that can obscure a client's understanding of the role each plays in their everyday life.

Stories of Struggle

In addition to creating opportunities for clients to tell their stories of suffering, it is equally important for them to tell their stories of struggle as well. These stories highlight the truncated, completed, failed, and successful attempts that often typify one's effort to cope with and overcome suffering. Addiction and recovery, as well as relapses, criminal recidivism, serial intimate relationships, drug use and dealing, and other illegal and legal activities are but a short list of behaviors that constitute attempted solutions to overcome, ameliorate, and/or transcend one's pain, hardships, and personal obstacles, that is, suffering. Thus, stories of struggle encapsulate the sum of all the efforts that one undertakes to overcome hardships and setbacks ranging from conquering personal emotional-psychological demons to escaping the life-altering effects of poverty.

Stories of struggle, while often painful, shameful, and (re)traumatizing to tell, are also vitally important to share in the presence of a caring and validating witness. With the therapist as witness, stories of struggle can and often do become hope-inducing by making it possible for clients to recognize their acts of resistance, resilience, and efforts to recover, even if all the initial efforts failed and were sternly unsuccessful. The purpose of telling these stories is to highlight the virtually inseparable connection between suffering and struggle while lauding the power embedded in the struggle—individually, collectively, and culturally.

Stories of struggle must be extracted from the vaults of clients' vast life experiences and told in detail, because they help to provide the rich sociocultural context often associated with a wide and varying range of self-defeating, self-destructive, and self-sabotaging behaviors that many clients may exhibit. All these behaviors are often major parts of one's stories of struggle to overcome suffering and to ultimately survive. For poor clients, regardless of race, and Clients of Color, regardless of class, the telling of stories of struggle is a major act of personal liberation. The

RACIAL AND CULTURAL STORYTELLING

act of telling and being witnessed with empathy and validation serve to combat devaluation, transform shame, and dismantle the metaphorical walls of hopelessness that are responsible for the spiritual death and demise of so many People of Color. The racially traumatized, as well as those suffering from other manifestations of sociocultural trauma and oppression, are born into conditions of lifelong perpetual struggle, and the acknowledgment, honoring, and telling of these stories are crucial to healing and transformation.

Some of the clinical prompts that can be used by therapists to elicit stories of struggle are:

1. Please tell me a story that typifies your group's [family's, your] struggle to overcome adversity in your life.

2. Please tell me a story about where the legacy to never quit or never give up comes from. Who in your life exemplified this noble act?

3. Please tell me a story about a time when the suffering you experienced as a POC was either overshadowed or counteracted by your instincts to survive or when your instincts to survive were overwhelmed by your suffering.

4. Where did you learn, or who taught you, about hanging in and never giving in or up? Or not fighting back and just accepting your fate?

5. Can you tell me a story about a time you struggled to overcome, and it just didn't work out because the burden was too heavy to overcome?

Stories of struggle are principally formulated and shaped by the (often relentless) efforts that one extends and expends to cope with, combat, and overcome suffering, whether they are ultimately deemed successful or unsuccessful. The strategies, venues, and vehicles typically employed to accomplish this feat can vacillate between functional and dysfunctional, growth enhancing and growth inhibiting, as well as effective and ineffective. Regardless of the experience and its valence, stories of struggle warrant acknowledgment and must be told, heard, witnessed, and ultimately validated as an integral dimension of the healing process. It is critical for therapists to create the physical, emotional, and psychological space for the telling of and listening to these stories. Granting permission for the client to tell their stories of struggle with vigor and a sense of pride and dignity can be empowering and transformative. For many racially oppressed and traumatized clients, the mantra that there can be no survival without struggle, and to be born a Person of Color is to essentially be born in a context of struggle, is an organizing principle that underscores the saliency of the entanglement of struggle and survival.

Stories of Survival

Stories of suffering and struggle are often complexly interwoven with *stories of survival*, which often highlight acts of heroism, tenacity, perseverance, and resiliency. Unfortunately, for many Clients of Color, suffering and struggle are a way of life. Thus, the frequency and normalcy of these experiences can contribute to a sense of oblivion that some clients have about the potent and pervasive role that these stories play in their everyday lives. Rather than survival being regarded as a celebrated feat, a marker of perseverance, or a testament to one's fortitude, it is alternatively perceived as merely doing what is needed or necessary. While it certainly can be both, recognizing stories of survival can be quite instrumental in magnifying, accentuating, and naming strengths that clients have but may not be aware they possess. The telling of these stories and the process of having them witnessed also help to affirm for clients that survival is an ongoing process, a journey on which there will inevitably be many predictable and unpredictable metaphorical stops along the road of life. It helps clients who have traversed great odds and barriers to recognize the extraordinary embedded in what they might consider to be the mundaneness of the ordinary. Furthermore, it can be a much-needed reminder that tremendous personal power can be embedded in carrying out that which is believed to be routine, pragmatic, or perfunctory.

It is crucial for clients harmed by racialized trauma and other ill effects of sociocultural oppression to tell their stories of survival repetitively as a grounding experience and a safeguard against recurring intrusive ideations about being an imposter. Often, internal questions about whether one is an imposter, that is, a fake or inauthentic version of who and what one purports to be, can create doubt about whether one has genuinely overcome the complexities of one's conditions or is just pretending to have done so. Those who must incessantly spar to extricate themselves from the firm grasp of racial trauma and sociocultural oppression are often inundated with self-doubt and lingering existential questions regarding whether their achievements, success in overcoming, and survival are real or merely the vestiges of imposter syndrome. Considering these issues, the notion of survival is fluid and an often-subjective process. It is not an endpoint or a rigidly fixed destination that one arrives at and becomes stagnant. Nor is it an individual accomplishment but instead one that is achieved only through the collective sacrifice of the group, tribe, or community to whom one belongs. For those who are targeted, traumatized, and oppressed, what is required to survive and what is demanded of those committed to doing it can shift dramatically over time. Consequently, stories of survival can and do also shift as life circumstances dictate.

The following list highlights a few sample questions that therapists might ask to invite the sharing of stories of survival:

1. As you think about your extended family's quest and struggle to survive living under oppressive racial, economic, and maybe even other conditions, what lessons did you learn about how to survive? Can you tell me about a time that jumps to the front of your memory as we talk about this?

2. What legacies and life lessons about surviving do you hope to leave for the next generation? Or hope that they might learn from knowing you the way they do? What ancestral and/or family of origin survival strategies and techniques were passed on to you or were not done so in a way that you would have liked?

3. Survival and surviving can be the flip side of suffering and struggle; what have your life experience, accomplishments, and setbacks taught you about the connection between setbacks [suffering], struggle, and survival? Can you tell me [a story] about a time in your life when you had to deal with these issues and did so successfully?

4. If you had to identify three key words or concepts that you would associate with surviving or survival, what would they be? Why these three? Can you tell me about a time in your life when one or all three words were critical to your survival?

5. For our next session, can you please bring in a song, poem, book, and so on that tells *your* story of survival in a way that you would want it told, or would tell if you had the opportunity?

The stories of suffering, struggle, and survival have been described here in a neat, orderly, linear, and sequential fashion for discussion and clarity purposes. However, during the process of therapy, these stories, when pursued, are usually far messier, more circular, and entangled. During moments of distress, some clients may not be able to neatly articulate the stories of their lives in the clearly delineated and compartmentalized ways in which they appear in this chapter. Regardless of the approach the client employs to engage in the storytelling process, it is crucial for the therapist to meet the client where they are and recognize that there are no rigidly prescribed rules governing how, or in what sequence, these stories must be told. Thus, if a client feels a sense of urgency and the necessity to start the process by focusing on their stories of struggle or survival, for example, it would be important for the therapist to sanction the client doing so. Rather than suggesting or coercing the client to adhere to telling the story in a particular sequence, it would be far more important for the therapist to grant the space for the storytelling to unfold, engage in deep listening, and meticulously track the themes associated with suffering, struggle, and survival. If at any point the storytelling became confusingly entangled or conflated with other stories in ways that appeared overwhelming or at risk of impeding or limiting the client's growth and well-being, it would be important for the therapist to then offer the framework of stories of suffering, struggle, and survival. Doing so would provide the client with a framework to help organize their thinking, gain clarity, and become more emotionally regulated. This type of clarity would facilitate a deepening of the storytelling process and the therapeutic alliance.

Demonstrating the ability to work effectively with and promote racial storytelling in therapy is an important clinical task associated with providing racially sensitive therapy. The skillful and competent mastery of this task is required of both the aspiring and accomplished racially sensitive practitioner. Racial and cultural storytelling is not aligned with a particular theoretical orientation or model of therapy. Thus, it is most effective when it is delicately and seamlessly integrated within a therapist's customary therapeutic approach. The effective implementation and execution of racial and cultural storytelling as a powerful therapeutic tool is not just a simple matter of mastering a technique (although this is massively important), it also requires substantive Self of the Therapist work or, as Hardy (2023) describes it, Selves of the Therapist work. Hence, as discussed in Chapter 2, intensive Self of the Therapist work is central to the process of becoming a racially sensitive therapist. A major dimension of this work must involve encouraging therapists, whether in training, beginning, or experienced, to participate in a process of and racial and cultural storytelling as a component of their clinical training and supervision. When these strategies are integrated into the clinical educational process, it affords the clinician the opportunity to learn the unteachable dimensions of the work by experiencing it.

Racial and Cultural Storytelling in Clinical Training and Supervision

As is the case with therapy, storytelling must also be a fundamental component of the supervision, education, and training processes of preparing racially sensitive therapists. It is important for clinicians to establish facility with cultural storytelling, which takes a broad sociocultural approach, as well as racial storytelling, which is a derivative of the former. The dichotomy between racial storytelling and cultural storytelling, to a degree, is an artificial one since culture includes race. However, as noted at the beginning of this chapter, the tendency to marginalize or deny the significance of race altogether makes it essential to punctuate racial storytelling to ensure that race is addressed substantively. The benefit of incorporating racial and cultural storytelling in all approaches to clinical training is twofold: (1) it allows clinicians to learn the intricacies of the storytelling process, by doing it; and (2) it is a powerful tool for promoting racially and culturally informed Self of the Therapist work.

Historically, most approaches to Self of the Therapist work have focused on encouraging clinicians to consider the ways in which their family of origin experiences may have impacted them as human beings and ultimately as clinicians. This work has and continues to be a long-standing and immensely valuable dimension of therapy training across many clinical disciplines. It has been a powerful clinical training tool for beginning and experienced clinicians, and regrettably it also has been quite limited in its scope. Unfortunately, most traditional approaches to Self of the Therapist work have either ignored the omnipresent cultural dimensions associated with it, such as race, gender, sexual orientation, and others, or only addressed these issues in a cursory and superficial manner. Even the genogram that is routinely used in clinical training programs and supervision as a Self of the Therapist tool often focuses heavily on intergenerational family dynamics, which is needed, and yet its overall impact is diminished by the scant attention that is often devoted to race and other cultural factors. While this traditional approach allows for the sharing of rich family of origin stories, discussions of racial issues are usually relegated to the margins of the family dynamics discourse, unless, of course, one of the following conditions is present: (1) the presenter is a Person of Color, (2) there is an interracial relationship or multiracial child within the family that is being presented, or (3) the facilitator is a Person of Color.

To compensate for the inattention that is often accorded to the genogram process, Hardy and Laszloffy (1995) introduced the cultural genogram as a tool to promote racial and cultural storytelling. The design of the instrument requires therapists in training and supervision to address issues of race, class, gender, and ethnicity, and other dimensions of culture, explicitly. For example, according to Hardy and Laszloffy (1995), participants are required to address a standard set of questions that are an integral part of the cultural genogram preparation process. The following is an abridged list of some of the required questions:

1. What were the migration patterns of the group?

2. If other than Native American, under what conditions did your family (or their descendants) enter the United States (immigrant, political refugee, slave, etc.)?

3. What were/are the group's experiences with oppression? What were/are the markers of oppression?

4. What issues divide members within the same group? What are the sources of intragroup conflict?

5. Describe the relationship between the group's identity and your national ancestry (if the group is defined in terms of nationality, please skip this question).

6. What significance does race, skin color, and hair play within the group?

7. What is/are the dominant religion(s) of the group? What role does religion and spirituality play in the everyday lives of members of the group? . . .

8. How are gender roles defined within the group? How is sexual orientation regarded?

9. (a) What prejudices or stereotypes does this group have about itself? (b) What prejudices and stereotypes do other groups have about this group? (c) What prejudices or stereotypes does this group have about other groups?

10. What role (if any) do names play in the group? Are there rules, mores, or rituals governing the assignment of names?

11. How is social class defined in the group? . . .

12. How is family defined in the group?

13. How does this group view outsiders in general and mental health professionals specifically? . . .

14. What are the ways in which pride/shame issues of each group are manifested in your family system? ...

15. If more than one group comprises your culture of origin, how were the differences negotiated in your family? What were the intergenerational consequences? How has this impacted you personally and as a therapist? (Hardy & Laszloffy, 1995, p. 232)

In addition to addressing these questions, participants of the cultural genogram process are expected to explore and discuss pride and shame issues associated with their respective culture, as well as their family of origin experiences. These foci often pave the way for them to delve into their stories of suffering, struggle, and survival. These processes are most effective and impactful when they are conducted and completed in group and/or dyadic supervision or training circles. Diaries, songs, digital recordings, video playback, short stories, and poetry are some of the many possible mediums that can be utilized to augment the storytelling process.

In storytelling that emanates from the cultural genogram process, therapists, on the pathway to becoming racially sensitive practitioners, must also be willing to answer five fundamental questions thoughtfully and substantively in their training programs and/or in clinical supervision. These queries often require interrogation of the Self of the Therapist and a willingness to be self-reflective and self-disclosing. It is through intensive processes such as these that therapists can further develop and refine the relational skills, therapeutic temperament, and clinical acumen necessary to integrate racial and cultural storytelling into the main work of clinical practice. The questions are:

1. What are the pieces and particles of suffering that have delivered me to do the [soul] work that I am committed to doing? What are the ways in which my oppressor/harmer is complexly tied to my clinical work, or my personal liberation, if at all?

2. How do I identify racially, and how does that provide a prism through which I see the world and believe I am seen? How does how I see the world and believe I am seen inform my approach to therapy? How

does it shape my views about help, health, healing, and harm, as well as suffering, struggle, and survival?

3. Who am I culturally? What is it that I now know about who I am culturally that I didn't know at another point in my life, and what is the impact of this new knowledge, if any, on my work as an aspiring racially sensitive therapist?

4. What is a truth about who I know my Self to be culturally that I have always known? How does what I have always known about who I am culturally inform [or how has it informed] me as a therapist?

5. In what ways, if any, have my suffering, struggles, and survival facilitated and impeded my ability to become a racially sensitive therapist? During the best version of my Self as a Therapist, what are the strengths and weaknesses I display in my evolution to become a racially sensitive therapist?

These racially and culturally based existential questions are critical for the aspiring racially sensitive therapist to answer, preferably in a context where others are bearing witness to the experience. Doing so enables and empowers clinicians to learn the unteachable dimensions of the racial and cultural storytelling process, as well as the potency of experientially based Self of the Therapist work.

Summary

This chapter asserts that racial and cultural storytelling is a valuable clinical tool for therapists to use in therapy when working with Clients of Color and other marginalized clients grappling with racialized and sociocultural trauma. Songs, spoken word, movies, genograms, and other methods are introduced as possible vehicles for fostering storytelling in therapy. Furthermore, three specific oppression-centric stories were introduced that both therapists and supervisors may use to structure and promote racial and cultural storytelling in therapy and beyond. The three stories (stories of suffering, stories of struggle, and stories of survival) were discussed as constituting a quasi-conceptual framework that could be employed to help inform and shape the storytelling process. In addition to its application to therapy, racial and cultural storytelling was also discussed as an effective training and supervisory tool that can help augment the Self of the Therapist work that is often integral to the preparation of effective therapists, especially those committed to the process of becoming racially sensitive therapists.

CHAPTER 6

Wandering and Wondering in the Wilderness: On Being White and Jewish in the United States

BONNIE BERMAN CUSHING, LCSW

It is always the same: once you are liberated, you are forced to ask who you are.

—JEAN BAUDRILLARD, *America*

Prologue

When I first started out as a therapist in 1988, I had but an inkling of the role that my various social identities and positionality played in the clinical work I provided. My social work education supplied me little opportunity to name—much less grapple with—the various spaces I occupied in our society and how they shaped my worldview and therapeutic practice. Subsequent traditional training, as well as working in community mental health, only reinforced an outward-facing focus on the problems presented by those I served—not my own limitations or their genesis and manifestations.

It was not until I was hired to assess the psychiatric fitness of inmates (99% of whom were indigent and of Color) for a work-release program in a New York City jail that I was awakened to how much I didn't even know that I didn't know about myself. Thus began my journey to find out how the stories I had been told about who I am, and the socialization and structures which supported that ignorance, had blinded me to the ways I walked, and worked, in the world. These stories, and the stories of all of us who aspire to be healers of trauma and relational breaches, are crucially important to the work we do and the lives we live. We need to interrogate how we see ourselves and how we are seen by others, and to unearth and challenge the unearned access and/or unfair barriers conferred by the hierarchies of our society. In the therapeutic, training, and organizing spaces we occupy, we must continually track how our multiple identities intersect, compete, and are triggered in our interactions with others in both the therapy room and beyond its walls.

I share the narrative that follows in the spirit of my own healing and desire to help others to heal. I was at first reluctant to share my messiness around these two identities publicly but, as I have learned, stories have an agenda of their own—and these insisted (with the assistance of my editor) on being told. I offer them up in the hope that they light a way forward for my fellow therapists as they continue to shine a light for me.

◊ ◊ ◊

Stories shape, scar, stretch, and sober us. Some accompany us into the world, embedded in our bones and biology. Frequently the ones that are the most impactful are the ones communicated covertly, sheltered below consciousness, silently dictating our alliances and behavior.

This chapter is about three of the many storylines that have shaped me—stories that have tutored me in what it means to be a Jew, what it means to be white, and what it means to navigate both at the same time. These narratives have a tumultuous, triangulating relationship with each other. My Jewishness and my whiteness frequently demand that I choose one self over the other, and the challenge of their integration can leave me feeling hopeless that I will ever find a home where I can live a fully actualized life that aligns with my highest values. The experience of trying to reconcile these identities is evident in the very writing of this chapter. I have struggled for some linear order and clarity—yet despite what has seemed like endless coaxing, it's been elusive. I can only invite you to wander around this circuitous and contradictory wilderness alongside me.

I have found one way, however, to loosely contain these contentious narratives by way of a story that captured me, heart and soul, when a little girl—the Jewish story of Passover. Of the thousands of Torah allegories recounted to me over the years, the one that has influenced me the most is the story of our exodus from Egypt and subsequent sojourn in the Sinai Desert. Its themes of freedom, betrayal, and redemption completely captivated me. Its overarching message, "Do not oppress an outsider, for you know the heart of an outsider, since you were outsiders in the land of Egypt" (Messianic Jewish Family Bible Society, 2014, lines 19–21) deeply reverberates within me to this day. Following this injunction and answering its call has become the most significant expression of my Jewishness and the primary form in which I worship.

The root of the Hebrew word for Egypt, "Mitzraim," is *tzar*, which means narrow or constrained. For a long time, I simply saw that as a reference to our enslaved status in Egypt. When I later read in the Talmud that an estimated four out of five enslaved Hebrews remained in Egypt (*Number of Jews*, n.d.), not only because they feared dying in the desert but also because they were so steeped in Egyptian culture that they were unwilling to leave, "constraint" took on a deeper meaning for me—one of the seduction and entrapment of assimilation and its accompanying loss of both faith and moral direction.

As I ruminate on the Passover story, I can't help but see a powerful parallel to my own experience of being white and Jewish. As a second-generation white Jewish American, I enjoy a level of freedom and security my grandparents could only have dreamed of. But this is not the destination—the Promised Land—that I have always longed for, for myself and for the world. Unshackled, yet still very much in bondage, it is the desert wilderness I now wander in. I am a descendant of Jews who accepted, gladly, the invitation to live white in this land. I have internalized whiteness, enjoy the privileges it has given me, and periodically enact its manifestations despite my best intentions and strongly held Jewish values. This has impaired my effectiveness as an antiracist organizer and educator and impeded my ability to form trusting, sustainable cross-racial relationships. This has compromised my humanity and disconnected me from what I believe, in my heart, it truly means to live a Jewish life.

Jewish to the Core

I have loved—and still wholeheartedly love—being Jewish. I love our rituals, our mysticism, our earthiness. I love the minor key we chant in. I appreciate how highly valued questioning is in our culture and religious traditions, and the centrality of family, especially children. I cherish our humor (oh, our life-sustaining, life-saving humor!), our warmth, and the unspoken kinship I feel in the presence of other Jews. Perhaps, most of all, I treasure the overarching precept to engage in *tikkun olam*, the repair of our broken world. Yet none of these reasons sufficiently explain the depth of my identification as a Jew. It is primary, immediate, essential. It is who I am. I grew up in an unequivocally, unapologetically Jewish home despite—or perhaps—because we lived in an overwhelmingly Christian town within a larger society steeped in Christian hegemony. The primary distinction wasn't that we were white in comparison to People of Color; it was that we were Jews in comparison to the Gentiles. We were different and, although it was never overtly stated, somehow special. There was pride in being part of a resilient people that, despite thousands of years of persecution and exile, were still here. The European Holocaust, having just occurred a little over a decade before I was born, hung like ash in the air, a silent reminder that security has always been a fragile and fickle state for us.

Perhaps in part to counter that sense of vulnerability, stories circulated regularly in my home of our striving and exceptionalism. How even though less than 0.2% of the world population was Jewish, 22.5% of Nobel Laureates were Jewish. That Jews had been instrumental in founding the NAACP, were Freedom Riders, were lawyers that represented the downtrodden. That we were contributors and champions of the arts. Whenever a Jewish person achieved something great, it was pointed out and celebrated.

At the same time, the transgressions of any Jew anywhere were equally notable. They were a *shonda*—a shame that represented and reflected upon all Jews. Their sins were our sins, and with those sins always came a visceral fear of retribution—especially if what they were guilty of reinforced the stereotypes of Jews as greedy or un-American. We needed to be vigilant about anti-Semitism surfacing. We could never forget what had been done to Jews throughout history simply because they were Jewish. We had a personal obligation to the uplift and continuity of our people.

When I was 12, I received a coffee table book, the title of which I no longer recall, as a Bat Mitzvah present. It contained photographs of the diaspora of Jews around the globe. I was surprised by the Black face of the girl on the book's cover and the variety of hues I found throughout its pages. The only Jews I had ever seen or known were white. It is testament to the ongoing segregation and racism within our own Jewish communities, and the power and influence of whiteness, that I had universalized my own skin tone to that of Jews worldwide.

My home was also patriotically American. With both sets of grandparents having escaped anti-Semitism in Romania, the fact that they now lived in a land of relative safety and endless possibilities was a blessing. My parents were progressive liberals who were civically active. They believed in the promise of this country, and they passed that belief on to me and my siblings. But there was very little talk of how that promise remained unfulfilled for People of Color in our country.

My grandparents were not accepted fully into white society. As part of the hordes of "dirty Jews" that immigrated from Eastern Europe at the turn of the twentieth century, they were naturalized citizens with the right to vote (unlike other groups of marginalized people), yet were socially shunned and legally excluded from many institutions and neighborhoods. They clung to the ways of the old country, a source of constant embarrassment to me.

My parents were born in the 1920s—the harshest period of anti-Semitism, so far, in the United States—a decade that gave birth to Henry Ford's *The International Jew* (2024), heard the radio rants of Father Coughlin (Hahami, 2022) and Charles Lindbergh (Margaritoff, 2020), and saw the immigration quotas of the Johnson-Reed Act (Diamond, 2020). They understood where Jews were positioned in the American society of their time. My mother warned me and my siblings that we would encounter people who thought less of us because we were Jewish—but that it was our obligation to teach them otherwise by acting above reproach.

Indoctrination Into Whiteness

One of the ways that my grandparents did assimilate into white American society was in their embrace of anti-Blackness. This was the first and perhaps most important prerequisite to admission, and they apparently absorbed it through osmosis. I have distinct memories while in elementary school of being my paternal grandmother's after-school "checkout apprentice" at our family's store. I watched my grandmother, day after day, kibbitz (chat) with the white schoolchildren buying candy. But whenever Black children would come in, her demeanor would shift dramatically. Her whole body would stiffen as she vigilantly tracked them perusing the candy shelves. When they came to the counter with their purchases, there was no smiling, no kibbitzing, no warmth. Once they would leave, she would return to her jovial self. I was both confused and distressed by this. Some of these kids were friends of mine. But I said nothing, fearing it would make her angry. Over time, I was taught by this person I loved and depended on that Black people were—for some unknown and unproven reason—not to be trusted. Perhaps more importantly, I was taught not to question biased behavior, lest I lose approval and love. As a result of this early socialization, silence became my default behavior. It has taken discipline and practice for me to break this pattern when witnessing racism.

My mother, despite her rhetoric about equality, also had a deep-seated mistrust of Black people. Her ongoing suspicions that our Black housekeeper Lizzie might be stealing from us was utterly perplexing to me. And, even from a tender age, Mom's resentment of my deep and abiding attachment to Lizzie registered. I witnessed my mother's cold, transactional treatment of her in ways I knew were just not right—but once again, my allegiance and reliance silenced me. My mother also harbored a deep fear of Black people—especially Black men. The uprisings of the 1960s magnified this significantly. We lived close to Asbury Park, New Jersey, one of the many cities throughout the country where racial rebellions broke out. Her outright terror of Black anger during, and following, that time had a lasting effect on me, one that has taken somatic work to begin to clear.

On the other hand, my father—having formed meaningful relationships with some Black soldiers in the World War II troop he was assigned—was committed to racial justice. I witnessed him speaking up and taking righteous risks on many occasions, such as when he weathered a townwide boycott (and my mother's ire) for hiring a Black salesman in the store. I recall countless arguments between my parents about racism and how we should be raised in the shadow of it. I both wholeheartedly aligned with my father's passion for justice and absorbed my mother's fear of Black enmity toward whites (just as I absorbed my mother's fear and anxiety about so many things). I still navigate that dance between my soul and my central nervous system to this day.

I grew up in the small town of Belmar, New Jersey, where half of the residents were Black. From infancy to age four I spent my weekdays at home with Lizzie while my parents worked. Weekends and after-school hours provided me lots of opportunity to play with the Black kids that lived in the blocks behind my family's 5-and-10 store. Along with my siblings, they were my earliest playmates. Although I certainly recognized the difference in our skin color, it was the fact that they went to church every Sunday and celebrated Christmas that was the most prominent difference between us. By second grade, however, I began to experience the racial chasm that was pulling us apart. The ease with which I gravitated to, and interacted with, Black people in my earliest years was slowly but surely replaced by the dis-ease of racism and, specifically, whiteness.

After my older brother started high school, we moved from Belmar—where he was attending school in Asbury Park—to Ocean Township, New Jersey. It was a chaotic time to move, as my father was terminally ill. What was the reason for uprooting us at such a time? Asbury High was majority Black, and Ocean Township High was overwhelmingly white. My siblings and I were told that we would be living in a "better" town so that we could attend a "better" school. We relocated to "safety" and were placed on the "right track." Again, nothing racially explicit was uttered and no questions were asked, but the implicit messaging was obvious and silently absorbed.

Saturated in Whiteness

So much of what it means to be white is difficult to pinpoint because it's about what doesn't happen to you, and what you are not. My mother did not clean other people's houses, as our Black housekeeper, or the housekeepers my aunts employed, did. I did not see the first appearance of my people in history books bound in shackles, nor people who looked like me rounded up by the police on the news.

What I did see were people that looked like me in all the teachers and administrators in my schools. I saw my shade in almost all the people in the magazines and books I read, all the people heralded in the history I was taught, and all the families I watched on television. In this way, I came to identify the face of authority, beauty, heroism, achievement, worthiness, and value as a white face—a face much like my own.

Growing up as a white person, there was never a hint that how I was received by nearly every institution and person—worthy of safety and credibility—had anything to do with the color of my skin. I assumed that "the talk" I received from my parents was a universal one: the sky was the limit; I could achieve anything my heart desired if I worked hard enough and played by the rules; the police were reliably there to help me if I ever was lost or in trouble. My subconscious conclusion, therefore, was that it was my personal intelligence, talent, charm, and/or work ethic that earned me this reception. And the other side of that coin was the subconscious, unspoken, and undisrupted belief that those who didn't have what I had, didn't receive the treatment I did, and didn't achieve what I achieved must have lacked sufficient intelligence, talent, charm, and/or work ethic. They hadn't earned it. There was some language around me being lucky and some instruction about the obligation to help others who weren't, but the critical role that being white served for me was completely obscured, as well as the unvarnished truth that the relative ease and advantages I had were gained at the expense of others.

Precariously White

Multiple times throughout our history, my people have escaped persecution and near annihilation only to migrate to a new land, assimilate into another host society, and frequently flourish for a time before being targeted once again. Ironically, our successful assimilation, our ability to become indispensable to the reigning power structure of each foreign culture, coupled with beliefs about Jewish conspiracies that have persisted for millennia, has to some degree provided the very justification for our eventual expulsion and/or murder. And it has also been the source of our moral undoing.

My lived experience embedded in American culture—and especially within the Episcopalian family I married into—let me know in no uncertain terms just how my way of being differed from "pure" white culture. I am too much—too direct, too loud, too emotional, too challenging. I don't worship the right God on the right day. I exist in a borderland wherein I am most definitely not a Person of Color, yet socially never deemed quite white enough.

White Nationalists do not recognize Jews as white either. In his article, "Skin in the Game: How Antisemitism Animates White Nationalism," African American activist Eric Ward (2017) explains, "Within social and economic justice movements committed to equality, we have not yet collectively come to terms with the centrality of antisemitism to White nationalist ideology" (para. 7). Ward continues, positing that a "well-meaning but counterproductive thicket of discourse has grown up insisting that Jews—of Ashkenazi descent, at least—are uncontestably White, and that to challenge this is to deny the workings of White privilege" (para. 24). It has been exceedingly difficult to hold both the truth of my racial advantage and the presence of anti-Semitism at the same time and not be called out in racial justice spaces for trying to escape being white. But we organizers for racial justice and equity need to grapple with the complexities of this dynamic, lest we play (as we are) into white supremacy's age-old strategy of divide and conquer. We end up fighting each other, instead of acting in solidarity against the real barrier to our collective liberation.

Singled Out Among Whites

In movement spaces I have occupied over the past three decades, I have heard People of Color add the adjective "Jewish" to "white" on more occasions than I can count. "My white Jewish professor," "my white Jewish boss," "the white Jewish shopkeeper down the street where I grew up." Each time I hear this, it activates my sense of vulnerability and defensiveness. And at each of these moments I try to remember this could very well be reflective of the lived experience of People of Color (especially Black) in urban areas, in the social service and academic arenas, the fields of media and entertainment, and more. Jews have been the slumlords, the merchants, the Hollywood producers, the lenders that were historically and, in many cases, intentionally positioned as the face of power and predation. Too many of us have cooperated in those roles. It is a stain on my people that goes back to Jews engaged in the slave trade and continues to the present day both in this country and through the brutal occupation of the Palestinian people by the State of Israel. Note: Since I wrote this chapter, devastating war has unfolded in Israel/Palestine, compelling me to acknowledge here the ongoing genocide of the Gazan people. I bring all of the complexity and complicity of my identities as a white, American Jew into this moment in history, taking whatever action I can to bring an end to the violence perpetrated on the Palestinians in the name of Jewish safety.

Yet what of the overwhelmingly Irish police that have been a militarized presence in Communities of Color for over a century? What of the overwhelmingly Anglo-Saxon Protestant politicians, bankers, and corporate CEOs that have occupied, and still occupy, the highest levels of our society? I have never heard their ethnic identities specified in our social justice meetings, conferences, or literature. Why are Jews singled out for more scrutiny than other ethnic groups within the white collective? Are we to be held to a higher standard? Are we somehow more culpable? Or is it possible that deep-seated anti-Semitism is operating in these spaces, too?

I myself hold Jews to a higher standard and agree that we are more culpable. Given our moral imperative and history, we should know better and, therefore, do better. As white-bodied Jews, too many of us have traded our values for the comforts of whiteness. To return to the metaphor of the Exodus, driven by our fear and existential insecurity, we have fashioned a Golden (more aptly, white) Calf to worship in this barren desert, falsely believing it will bring us lasting safety.

Simultaneously, anti-Semitism—fueled by centuries of Christian bias—is very much alive, well, and growing in this country. Just as those of us devoted to social justice need to address the impact of sexism, heterosexism, ableism, classism, and so on, we need to talk openly about the anti-Semitism that exists within our own collectives as well.

I do recognize and own that many of us, including me, find ways to assert our Jewishness within the movement—and I suspect this assertion can, and does, invite tension. In part, I believe this emphasis on our Jewish identity is preemptively defensive, in part an attempt to deny our whiteness (or alter its hue) and in part an attempt to put forth a false equivalency that we have been/are equally persecuted. All these parts ultimately add up to undermining authentic and effective solidarity.

There Is Hope for Healing

Understanding that this wandering and wondering cannot be done in isolation, I have been feeling my way through the wilderness with other white Jews. At times, I encounter resistance, denial, and/or outrage. At other times, I've found synergistic kinship.

Transcending Jewish Trauma (TJT) (Katz, n.d.a) has been immeasurably helpful in doing the necessary work of "righteous fusion" as white, Jewish, and antiracist. This website, along with participating with other white Jews in the "Jewish Justice Circle: Awakening to Whiteness" workshop, an educational component of the Jewish Bridge Project (Paradise, n.d.), has provided me and a growing cohort with the framework, tools, and fellowship to survive and thrive as activists in the desert.

TJT (Katz, n.d.a) addresses the personal, ancestral, collective trauma and internalized oppression of assimilated, white Ashkenazi Jews living in the United States in the service of being more whole and more effective in our solidarity work with other marginalized groups. It provides a road map that honors our loss and multigenerational trauma, acknowledges the costs of assimilation into a culture intentionally engineered to establish and maintain white supremacy, and reckons with the ways in which we have internalized and become complicit with whiteness.

Jo Kent Katz (n.d.a), author of TJT, identifies factors which impact the degree that ancestral trauma may inform our current patterns of behavior, among them how many generations our families have lived in the United States, our history of generational trauma, our immigration story, and our connection to religious tradition. Examining this history and holding it with compassion for both me and my ancestors is critical to my process of healing.

Also critical is interrogating those inherited patterns of internalized whiteness for the sake of developing new patterns—ones that are aligned to the antiracist, antioppression principles I believe in and try to follow in my work and daily life. Over the years 2010–2012, Jo Katz (n.d.b), in collaboration with others, developed "A Map of Internalized Anti-Semitism for White Ashkenazi Jews in the U.S." that serves as a GPS in the wilderness. In the center of the map are the dual engines of Terror and Sense of Otherness. Emanating from them are the Drive for Security, Drive for Acceptance by Way of Perfection, a Sense of Powerlessness and of Not Belonging, Self-Hatred, Denial of the Existence of the Oppression, and Desire to Control (Katz, n.d.b). Each one of these "pistons" is further unpacked, specifying coping behaviors that can be dysfunctional as well as antithetical to the project of collective transformation. Many of these behaviors coincide or toxically harmonize with the manifestations of internalized racial superiority. I see my family's story, their journey, and their striving, located on this map. I recognize my own story mirrored and mired in it, too.

Liberated and Liberatory

In his online editorial, "A Revised Jewish Understanding of the State of Israel," Rabbi Michael Lerner (2023) opines,

> Judaism has always had within it two competing strands: Love Judaism—a Judaism of love, social economic justice, and compassion that envisioned a world of peace and justice and affirmed the possibility of healing the world and transcending its violence and cruelty. . . . Settler-Judaism—a tendency to see the world as dominated by evil forces and to believe that only power over others could ultimately provide salvation for the Jewish people. . . . The supremacist ideas of Settler-Judaism create a religious ideology that can only appeal to those stuck in the sense that we are eternally vulnerable. (paras. 8–9)

Although Rabbi Lerner was addressing contemporary Israel in these remarks, I feel his paradigm is equally applicable to the dynamics of assimilated white Jews here and now in the United States. Compassionately excavating the part within me that feels eternally vulnerable facilitates my ability to pivot from my internalized Settler and to resource the love and inspiration my faith can provide me while remaining curious, connected, and engaged.

I realize that the struggle is not about choosing, at any given moment, between being white or being Jewish (as if that were even possible). It is between what kind of white person and what kind of Jew I intend to be. I aspire daily to be a white person committed to decolonizing the whiteness within me and to using the positional power and access being white affords me as a force for justice and equity. I aspire daily to be a Jew committed to healing my intergenerational trauma and to drawing on the spiritual values and fortitude of my faith in the service of dismantling racism and all the other oppressions—including anti-Semitism. It is my devotion to antiracism and all other oppressions that provides the connective tissue between these identities and that leads to alignment and wholeness. It is this alignment and wholeness that now guides my clinical work as I continue my journey toward becoming an ever-evolving racially sensitive therapist.

Wandering through the landscape of my white and Jewish identities has deposited me in a decidedly different place in the therapy room. The clinician I was before setting out on this journey has been transformed by what I have discovered about myself—or, more accurately, my selves—and has added layers of nuance to what I track internally as a therapist and see operating within and between the clients I work with.

My appreciation for the profound influence of our socialization into the hierarchies of worth that form the caste system of our society—and how the internalization of those multiple hierarchies plays out relationally—has deepened because of my exploration into my own history and the history of my people(s). More than perhaps anything else, going on this quest to better understand how possessing (and being possessed by) these identities impacts the way I live my life and do my work has helped to translate theory I have understood intellectually into clinically valuable practice.

Interrogating why and how I switch, sometimes at a moment's notice, from a position of privilege to one of subjugation has provided me with critically important information and a sorely needed pause in which to manage my triggers, activations, and reactivity. It has also widened the portal through which I enter conversations with my clients (particularly, though certainly not exclusively, those who are white and Jewish) about power, privilege, and oppression—something I had been trying to do for some time, but with considerable awkwardness and less-than-optimal skill.

Tracing the identities and their designated social locations with my clients through their family and multigenerational histories, traumas, and narratives of resistance and resilience has contributed to more presence, vulnerability, intimacy, and healing in our work together.

Traveling this path of "selves-discovery" has been humbling. I have had to build a surplus of courage and apply a large dose of self-compassion to continue this ongoing project of excavation. That, in turn, has expanded my capacity to offer compassion to, and inspire courage in, my clients. I know I could not nurture this depth of work with others without having initiated my own wandering and wondering. Braving the wilderness, and continuing to do so, has broadened my life, my vision, and, therefore, my work as a therapist. I will continue to wander in the desert—stumbling and falling at times, yet always rising again to move in the direction of Love. I will wander, but never alone. This desert I travel is far from the Promised Land, but it is a place that holds promise, both for me and those whose lives I impact as a therapist.

I wander—but I am not lost.

CHAPTER 7

From Shame to Pride: MY Mother/your mammy and the Making of a Racially Sensitive Psychologist

VANESSA M. BING, PhD

It has been close to 20 years since the passing of my mother, a woman born in the South in the early 1920s. A woman who, in the eyes of society, had very little to offer: she, a domestic who failed to complete school beyond an eighth-grade education, and who cleaned the homes and spaces of individuals and business entities. What could she offer her six children? What could she offer the world? That woman offered me plenty—although it took several decades for me to learn these lessons or recognize the values of what her "simple" upbringing was able to give the world and offer to her daughter.

Over many years, her youngest daughter would earn a doctoral degree in clinical psychology, would become a tenured professor of psychology at one of the largest public university systems in the United States, and would become a practicing psychologist providing therapy to individuals and families for more than two decades. This was made possible by integrating the many lessons learned about compassion, care, responsibility, equity, fairness, and commitment to making the world a better place.

Humble Beginnings

My mother migrated to the North to seek out better opportunities. She, and many of her siblings, came to cities such as Baltimore, Washington DC, Camden, NJ, and New York City, seeking opportunities to work, make money and live a better life. That better life was not especially evident to me while growing up. We lived in the public housing projects run by the New York City Housing Authority (NYCHA), a sprawling complex of more than 500,000 residents across five boroughs of New York. Established in 1935 as an enclave that offered modest, "affordable housing for low- and moderate-income New Yorkers," it is currently "home to 1 in 17 New Yorkers" (NYCHA, n.d., para. 1).

In its heyday, NYCHA homes boasted an affordable community for blue-collar workers, including teachers, police officers, and nurses—the essential employees who kept the city running. The size of the complex is overwhelming. It has been noted that it would be ranked the 35th largest city in the United States because of its population of residents, larger than cities such as Atlanta, Sacramento, and Miami. However, this "city in a city" that was once a jewel became a depressing environment in which to raise families. NYCHA has been in steady decline for several decades. As an example, in 2022, allegations were made that traces of arsenic were found in the water at one NYCHA complex. This made local headlines and resulted in a series of tests conducted by the NYC Department of Environmental Protection. During the testing period, residents were advised against using the water in their homes for cooking or drinking purposes (Smith, 2022). Ultimately, a memo from the CEO of NYCHA indicated that the initial testing was incorrect and there was no evidence of arsenic present (Russ et al., 2022). However, this provided little consolation for residents who have had to endure many problems over several years. Del Cerro (2023) reports some of the daily outages that residents frequently endure, including hot water, heat, and water outages. NYCHA, by its own admission, recognizes the need for changes in its facilities to improve the quality of living for individuals residing in public housing. Their 2023 fact sheet cites the "impacts of decades of federal disinvestment from public housing," which led to deterioration of their public buildings, and notes "more than $40 billion in major repairs needed" (NYCHA, 2023, p. 1).

Growing up in the 1970s, there was nothing but urban blight in my community. Squalor was everywhere. My recollection of life in the projects, as we called them, was replete with images of urine-filled elevators, garbage strewn about in the stairwells, clothes hanging out the window, floors covered with dirt, and noise permeating from the streets and the walls. The smell of the garbage that littered hallways, stairwells, and trash compactors was ever-present, as was the presence of roaches that Raid spray could never dissipate. This is where I lived with my mother and five siblings. As a very young child, I did not think much of this. It was simply home. And my mother would remind my siblings and me of the importance of keeping our home clean. It mattered not what went on outside; what was important was how we maintained our home on the inside.

My mother took great pride in maintaining a clean home. Perhaps this was to be expected of a woman who worked as a domestic. She was an impeccable homemaker who knew how to clean a home, scrub floors, and wash dishes until they shone.

I didn't think much about my home in the projects. It was a community where I had friends who also lived in the projects, whose parents also held menial labor jobs. My greatest concern as a child was the danger that loomed related to the increasing drug use and abuse in my community. People would rob and steal from their neighbors just so they could get a hit. My childhood was never idealized, nor did I have images of a home with a white picket fence. The closest thing to that image was the home my paternal aunt had in Jamaica, Queens, where we visited occasionally. Outside of that, I never saw anything resembling a white picket fence and never longed for such a home. I never knew that my neighborhood was such a problem until I entered white spaces.

Intelligence and Whiteness

As a young child, I was identified as gifted and talented and after third grade was taken out of my neighborhood elementary school and transferred to another school in my community that had a designated gifted and talented class (there was only one). I would move from my elementary to a middle school program for gifted children. Middle school (or junior high school as we called it then) took me from the immediate comfort of my neighborhood, as my new school was sandwiched in between three different communities—Chinatown, Little Italy, and "Jew town," the latter being a very pejorative term for the Jewish community in Manhattan's Lower East Side. It was fascinating to attend school with Asian Americans, Latinos, Jews, and the other white ethnics (largely Italians and Irish). What "a gorgeous mosaic" (*New York Times*, 1990, para. 1), as former New York City Mayor David Dinkins once proclaimed. As I became exposed to a greater diversity of people, it was wonderful to cultivate friendships with different people. But it was also when I began to hear terms that seemed to separate out Blacks from others. "Negrita," "Schvarta." Although I was initially fearful of attending this new school, it became a comfortable environment that fostered academic excellence and that led me to gain admission to one of New York City's elite specialized high schools—programs for which you had to take an admission test that covered language arts and higher-level mathematics.

My mother, with her eighth grade education, consistently encouraged me to excel in school. Whenever I performed well and received accolades, she would beam with pride and express much enthusiasm. Little did I know that I held the hopes of a people in my mother's eyes. I held the dreams that she and so many African Americans of the Northern Migration held. My mother had what folks would call "good common sense." She wasn't educated in the formal academic sense but was deeply educated in the ways of the world, largely from her upbringing in the South where she received the lessons of Jim Crow. She often told my siblings about the importance of education, had our home filled with books and magazines to ensure that we were reading, and we always had a complete set of encyclopedias where we could find interesting facts and tidbits about a range of topics. Reading was indeed fundamental.

In many ways there is real irony in the fact that I could learn so much from someone who society teaches us has little to nothing to offer. A poor, uneducated Black woman from the South brings no added value to life and has nothing to offer the world. How could she? She doesn't possess the intellectual acumen to bring any value to society; if anything, she reflected one of many stereotypes assigned to Black people that made us worthless. Blacks were frequently depicted as treacherous, dishonest, submissive, and lewd (National Museum of African American History and Culture, n.d.).

Notions of Black women as dishonest, unchaste, and deviant were ever present (Berry & Gross, 2020), and women typically fell into one of three categories: the mammy, the jezebel, or the angry sapphire. My mother had the mammy image.

Early Life as a Domestic

My mother worked outside of the house from the time she was a young woman in her teens. She was raised at a time when women who worked outside the home were excluded from the commonly held ideas of respectable womanhood, as those with respectability were generally white women who could afford to stay at home (Berry & Gross, 2020). As a young girl, she spent time in other people's homes cooking and cleaning as she, unlike her siblings, could not tolerate the sun long enough to pick cotton in the fields of the South.

As a little girl, these images, and stories I heard, caused me to feel discomfort and would later become a source of real embarrassment. As a child, I cringed hearing the stories of her long hours cleaning the homes of white people, and when I got older, I could not understand why my mother would leave the South, only to travel north and continue with the same menial jobs. In my youth, I could not understand why she would continue to take on jobs in service to others, jobs where she relied on the generosity of others to help keep food on the table through the potential tips that she might earn.

My mother was an absent figure for most of my formative years, but not in the traditional sense. She was definitely home—cooking and cleaning for her family—but her hours at home were out of sync with mine as a school-aged child. I recall coming home from school during my elementary school years around 3:15 p.m. when I barely saw her as she raced to work for the 4 p.m. to midnight shift at the hotel where she was employed. I hated her job because it took my mom away from me. As a 6-, 7-, or 8-year-old, it was hard for me to understand that she had to work this job. I have clear recollections on many a night, my mother complaining about the poor or nonexistent tips that would be left for her. Perhaps one or two dollars if she were lucky. Many guests never left a tip at all. In my mind, my mother was cleaning toilets, bathtubs, and beds for people who gave no thought at all about the service that was being provided to them. They just expected to be served. However, from this I learned the importance of valuing the service that all laborers provide.

My mother was a maid. When she wanted to make it sound better than it was, she would call it "chambermaid." It was an honest paying job, but not one that I could be proud of as a child (or so I believed). This would only become emphasized when I entered the predominantly white space of my high school.

The Shame of the Domestic

The mammy image is one that was seared in my brain long before I even understood what it meant in a sociopolitical sense. The caricature of the full-bodied Black female could be seen on every box of Aunt Jemima's pancake mix and syrup bottles. The image is an offensive depiction of Black women who were in service to others. These images were largely conceived of during slavery and made popular through minstrel shows. Enslaved Black women were, for the most part, highly skilled domestics who worked in the homes of white families and served as the primary caretakers of white children. The tropes that developed from these images were that of a woman who had undying loyalty to her slaveholders, serving as their caregiver and counselor of sorts (National Museum of African American History and Culture, n.d., para. 4).

I resented the fact that my mother assumed this mammy role throughout her life, not simply in the homes of the white people in her native state of Virginia as a young woman, but even when she came to New York City to find better opportunities. How was it that New York City offered no better opportunities for my mother? Was it a racial thing? Or simply because she had less education? At the time, I did not realize how the two were inseparable.

My mother was unable to attend high school because she had no transportation to a school for "colored children" that was more than two miles away from her home. An elder aunt who was successful in graduating high school was only able to do so because she left Lancaster, VA, and stayed with a relative in Baltimore. My mother was not as lucky and eventually had to leave Virginia altogether in the hopes that her life would be a little better.

My mother, like so many others, was part of the Northern Migration that brought southern Blacks to northern parts of the United States.

As I got older and continued to demonstrate strong academic potential in school, I would be taken away from my local school and all the familiar faces of the Black and Brown children with whom I attended and thrust into an environment where white children and Asian Americans began to fill up the classroom seats. By the time I entered high school, an elite and academically rigorous public math and science high school, those Black and Brown faces would be almost nonexistent. That was the first time in my life when I found myself cloaked in shame the majority of my days, and felt the need to wrestle myself away from everything that brought this shame: my terrible neighborhood, my roach-filled apartment, and my domestic "mammy" mother who made no more than minimum wage.

I attended high school with children whose mothers and fathers were doctors, lawyers, engineers, and diplomats. This was a great departure from my mother, the domestic, the woman who represented many of their nannies and mammies. Their lives were a far cry from my life of abject poverty. Then, when I became more attuned to the different socioeconomic strata, the shame only grew. The mammy image became even stronger—seared in my brain. The neutered, asexual figure who always put the needs of her white bosses and their families/children first. As Ruby Hamad (2020) so eloquently states in her book *White Tears/Brown Scars*, the mammy was a way of neutralizing Black women, presenting them as obedient, grateful, and lacking agency. How could I be associated with a mom who represented an image that I routinely saw on the Aunt Jemima pancake mix box and syrup bottle that I would routinely see in our cupboard? The more I saw that image, the more it left an indelible mark, and the more I knew I had to move away from it, and everything associated with it. This required me to negate my mother and her so-called job. I learned to feel shame for a woman who put her children first and worked any way that she could to keep food in our mouths. I was taught to disparage my mother and all the women she represented who did backbreaking work daily.

This internalized shame for my life would consume me and extend to my physical home and neighborhood. This feeling was further punctuated when one of my high school classmates reminded me of my exact placement in society, letting me know exactly who I was and where I came from.

Entering Predominantly White Spaces and Internalizing Racism

When I finally entered Stuyvesant High School, I immediately knew that I was "no longer in Kansas." Stuyvesant High School was a selective public high school that only admitted the best and brightest students in New York City. At the time of my attendance, it comprised largely white and Asian students and a little less than 10% were Black. Indeed, statistics comparing enrollment at my high school from 1976 to 2017 reveal significant gaps. In 1976, 14% of the enrollment of my high school was Black and Latinx students. In 2017, that number declined to a total of 4% (Shapiro & Lai, 2019).

In 2023, 762 offers were made to students who were successful on the Specialized High Schools Admissions Test, the exam needed to gain entry into the specialized high schools. Of the 762 offers, only seven were made to Black students, a decrease from 11 in 2022, and eight in 2021 (Closson, 2023). If all seven students accepted were to attend, that would constitute less than 1% of the student population. This is particularly significant as the selective schools are part of the city's public school system where Black and Latinx students make up more than two-thirds of the student population. Yet in 2023, only 10% of offers made by the selective schools (three schools in total) were made to Black and Latinx students (Closson, 2023).

Coming from my mixed-race elementary and middle school, I was immediately uncomfortable amid this sea of white faces. I immediately took note of the clothes that they wore—Calvin Klein jeans and Izod Lacoste were all the rage—I had nothing like that in my closet. The sheer numbers of whites alone made me feel like I did not belong. When I shared this with my mother, she offered little more than this: "As long as your clothes are clean, nothing else matters." I was fine.

When entering the cafeteria at school, the disparity was obvious at a glance, especially the "ink spots" in the room where all the Black students sat together. Tatum (2021) describes at length this phenomenon of all Black children (as well as the other ethnic/racial groups) congregating in their safe spaces. That gathering, however, was an enigma to me, as I spent my elementary and middle school lunches with friends of various races and ethnicities, sharing lunch together.

At my new, predominantly white high school, it appeared that I had to choose a side. What would it mean for me to join all the Black students when a couple of my Asian friends from middle school also attended Stuyvesant? Why would I separate myself from them and leave them behind? Would I be at a disadvantage as I tried to navigate these new spaces if I defaulted to what was familiar? Should I try to befriend some of the white kids? Ultimately, I ended up spending most of my lunches with a mixed group of students and was left feeling very self-conscious about the fact that I was not sitting alongside my Black peers. Was I a sellout for not sticking with my Black peers? Why had this all become so confusing? In fact, many of those Black students were actually not at all like me. A number of them came from more middle-class backgrounds, hailing largely from the distant boroughs of Brooklyn and Queens where they lived in houses. Generally, they did not come from the NYCHA projects of the Lower East Side or the poorer areas of the city. Suddenly, both my race and social class became a problem.

Lessons of White Supremacy: When Friendships Yield Shame

I learned to befriend white people, or rather, I learned to be conversant with white students (even if we were not always talking about the same thing). My mother often reminded me not to be afraid just because people were different from me. I took that to mean that I had to go along to get along and learn about a culture and worldview that seemed so very different from mine. I heard stories about people's summer homes in Sag Harbor or the Hamptons and realized for the first time that people had multiple dwellings!

The very first time I dared to bring one of my new high school friends into my neighborhood, I was quickly reminded of our differences and my station in life relative to theirs, and how unacceptable impoverished living was to the elite whites of the world. Although I never actually dared to invite anyone into my actual home, the lesson of bringing someone into proximity proved to be sufficient. Wanting to learn to play tennis (a thing that several of my white classmates frequently talked about), I invited a classmate to meet me at the public tennis courts that were situated across the street from my home. The park, one of the few perks of living in the public housing projects where I resided, was a place where people, rich or poor, came to play (although those with money never stayed after dusk).

On that particular day, Marcy met me at the park, which was a stone's throw away from my NYCHA apartment. She asked where I lived, and I pointed to my apartment building that could be seen across the highway overpass that separated my apartment building from the greenery of the park. Marcy gasped and uttered, "You live *there?!*" I was stunned by the emphasis placed on "there." It was clear even to me that she looked upon the apartment complex with contempt and disdain, and it was incomprehensible how someone could live in such an ugly and toxic environment. That was the last time I met with Marcy in my neck of the woods.

As I reflect on that day now, I not only remember the image of Marcy and her shocked look upon seeing where I lived, but I also remember the silence that fell upon me. Where was my righteous indignation about Marcy's critical response to my family's residence? Why was I unable to push back on her and make her aware of how insensitive and crude her comments were to my ears? Where had my voice gone? Why had I chosen to be put in my (lower socioeconomic) place and to act only as the good little Black girl who didn't push back? Where did my voice go?

This is what Hardy (2013) refers to as "voicelessness." The loss of a voice is a consequence of systemic racism, and it silences Black people. We lose the capacity to defend ourselves against a barrage of unwelcome and unjustified debilitating messages. My voice grew more and more silent in my largely white high school, a school where I was cornered, more than once, by white girls who would ask me if they could touch my hair and asked whether it was true that Black people never washed their hair. Seemingly, the reasons these girls in school could very comfortably ask me such inane questions is because whiteness and white bodies are centered in our culture. I was the different one and therefore had to explain myself.

I remember going home that day in tears and later telling my mother about that experience. She would simply suggest that I give that "no never mind" and understand that those girls were simply ignorant. Lesson learned: forgive others for their lack of knowledge.

With the various kinds of questionings I endured, I am reminded of what Black feminist scholar Patricia Hill Collins (2020) referred to as the controlling images placed upon Black girls and women that affect their being. Collins coined the term "controlling images" to articulate the socially constructed images of Black womanhood that were cultivated in times of enslavement and structural racism. How had these images seeped into my own pores? This became evident as I began rejecting my own mother and everything that she represented: a poor, uneducated Black woman whose simplicity allowed her to be ignored, ridiculed, and overlooked.

With each passing day I grew to hate the high school I attended. The constant reminder of being poor and Black was unsustainable. I would then come home and complain to my mother (assuming she was not rushing off to work). She insisted that I had to stay in that school because "education was everything" and would lead me to greatness. One of her overused expressions was "everything you touch turns to gold." I heard this as something straight from a children's book or fairy tale. Who was she kidding? I went to a high school where, even though I had to pass an admissions test to gain entry, I was still made to feel like I was less than nothing and did not belong. I could not swap stories of my weekends in the Hamptons nor speak with great pride about the impressive job my mother or father had. It was in this environment where I learned to hate everything about myself—my hair, my home, my community.

This was a school where I had to endure the indignity of having my classroom seat rearranged (moved to the front right below the teacher's desk, moved to the rear of the classroom where there was no one to my left or right) to ensure that I wasn't cheating on exams because I consistently scored in the top 3%. Why did I have to endure this, and how would I get through to my senior year? My mother simply reminded me to "stay the course" and understand that this race was mine to lose. She let me know that it was important that a child like me not drop out of an elite school, as this experience "was bigger than me" and a right that many of my ancestors died for. Lesson learned: patience and endurance.

Internalized Devaluation

My experiences in predominantly white spaces that occurred at the start of my high school years were responsible for the development of my internalized devaluation. Hardy (2023) defines "internalized devaluation" as an "unconscious process" that "relies on the incorporation of negative racial valuations into the mainstream of one's psyche" (p. 124). He sees it as akin to an untreated cancer as it attacks and assaults one's sense of dignity and how one perceives oneself. As I moved through my high school years, there was an eroding sense of who I was and who I was capable of becoming. I felt only disdain for everything associated with being Black and poor. I could not figure out how to fit into my predominantly white environment where I had little in common with my peers. I had little involvement in the life and culture of my school, because I tended to leave school daily to go to my after-school job to make a little extra money to buy myself the things that my mother could not afford.

I had a mother who was a maid, who became a greater source of embarrassment. She represented "the help" that many of my white classmates had at their homes, tending to their every need. My mother, because she worked long hours into the evenings, was barely around for me, even though she always prepared dinner and made sure all her children were fed before she left for work. I was unable to appreciate this because I could only think about the work that she was about to commence and how this brought me shame.

When I look back on this now, more than 40 years later, the shame I now feel is for a racist system that allowed me to overlook the power and strength of my mother. My mother ultimately taught me many lessons of kindness and human decency, strength, and integrity, lessons that were far more powerful than anything I could have learned in academic spaces, and far more meaningful in moving me through life.

Life Lessons From My Mother

Lessons in Community and Compassion

My mother taught me lessons in the importance of community and compassion. My mother did not really see the difference in people and understood that, in a real way, we were all responsible for one another, that each of us can play a small role in making a difference in the world. This was evident when my mother brought home a young white child ("JD") one day from her job. The child's mother was a sex worker and had somehow managed to keep Child Protective Services off her radar. I was puzzled why this little white boy appeared in our home one day—an apartment that was already way too small for the six of us. My mother reminded my siblings and me of the importance of coming together and lending a helping hand, regardless of how much we actually had. The fact that we were of the working poor class was irrelevant. We were housed, fed, and clothed. Thus, if this young child could not be housed, fed, and protected because his mother had to work, it was our job as a community to lend a hand. I was probably around age seven at the time and could not fully grasp the scope of what my family had taken on. This, however, became "really real" when Child Protective Services ultimately became involved when JD's mother was murdered by her pimp, and the child had to be placed in the care of the state. This was indeed a tragic story, but my recollection of it is one where my mother, and by extension her family, came together to take care of a three- or four-year-old boy who suddenly lost the only parent that he knew. The question of race never even entered the equation, although one might surmise that it was easy for my mother to step into the mammy role for this young white boy (even if his white mother did not fit the stereotype of who a Black domestic would provide service to). Care, compassion, and community service and outreach were the pivotal lessons that were conveyed.

Lessons in Strength and Fortitude

My mother repeatedly, and without uttering any words, provided lessons in strength and fortitude. My mother never once complained of being tired (although she had to have been). She worked long hours cleaning hotel rooms, always prepared food for her children before leaving for work, always cleaned the house and provided instructions for what we were responsible for, and did this every day of the week. What she did give voice to was the need to work hard and never give up, even when you think you can't go further. She would launch into stories about how our ancestors managed adversity and pressed forward when they felt they did not have more to give. These stories reminded me of how strong Black people were and how this mental strength gave us all that we needed to overcome obstacles. I often thought about this as a child struggling to fit in and could call on this inner strength to get me through.

Lessons in Work Ethic

Even while the role of a domestic was never lauded in society, Black women assumed the role and approached it with pride. I grew up often hearing "an honest-paying job was nothing to ever be ashamed of." My Black mother, like other men and women of her generation, understood that holding a job as a domestic was nothing to ever be ashamed of. This reflected, as bell hooks (2015) describes in *Sisters of the Yam*, a philosophy of work that focused on the commitment one makes to any task, no matter how big or small, and the importance of getting the job done, and doing it well. This worldview speaks to a broader work ethic that my mother, and many women in her generation, understood. They knew how difficult it was to take on what was considered by white folks an undesirable service role, where they would daily confront the inevitable onslaught of racism. Rather than focusing on the job's title and level of income assigned, my mother focused on the value of working hard at whatever you do. She taught me that there was an intrinsic value to be achieved in doing a job well and a level of pride one takes when one has completed a task to the best of one's ability. The less than tangible rewards that she received in a menial paycheck or tips did not matter.

Like many of her generation, my mother was working for something much bigger and more valuable. The extrinsic rewards of money and material goods did not faze her. She knew how to go without material goods. She had a greater investment in providing her children with opportunities for their future growth. Although Mom may not have received the dignity and respect that she deserved as a hard-working person, her efforts were about her children's survival and creating the pathway for their future.

Lessons in Patience

My mother used to say, "life is long." I didn't really understand this as a child, but as I grew older, I reflected on this, many times over. We have many chances in life to achieve our objectives, to change our goals, and to create new opportunities. What was needed in many situations was simply patience; having faith and belief that time would help move us along, and that we would arrive at certain junctures right on time.

Cultivating the Tools to Withstand White Supremacist Ideology

While it is clear to me now that my mother had powerful lessons to teach me and the rest of my siblings, as I reflect on the early period of my life, I am saddened that her lessons were lost as I internalized the value of wealth, status, elitism, and tangible, material goods. I feel shame now in failing to embrace my mother during those early years because I allowed individuals who represented a supremacist culture to inform me. I don't, however, believe that I was the only one so afflicted.

As a child, I was not armed with the resources to understand the impact of what Hardy (2013, 2023) refers to as voicelessness, psychological homelessness, and internalized devaluation. Even as a child raised in one of the most cosmopolitan melting pots in this country, I was unable to escape the remnants of Jim Crow. While I did not see the "Whites only" and "Blacks only" signs in my day-to-day experiences, I experienced the weight of years of oppression against African-descended people. How do we counter the negative messages that have infiltrated the corridors of our school buildings, neighborhoods, and communities?

Reflections on the Lessons Learned

As I reflect upon the lessons learned from my mother, it's a broader message of the unrelenting strains of racism in America. I learned to feel shame for a hardworking woman who instilled values of love, care, compassion, and selflessness—recognizing that there will always be others out there who are barely surviving but for the grace of God. I internalized the values of a white-body-centered supremacist culture, one that informs us that those lacking formal education and possessing darker skin have little to no value in society. And even when one dares to enter the halls of academia, one must do so with caution if there is any hope of maintaining a core sense of dignity and integrity.

The culture in which I was raised informed me that my eighth-grade-educated domestic mother had nothing to offer and that I should feel shame and embarrassment for that to be part of my lineage. When asked, "What kind of work does your mother do?", I learned that I should lower my eyes and avoid speaking about her job and find a way to change the subject, that I should not hold my head up with pride for a strong Southern woman who sacrificed her entire being to ensure that her children would have an elevated status in life, a woman who, even though she faced one adversity after the next, had love in her heart and could tell her daughter "You can be anything you want to be" and "Everything you touch turns to gold."

What was golden was the strength that I learned from her, the tenacity that I internalized, which initially only masked the internalized shame. Be strong—don't let them see you sweat, was the ultimate message.

Journalist Brea Baker (2022), in her interview with Dr. Imani Perry, author of *South to America: A Journey Below the Mason-Dixon to Understand the Soul of a Nation*, reminds us that there is much we can learn from the women of the South. Perry's (2022) book provides examples of the "protective sensibility" held by many folks of the South that allowed them to navigate a racist country. In her article, Baker (2022) highlights that the experiences of women in the South taught them to "easily diagnose the problems with American society while visioning something better" (para. 1). My mother maintained a vision for something better, though, arguably, her life did not change for the better because of white supremacist standards. She continued to live in public housing, earning meager wages until she could no longer work, but was forever the eternal optimist. She took immense joy in watching her children become formally educated and excelling in life. Whether they became a clerical assistant, administrative assistant, physical therapist, or psychologist, she knew that they had all exceeded her experiences and defied the odds by not only existing, but standing tall in a racist society that forces us to shrink our beings.

Mammy's Daughter and the Making of a Psychologist

As I reflect on the early years of my life, I often contemplate how my early experiences transported me into the helping profession. The constant image of my mother being a caregiver certainly provided the strongest possible lesson in the importance of helping others. However, it has been the juxtaposition of my financially impoverished life with the life I encountered through my high school experiences that fostered a curiosity and questioning of the challenges that we all endure.

The lessons of racism that informed my mother's life that were shared through stories of her mother, her grandmother, and all those before her were experiences that I carried in my body. I experienced the shame of a family with deep Southern roots trying to make it in a very challenging city where the rich lived very well and the poor were left behind. My internalized shame and devaluation would soon become the very tools that enhanced my clinical insights, skills, and abilities. They armored me with experiences that ultimately encouraged strength, resiliency, and empowerment of others.

Additionally, the experience of feeling like an Other would ultimately fuel my desire to support marginalized and minoritized clients to feel whole and valued—irrespective of the negative messages received from society. Awareness of othering can also lend support to the role of the psychologist-activist (Nadal, 2017), who participates in political activism as a means of advocating for those historically marginalized groups. Awareness of and sensitivity to the many ways in which marginalized groups may be mistreated, shunned, and rendered voiceless by society can enhance the effectiveness of a clinician.

While I spent many years (decades!) studying in multiple and varied spaces, there was not one where I had a sense of being at home. These experiences made it easy to feel like an Other. It also sensitized me to work compassionately with those who also experienced othering.

Finding a home required me to identify spaces that contained individuals who understood where I was coming from, and who understood my struggle to transcend the fixed boundaries of professionalism that obliterated my culture and those of other People of Color. I then began to embark on soul work.

Soul work has been defined by Hardy (2023) as internal work where there is "a focus that helps to restore all the parts of one's being that have been nicked, bruised, and decimated by the forces of racial trauma and oppression" (p. 105). My soul work had everything to do with my internal struggle of managing my multiple identities—being an African American woman, born and raised in the public housing projects of New York City, raised by a mother whose primary occupation was that of a domestic, and being educated in spaces where I frequently received messages that I did not belong, but somehow (perhaps underhandedly) found a way to achieve something that I never should have. Having earned my place in a competitive graduate program where I earned my doctorate in clinical psychology, I was frequently expected to leave those early parts of me behind to join an elite profession where people who looked like me represented only 3% or 4% of the population. I was taught the language of my discipline and was expected to practice what I learned, even if it felt conflictual for me. Conflictual because I was not always in agreement with the approaches employed. Conflictual because it demanded that I be a blank slate, which required that I leave very colorful aspects of my personality aside. Conflictual because the rules of the profession required me to suppress and/or subordinate the anger I often felt and rise above it all, in the face of microaggressions and microassaults, and to always comport myself as a professional. The ethics of the profession demanded that I have very strict and rigid boundaries in engaging clients and patients, which translated into, for example, resisting hugs and not accepting even the smallest of gifts from appreciative clients (or else be subjected to accusations of unethical boundary violations). Ultimately, I was required to look at who I was becoming and what I was leaving behind, in order to fit into spaces that demanded a certain posture. My experiences help me to appreciate that many clients, especially those among the marginalized, come to therapy with many of these same hidden and unspoken struggles that may not ever get acknowledged or addressed clinically.

In the clinical realm, where I have incorporated Self of the Therapist approaches, I have learned to effectively use self-disclosure to support the emergence of clients who have been made to feel a sense of shame because of their family of origin. Watts-Jones (2010) takes the position that therapists have both a professional and personal presence in the consulting room. I use my person as well as my role of clinician to draw parallels and connections to the unique struggles and pain presented by a range of clients, especially Clients of Color, individuals who have been taught, despite their accomplishments, that they are still not enough and fail to measure up. As I reflect on the shame that I was taught to have, I can imagine how liberating it would have been to have a professional (therapist or even educator) disclose to me that they too grew up in oppressed circumstances and were taught to feel the shame that I felt. Unfortunately, such liberating practices violated the norms of what was considered traditional psychotherapy.

My soul work and my efforts to become a racially sensitive therapist have afforded me the opportunity to critically rethink the efficacy of traditional practices. My efforts to become a racially sensitive therapist have given me permission to examine difficult feelings within myself while also allowing me to create space for others to examine their experiences with internalized shame, devaluation, and whiteness. I am much better able to help clients explore how the various frames and structures of oppression have also held them back. This is true for white people as well as Folks of Color. I have been able to explore with white clients why they chose to work with a Black therapist. What is it that they hoped to accomplish? What need were they fulfilling? Reflecting on their own intentions and ideas (or even fantasies) about working with a Black clinician can yield powerful insights for white clients and can model the depth of connection that is possible between individuals from disparate backgrounds.

The use of racialized conversations and dialogue that explicitly address race are also important components of therapy that I have learned to incorporate in my work. It has been my experience that opening the therapeutic process to discussions of racialized matters can be transformative. Talking about race grants permission to all to free themselves of the constraints that white culture imposes upon us all. Clients of Color I have worked with come to understand how their voices are often suppressed as they move through various phases of life. Granting permission to address those issues is liberating and creates the possibility for enhanced discussion. Additionally, when white folks are offered a relatively safe platform to address their own internalized biases, this can allow for personal growth and greater connection. Creating such space for authentic sharing of ideas and feelings opens up the opportunity for white clients to wrestle with their own internalized racism or their internalized values of white-centered cultures. Bringing greater authenticity into the therapist's consulting room encourages a level of disclosure and intimacy that might otherwise not be available. We are raised in a culture that stymies all of us in interrogating the centrality of whiteness. Whether a person is Black, white, Latinx, Asian/South Asian, Middle Eastern, or any other racialized group, raising the specter of whiteness and how it affects us allows us all to explore suppressed feelings.

Telling my own painful, shame-laced racial story has helped me become more adept at using racial storytelling as an effective therapeutic tool. When used effectively, racial storytelling can reveal much about a person's inner conflicts and struggles. Unfortunately, many clinicians may avoid explicit discussions of race as these discussions can be fraught with misunderstandings, inadvertent microaggressions and microassaults, and polarization.

Hardy (2016) notes that "the prevailing views regarding racial conversations are either that they should be avoided completely, or they should just happen spontaneously" (p. 125). He adds that neither approach is especially effective. Hardy (2016) suggests a model that requires the understanding of our privileged and subjugated selves (the PAST Model). The model presumes that we each have multiple identities, of which race is one. Race (or racial identity) is either associated with value and privilege or is devalued and relegated to positions of inferiority and subjugation.

My work as a practitioner incorporates the use of my social location and awareness of both my privileged and subjugated selves. I hold the privilege of being an educated professional psychologist, while parts of my internal world may hold tightly onto my subjugated self—the poor Black girl who felt ashamed and unacceptable in the predominantly white education spaces where I found myself. By supporting clients to reflect on their various identities and privileged and subjugated selves, I encourage sensitive discourse that brings alive discussions of race, social class, and identity into the practice.

Effectively, I have learned the importance of bringing myself into the clinical work, addressing racialized experiences and the trauma from these experiences, and supporting those from marginalized backgrounds to combat their internalized devaluation and their voicelessness. These have become the hallmark of my work and had their origins in being the child of a Southern, African American domestic mother whose value and worth were denigrated because white supremacist culture deemed her unworthy.

Conclusion

My journey to become the professional Black woman that I am today began with the journey of being lifted by a woman who understood how important it would be for me to feel valued and appreciated. She knew, without ever saying it explicitly, that the centrality of whiteness in the United States would be persistent and pernicious. Messages of white supremacy would follow me through my educational journey to become a psychologist and would instill moments of significant doubt. Nonetheless, my mother's strength and sacrifice would allow me to emerge victorious, knowing that I stand on her shoulders. I can never repay my mother for the love and sacrifice she made for my siblings and me, and for the powerful messages she imparted in her quiet ways. Her strength allowed her to endure the disrespect of others while she kept her eyes on the prize.

While it has been close to 20 years since the passing of my mother, I have carried her with me daily. Through the various indignities and assaults on my person, I have held on to the belief that my mother shared many times: "Baby, you can do anything you want." Well, Momma, we did, and we continue to fight the good fight. I embrace my privileged as well as my subjugated selves and know that by internalizing your values, I have become a respected clinician and healer. My mother, your mammy, my shero!

CHAPTER 8

Unpacking My Invisible Racial Luggage: The One I Brought From Colombia and Failed to Unpack

GLORIA LOPEZ-HENRIQUEZ, DSW, LCSW

I arrived in the United States more than 40 years ago. I was 25 years old with concerns and dreams about my future and my young family's as well. What was in front of us was unknown, and we had very limited resources available to help us navigate this daunting new environment. I had no idea this country would become the place where I spent the most time in my life, where my children would become adults and my grandchildren would be born.

Among the few possessions I brought with me was what Sylvia Zamora (2022) called "racial baggage," an invisible suitcase carrying my racial history, my lifelong racial socialization, norms, and practices I was exposed to for the first 25 years of my life. The moment I entered the United States, I was required to identify my race in official documentation. I did not know what box or boxes to check concerning my racial identity. In these forms, there were no spaces for Mestiza, *morena clara* or *triguena*, the racial/ethnic *color de piel* classifications with which I was familiar. This question's framing activated my near-invisible racial baggage. After all, this was the only source to look for answers regarding race, but to no avail. This was how my racialization process in my host country began. In the blink of an eye,

I became "other Spanish/Hispanic." Regarding nationality and racial identity, I had no other categories to select besides "some other race."

For many years, I did not consider the relevance of unpacking this racial suitcase; I put all my energy into understanding who I was becoming, racially speaking, in my new context. I felt an urgency to understand this country's racial hierarchies and my position within that hierarchy. Except for the unexpected piercing of my racial baggage, I had not seriously considered exploring how my premigration racial ideologies were and continue to be impacted by immigrating to the United States. Following many essential cross-racial experiences and meaningful multicultural race conversations, I was pushed to recognize that my past racialization, the one before immigration, deserved as much attention as my racial development since I came to this country. I believe that my immigration experience has impacted and transformed, and continues to impact and transform, my understanding of race and racism in my home and host countries. Leaving my preimmigration racialization unpacked continued to threaten and derail my path toward greater racial awareness and sensitivity in my racially informed clinical work.

There are three preestablished racial beliefs and attitudes that came in my racial suitcase that threatened my racially informed clinical work: (1) my Mestizo privilege, (2) my anti-Blackness and white superiority attitudes and prejudices, and (3) my colonial racial mentality expressed in my internalized inferiority, which is the girdle supporting it all. These aspects of my racial ideology are not separate entities; to the contrary, they overlap and inform each other quite significantly.

Exploring these three dimensions has been vital to my growth and understanding of myself as a racial being. This is an ongoing reflective process, moving back and forth between my evolving racial ideologies, memories, discourses, and practices across time and space, uncovering many contradictions, inconsistencies, and tensions in my racial development and, therefore, in my relationships with others in both my native and host countries.

Mestizo Privilege

I identify as Mestiza. I was born in Colombia, in the city of Bogotá, located in the middle of the country, on top of the Andes. The Muiscas or Chibcha people were my original ancestors. The central part of the Chibcha/Muisca civilization was concentrated in Bogotá and its surroundings. My paternal grandmother, whose mother carried some of the stories of the genocide of our ancestors during the Spanish conquest and colonization, gave me the first direct ethnic/racial talk at the age of about seven. She said that we came from the union of a Chibcha princess and a Spanish adventurer. I remember liking my connection with the princess and having a visceral reaction to the realization that I carry the colonizers' blood. How can I reconcile carrying both the oppressed and the oppressor, the colonized and the colonizer, the victim of rape and slaughter, and the rapist and the killer in me? How does a seven-year-old answer such a jarring existential question? I did it like children often do in similar circumstances. I remember developing a strong emotional connection with my Indigenous roots where Chibcha princesses existed, and disdain and hatred for Spain as their colonizer. However, my young seven-year-old answer to this dilemma was firmly undermined by some family members' racial beliefs and attitudes and the racial climate of the society where I grew up.

My Indigenous identity was nurtured officially by school trips and the stories of the original inhabitants' sublime past. However, the devaluing narratives I heard about my ancestors' survivors contrasted dramatically with my history lessons. I know now that many descendants of those ancestors still live around Bogotá and are called campesinos, an old-world Spanish word that means "those who cultivate" (Woods, 2019). As a youngster on my trips to the city's outskirts or the little towns nearby, the campesinos I encountered looked like my paternal great-grandmother. But even then, I disconnected these folks from the Muiscas/Chibchas of my imagination. Somehow, this Indigenous group and the campesinos I met had nothing in common; I was wrong, they do. My confusion was created by the cross-generational results of a nineteenth- and twentieth-century sociopolitical agenda to homogenize the nation-state with no space for pluri-ethnic identities, with devastating long-term effects. "Categories [such] as *peasants* and *artisans* were used to erase any cultural or spiritual communal cohesion, and consequently, all indigenous claims to land or other rights went unheard" (Sanchez Castaneda, 2018, p. 13).

The maternal side of the family negated my paternal grandmother's story. I was told that my grandmother was *inventando cosas*, in other words, lying, and that we were primarily descendants of Spaniards. The narrative about our racial heritage from my maternal side closely aligned with what I heard a lot more frequently, sometimes directly and more often indirectly, that moving toward whiteness was a more desirable and civilizing choice; that the *blanqueamiento* of our bodies, our minds, and souls guarantees a better future. *Blanqueamiento* is not only an individual attitude but a social, political, and economic practice used in many postcolonial countries, like Colombia, to "improve the race" (*mejorar la raza*) toward a supposed ideal of whiteness (Vásquez-Padilla & Hernández-Reyes, 2020). Marrying someone with a lighter skin tone was and continues to be a way to *mejorar la raza*, and marrying someone of darker skin did the opposite. After an Afro-Venezuelan friend who came for a visit left, my mother told me that she did not want him to be my boyfriend because she did not wish to have Black grandkids.

I grew up in this context of contradiction and inconsistent racial narratives and powerful anti-Black and anti-Indigenous and white superiority bias, both informed by a colonial mentality, both coexisting with a racial discourse of color blindness.

Anti-Blackness Bias and Its Ramifications

It should not be surprising that I began identifying as Mestiza in my teen years. A quick look online at what Mestiza means led me to 10 definitions pointing to a woman of mixed race, in Latin America, especially one of Indigenous and Spanish descent (Cambridge Dictionary, n.d.). This is the definition I carried with me for most of my life. For years, I did not question why my African racial roots were missing from my and others' understanding of Mestiza. I disowned my African ancestry because I could not recognize it in my surroundings, body, community, and history. I inherited this historical amnesia—*El Incómodo Color de la Memoria*—the uncomfortable color of memory, as Javier Ortiz Cassiani (2019), an Afro-descendant Colombian historian, describes in his book.

Although Colombia is home to one of the world's largest populations of people of African descent outside of the African continent, Black Colombian residents represent just 1.5% of the urban population in Bogotá, a city of about 8 million inhabitants. The rest of the population comprises migrants from across the country, mainly descendants of Spaniards or Mestizos (Escobar, 2016). Consequently, I lived in Bogotá for 25 years and had limited contact with Afro-Colombians growing up.

My country is a country of regions. I heard that repeatedly growing up, but I was never told that the regional division has distinctive skin colors. There was and still is much racial diversity, but it was and still is profoundly segregated. "In fact, it is scarcely an exaggeration to suggest that Colombia is dominated by a form of semi-apartheid that relegates the Afro-Colombian and indigenous sectors of the population to the periphery of national life, both geographically and politically" (Lobo & Morgan, 2004, p. 83). I was born and grew up in the most racially exclusive parts of the country around many light-skinned Mestizos far away from the Atlantic and Pacific coasts.

But, while living in the same city, I was exposed to widespread racial stereotypes about Afro-descendants everywhere I went. In the bathroom of the university I was attending, where there was a small group of Afro-Colombian students, one morning I found writing on the wall that said, "contribuya con el aseo de la ciudad, mate a un costeno" (meaning an Afro-Colombian); what in essence translated to "help keep Bogotá clean, kill an Afro-descendant." I felt disturbed, but later, I dismissed its clear racial message to exterminate our Black citizens to have a cleaner city, meaning a whiter city, by concluding that it was probably a joke in poor taste. I superficially considered the impact on the Afro-Colombian students, but I did not turn to look at those who were spreading such racial hatred, which I knew in my heart were people who looked racially like me. But I was light years away from any self-interrogation about my participation in the oppression of my Black *compatriotas*. In addition, part of my racialization in my country was not verbally acknowledging racism in all its expressions; talking about it would create a conflict we, as a country, did not even recognize we had.

Something is evident in the unpacking of my racial baggage: coming to the United States brought to the surface my anti-Black bias, with which I have the most difficulty coming to terms. From the very beginning in this country, I chose white neighborhoods to raise my family and kept my distance from Black and Latino communities. I thought that white communities were safer for my kids, and what I did not say aloud was that Communities of Color were dangerous places to me. Not connecting with the Black and Latino communities left me without a concrete grounding to branch out into new areas of racial growth. Living in a community I desired, that unfortunately barely tolerated my presence, created a climate of survival for me and my young family. Surviving is a dangerous context for developing a racial self because it pushes you toward those in power. I was not white, but was close enough to it to help make my life easier.

My racial ignorance and denial were shaken as I began my professional life. I was very unprepared when I entered Brown and Black places to work. Early in my counseling career, for instance, I worked in a therapeutic community where several of my colleagues had been in recovery from drugs and alcohol abuse for several years, and at least half of them were Black. We had weekly supervision with an Argentinian psychiatrist who appeared to be as racially ignorant as I was. Several times during those sessions, I remember feeling verbally attacked by one of my Black colleagues. I still remember the intensity of his anger when he was speaking with me, but I never understood what it was about me that triggered such intense expressions of anger. Unfortunately, my supervisor was ineffective in unpacking what was going on relationally between the two of us. Without a resolution, we kept our distance and tolerated each other enough to work together. Months later, in another supervision session, I told the group I was not attending the following supervision session because that day was the closing on my new house. My Black colleague questioned the fairness of a new immigrant like me buying a home when I had just arrived in this country a few years before. He followed this question by assertively stating, "That would never happen to people like me." His voice carried some anger, but mostly sadness and frustration. I remained silent. However, I did find myself privately wondering whether because of his long history of drug use if he had likely missed taking advantage of the opportunities to attend college and have a career.

Retrospectively, I can see my negation of his experiences as a Black person, while simultaneously assuming a blaming-the-victim stance. I had an unwillingness to examine how my Mestizo privileges, created and nourished in my country of origin, were translated into an uncomfortable, albeit beneficial, closeness to whiteness. Some nuggets of unearned white privilege were bestowed upon me once I stepped foot in this country and embraced elements of whiteness. Fortunately, my preimmigration racialization principles of denial and silence around issues of racism and my Mestiza racial privileges were tested repeatedly, helping me to move ahead in my racial identity process.

During a race conversation with a group of Women of Color, I was asked by one of the group members, a Black woman, what my interactions were with Blacks in my country of origin. I responded that I had few recollections of interacting with persons of African descent in my country. She took a moment to digest what I said, then expressed her disbelief. I tried to explain that I come from a country separated by regions and that the area where I was from had very few Blacks. In my memory, partly learned at school and partly learned in my few travels across Colombia, most African descendants have historically lived on the coasts of my country, and I added that to my response.

I felt embarrassed. I immediately doubted the veracity of my answer because it came from old, unexplored racial memories. I was probably wrong, I thought. With the insidious anti-Blackness I was exposed to growing up, I probably did not see Black people even if they lived next to me in Bogotá. I felt embarrassed because I knew my reply to the question had a hard landing on the minds and hearts of the Women of Color in the group. I had given them an answer based on what I remembered or imagined about my interactions with Afro-descendants in my preimmigration life. However, my answer lacked the flesh, blood, and heart it deserved; it was a skeleton of an answer. I also felt humiliated, but I was unsure where these feelings came from. After reflecting, I realized my response to my colleague's question was a denial of Black presence in my city, which minimized, marginalized, and devalued their presence and existence. It took me several months to identify how my response came from a place of racial privilege based on skin color and my close identification with being something I was not, nor could ever be—white! It was a painful and, at times, humiliating reminder that the invisible baggage that I had happily and naively dragged from Colombia to "America" was finally being unpacked. I was growing closer to the racial human being I wanted to become.

Colonial Racial Mentality

My Mestizo privilege, the privilege that protected me from most race-related discomfort in the city where I grew up as a light-skinned Mestiza, was the first item in my racial baggage to be questioned the moment I entered this new context with new racial norms and practices. I felt the loss of racial status in my body as I entered the U.S. airport and was interrogated by the immigration authorities. I felt their condescending tone in the questions I barely understood. My lack of English skills appeared to be a great source of frustration for them; I was making their work difficult, and I did not deserve their efforts to accommodate my limitations. I could read it in their faces, in the way they did not look at me but only at my immigration papers, which, luckily, were all in order. That was my first encounter with the reality that, racially, I was no longer privileged; I had fallen to a lower category I did not recognize. But even with that sense of loss of racial status, my light skin and that of my partner continued to protect us during the months and years after our arrival, except when we had to speak. It was then that our lack of English skills and heavy accent would locate us in the immigrant, non-English-speaker, likely undocumented, category, as the following story illustrates.

Once in this country, we moved to a suburban, white college town. My partner and I were coming home when another car hit us from behind. It felt like a fender-bender type of collision. When my partner opened the car door to meet with the other driver and evaluate the damage, a police car arrived, and a loud, white officer came out of his vehicle and approached the other driver. The driver and his partner, an older South Asian couple with darker skin, dressed in traditional clothing, were ordered to get out of their car. The police officer screamed and yelled at them as if they were children. Our fear, combined with our poor knowledge of the English language, did not allow us to understand what the police officer was ranting about. We were puzzled by what we saw as an over-the-top display of police authority, but we kept quiet. We were afraid of being questioned and treated the way the other couple was treated. It was clear that the couple felt humiliated but, like us, did not say a word. Finally, the police officer came to our car, asked my partner to go with him to see that nothing had happened to our car, and told us to leave. We were relieved but deeply shaken by the experience.

For the rest of our trip home, my partner and I anxiously conversed about what prompted the police officer's aggression toward the other couple. Was it their ethnicity, traditional clothing, poor English skills, and apparent immigrant status? We shared all these identities with the South Asian couple. Why was the police officer so aggressive and demeaning with the other couple and so dismissive with us? We were almost invisible to him; he did not even ask for our driver's licenses and registration card. Did he pick up that we were also immigrants, and because the other couple caused the accident, all his rage went to them, leaving us to witness and learn the lesson: this happens to people like you when you don't obey the law? But the question that never entered our conversation was whether our lighter skin color saved us from becoming a second target for the white police officer's rage. Why didn't I see the brutality of the assault on the South Asian couple as racially motivated?

Regardless of our ethnicity, recent immigration status, and poor English skills, we moved into white spaces without many difficulties after arriving in the United States. I was oblivious that the benefits we received, such as renting a house in a white neighborhood, registering our children in the school, and entering postgraduate education, were facilitated because of our proximity to whiteness. My unexplored preexisting racial beliefs were confirmed then; I could continue living my life without paying attention to my racial being because I was very close to racial normalcy, that is, close to whiteness.

Complicating this picture, I want to add that an additional component in my racial suitcase was likely activated. I came from a country where thousands have been killed or disappeared because of their political beliefs, and we, as college students in the 1970s and '80s, were primary targets of the armed forces. I experienced the fear of prosecution because of my political ideas, but not because of my skin color. Somehow, however, when I immigrated to this country, I was not afraid of the police force. I assumed that in this "civilized," enlightened country, police did not abuse their authority. I told myself that happened in countries like mine, not here. I assumed the police force was inherently superior to the police in my country. This piece of colonial mentality—again part of my racial baggage—colored the way I assessed the white police officer's aggression toward the South Asian couple as over the top, but not as the racial attack that it likely was.

Class Conscious, Yet Oblivious to White Supremacy

During my earlier conversations about race, I began to hear U.S. white folks of my generation describing their early racial memories. At that time, I did not see any similarities between their stories and mine. My budding racial awareness did not allow me to identify how much denial, blindness, and ignorance I shared with them. But the closer I listened, the more I ultimately heard. I could no longer dismiss what we had in common: we both struggled to remain in conversations and self-exploration regarding our racial privilege. At those moments, we would divert our exploration to our oppressed identities, social class.

I grew up in the 1960s, a decade of challenges and revolutions everywhere, including Colombia. I was born in a country with Indigenous roots, colonized originally by Spain and recolonized some centuries after that by powerful global economic interests and policies. At 16 years of age, I was part of a collective fighting for social change in my country, but the social change we were fighting for did not include racial liberation. We knew how the colonial and neocolonial forces kept our country and the rest of the Global South poor and dependent. Still, we could not see how much darker the skin color was of the countries in the Global South compared to those in the Global North. Unfortunately, I don't remember having any discussions or conversations with my *companeros de lucha* where we identified those colonial and neocolonial forces as being informed by white supremacy. Yes, we were aware of the U.S. racial conflict, but in our imaginations, we were nothing like the gringos in the North; after all, we thought we were a racially mixed society without the kinds of racial prejudices and the Jim Crow laws that made the United States genuinely racist. Somehow, we were not able to see what was in front of us but veiled: that social class and race follow the same rigid hierarchical order in Colombia because race, ethnicity, and class have been historically and profoundly socially intertwined; that is, upper-class whites at the top, middle-class, mixed-race people in between, and poor Indigenous and Blacks at the bottom. It became more evident to me that a very similar hierarchical order existed in the United States, with even more wealth and power as a driving force. This transformed the naive views from back in my youth when race and racism were not organizing my social understanding. My current ideas closely resonate with the results of the Project on Ethnicity and Race in Latin America (PERLA) by Edward Telles (2014), who states, "These data reveal that, in the case of Colombian society, social classes have skin colors" (p. 125). My *companeros* and I were correct. Thus, the class inequality in Colombia was extreme and long-standing, and what we missed from our privileged Mestizo/anti-Blackness bias and colonial racial mentality was the role that race and racism had played in such inequality. My racial blindness, ignorance, and collective denial, although invisible to me, informed my preimmigration racial self-concept and organized my way of thinking regarding those around me and my larger context, and it continued to do so after coming to this country.

Racial blindness or denial comes from some place. Experiencing the direct consequences of poverty in my family and community ignited and supported the development of my class awareness and consciousness. In a city like Bogotá, then and now, I did not have to go far to see how the prettiest, cleanest, and best-preserved parts of the city where men, women, and children exuded privilege belonged to the upper crust. This view was in stark contrast to the places and persons where folks like me and my parents lived. Rubén Blades's (1979) song, "Plastico," which I danced to with much passion during those days, describes what I thought and felt about the pretty people living in the pretty places in the city of my youth. Looking at the startling differences and feeling angry about the jarring inequality pushed me to search for answers to fight for class equity and justice. Unfortunately, I did not have the same contextual fertile grounding when exploring who I was as a racial being.

In contrast, my subordinated social location as a poor person fueled my class sensitivity and informed my understanding of class and class struggles; the dominant color of my skin and ethnic Indigenous roots did the opposite of developing my racial consciousness. A light-skinned Mestiza like me, born and raised in Bogotá, was provided a racial bubble of sorts. I grew up thinking of and describing myself as "racially normal," a Mestiza, *con color de piel morena clara o triguena*. As the capital, Bogotá has traditionally been the bastion of white Colombia, the home of the political elite. But Bogotá is also considered a Mestizo city, where my poor family, community, and I found the city a racially comfortable space.

Unexpectedly, my immigration to the United States provided the fertile ground to question my lighter skin privilege and internalized whiteness and better understand who I was becoming racially. It also opened my eyes to the contradictions and conflict between the process of racialization in my country of origin and the continuation of this process in my host country. The unpacking of my racial baggage, the painful and rewarding process I describe in this essay, was also necessary. Not knowing what I was mindlessly carrying in those invisible bags had the potential to derail my path toward greater racial awareness and sensitivity in my clinical work. As noted here, I firmly believe that my past racialization, before immigration, deserves as much attention as my racial development since I came to this country. My racial past and present are inseparable in my mind, heart, and body. They are also inseparable in my work as a social worker and clinician. When I now reflect on the earlier stages of my training and particularly my clinical work, I am left with a deep sense of shame, remorse, and grief. I now realize that the racial baggage that I failed to unpack early on had significant implications for all the clients I worked with, regardless of their racial background. In retrospect, I think of all the sessions when I failed to hold white clients accountable for all of the "just between us" racially insensitive and racist comments they made about African Americans, Puerto Ricans, and Mexicans. Instead of challenging these comments, I think I was relieved that I was regarded as different, and therefore acceptable and exempt from their obvious racial animus. I now think about how objectionable and repulsive these issues are to me now and how easy they were for me to ignore earlier in my career. Unpacking my racial baggage, which has included working with Supervisors of Color and racially sensitive white practitioners, as well as critically exploring my racial background, has dramatically shifted how I work as a clinician. In my contemporary work, I recognize the value of encouraging difficult conversations about race and racial identity regardless of who the client is or the presenting problem that brings them to therapy.

As a practitioner, coming to terms with my story has paved a way for me to see and understand that race is an integral part of who we are and how we walk through the world, and yet it can be simultaneously shielded from our awareness. I now understand that as a clinician, if I am not actively curious about race and its impact on clients' lives, regardless of their racial background, it can remain in the background, unseen, unaddressed, while remaining powerfully significant. This newfound perspective has been elucidating and liberating in my clinical work with poor immigrant Latinx youth, whose complex identities and life experiences as poor, Youth of Color, and immigrant are often unfortunately simplistically reduced to "migrant youth." As a result of my own racial evolution and enlightenment, I have a keen understanding of why it is critical for therapy to create ample space for them to explore how their skin tone, physical features, hair texture, and their proximity to whiteness and Blackness are complexly entangled with their immigration experiences, but also how they are treated both in and outside of their respective families.

I lived for 25 years in a racial context that promoted a culture of denial about racism based on the idea that as mixed-race, or Mestizos, we could not be racist. Once I became the target of cultural and other kinds of discrimination in the United States, my anti-Blackness bias and Mestiza privileges became even more obscure to me. It has been a complicated and humiliating process to come to terms with the fact that I could be the target of racial discrimination and at the same time, I can racially discriminate against others. As a bilingual, bicultural, light-skinned Mestiza clinician, I want to continue making space for Latinx and other clients in my practice to explore both.

Without unpacking my racial baggage, my efforts to have meaningful race relationships and substantive conversations, something I am fully committed to clinically and personally, were significantly impaired. For example, it was not until I embraced my deeply rooted internalized anti-Black biases, explored, and worked hard to deconstruct and dismantle them, that I could then do the type of intensive racially sensitive work that many Black clients deserved to receive from me and all other clinicians. Similarly, my work with all other clients was also stifled by my failure to see and treat race as an integral and integrated dimension of their lives as well. Thus, allowing myself to earnestly and retrospectively explore my racialization process and its impact on the development of my racial self in the United States transformed me as a therapist. While I remain a work in progress, I am comforted by the fact that the racial unpacking process to which I have been committed has empowered me with a sense of humility, deep respect, and sensitivity to assist those I serve to unpack their racialized baggage.

CHAPTER 9

At the Intersection of Whiteness, Trauma, and Relationship

SHARON RC LEE, PsyD

My dad's toast at our wedding should have opened my eyes to the work I needed to do on my identity as a white person in a multiracial, multicultural relationship, but I didn't get it at the time. My dad, who was notorious for saying inappropriate and embarrassing things loudly and without any self-awareness or self-consciousness, did not discuss his toast with me ahead of time, of course. As he picked up the microphone, my stomach lurched in dreading anticipation. Unforgettably, he started, "Our families are *exactly* the same." Long dramatic pause. I looked around the room, which was half filled with Thai families and half filled with my largely white family and friends. He went on to repeat this phrase emotionally a couple of times. I believe he thought he was saying something quite progressive. Like he was saying, "Even though Tom and his family are different, I don't look down on them. I don't see the difference because I see us as exactly the same." Ugh. I froze with embarrassment and horror. It felt wrong, although at the time I don't know if I could have articulated why. It's the kind of racist statement that was hard to question at the time, because it relied on what we have all been trained to believe and understand by white supremacy, that white culture is the standard by which all others are judged.

The wedding, somewhat reflective of our identities, was a mixture of traditions of Thai culture, Thai Buddhism, and nondenominational Western spirituality. Tom and I were born in the same hospital in Kansas City, Missouri. My family is white, immigrating to the United States mostly back in the 1600s from England and Germany and the 1800s from eastern Europe. Tom is first-generation Thai American, though his father is ethnically Chinese. We had planned to get married several years earlier, but Tom's parents had made it clear that they didn't support that decision. They didn't approve of the timing we had chosen because in their minds there is a proper order to things, and you don't get married before you are done with schooling. But they have never talked about their feelings about the fact that Tom was marrying a white woman. Our understanding is that Thai people have a view of white women as fat and lazy. Although they never said these words directly, we have suspected that race had to be a part of their discomfort with our relationship. While interracial marriages are more common now in Thailand, back then, it was rare to see a white woman with a Thai man. One of their objections we could do something about, the other we couldn't. So we delayed our wedding until Tom was done with graduate school and then hoped they would accept our marriage.

Our parents embodied the cultural and racial divide our relationship represents. While our dads were both doctors in Kansas City who knew each other professionally, their relationship didn't seem to grow beyond that over the years. My dad was a grandstander who frequently broke into uninvited song and dance. Tom's dad has a reserved presence and a surprising and understated humor. Tom's mom, and my stepmom, Marilyn, never seemed to have a way to understand each other. Marilyn was hard of hearing and Tom's mom spoke English as a second language, making comprehension a challenge at times. Marilyn was always buying things at garage sales and thrift stores and piling them around the house to be forgotten, while Tom's parents' house was and is always impeccably clean and orderly.

When we would get them all together, they seemed to mystify each other. My parents, white, privileged, and self-centered, didn't know how to be culturally attuned or even curious. They were loud and took up lots of space. In their older years they became more racist, culminating in my dad working on an "Obama notebook," where he thought he was going to crack the case of Obama's birthplace. I am still not sure if their racism got more outwardly expressed and sharp as they aged or if I just didn't see it growing up. But they seemed to have the kind of racism where some People of Color could prove themselves to be "one of the good ones." They had friends who were People of Color, and they still had racist ideas that shaped their perceptions of people, the news, and political events. Tom's parents are always quiet around white people, but when they are with their Thai doctor friends, they are the life of the party. It's karaoke, frivolity, food, and laughter. With my parents, Tom's parents would try, but their impulse to withdraw was palpable to Tom and me. I don't think my parents ever clued into how uncomfortable they made Tom's parents feel. They didn't have to. Tom's parents were the ones who were required to tolerate my parents' self-centeredness. And that is exactly what white supremacy teaches us they should do.

Tom and I had a certain way of talking about race in our relationship for most of our time together that was defined by noticing differences between us, often with humor. We weren't, however, really talking about power or about white supremacy with any kind of intimacy or vulnerability. It wasn't until the murder of George Floyd, when we both felt called to deeper personal exploration of our own racial identity, that we started having more intimate conversations about how race has shaped us. Before that time and especially before the 2016 presidential election, I was busy being a working mom, trying to keep up, climb the ladder, get it all right; I was complacent about the state of our culture. I bought the idea that Obama's presidency was a sign that we as a country had arrived at some new level of racial healing. We were the kind of well-meaning progressives that Martin Luther King Jr. (2018) talked about as being the most dangerous kind of white liberal. Tom is obviously not white but admits that he was "silently, obliviously complicit." We sat back, focused on our family, and slowly worked through our own healing. I believe it has taken time to get to these conversations because we had to know how to face ourselves and each other and deal with our emotions and traumas.

When we were 17, Tom and I fell in love. What I saw in him was stability, family, culture, and most importantly, kindness and gentleness I hadn't known before. What he saw in me was irreverence, drive, passion, and freedom. Our dynamic from the beginning was that I was on a mission to save myself from the trauma I experienced in my childhood and escape the Midwest, and Tom was my wingman. My healing took up a lot of space in our relationship in those years. I took up a lot of space in our relationship. I often feel awed that we survived those early years because I came out of my family fragmented, and he was trying to be obedient, something he had been taught to do in his family. We were both taught in the white midwestern culture we grew up in that his experience was less important than mine because of my whiteness. So for many years, while I was trying to heal, that setup felt comfortable to us both. That's an admission that I don't like to make because I can see now how it contributed to Tom's culturally sanctioned invisibility all those years. It's painful to think that my healing and my whiteness required him to be small, at least with what we knew at the time.

In the early years, Tom made it easy for me. This is what white culture demands, that white people's needs be centered. But it was also such an easy fit for both of our psychologies. We both viewed him as easygoing and laid back, which also translated into not having needs and being compliant. There is an aspect of Thai culture that also implicitly demands compliance and to reflexively wave off one's own priorities and say, "It's all right." I was so full of desperation and survival drive; I had enough drive to get us both out of Missouri and into a whole new life. I feel such a mixture of shame and pride at our origin story. We were so unformed, like amoebas. And yet, we found a way to cling to each other and survive. We had a long phase of this dynamic where our relationship was organized around my healing and needs.

Recently, I was talking with my very savvy 18-year-old and Tom about writing this piece and all the different ways to approach it. Jo asked me, "Mom, do you think that the stereotypes about Asian men being weak and passive might be part of the reason you chose dad?" My gut sickened with shame. After a pause to reflect and take stock internally, I had to say, "I think so." I looked at Tom apologetically. Later, I asked him, "How is it to hear me say that? Does it hurt you?" He said, not really. It wasn't a surprise to him. "At least we are talking about it," he said to me. But the truth is also that by the time I was 17, I was afraid of white men. I had been abused, mistreated, and oppressed by them my whole life. Tom's kindness and gentleness was life changing for me. I didn't know it consciously at the time, but I was looking for a way out of the oppressive white patriarchy I grew up in and thought I found it in Tom.

When Tom and I were ready to build our family, we chose Portland, Oregon, as a place to raise our kids. We were still looking for a home, but now we were looking for our home. I remember in our discussions we had some talk about how Portland was a very white town and how this was a downside against other places we were considering. At the time I knew nothing of Portland's history or why it is such a white town. Over the last five years or so, I have learned about its disturbing history, that the city I love and chose as my home was born of white supremacy and genocide. It is no coincidence that Portland is so white. Now I know it was very intentional in the minds of the white people who founded Portland that they did not want to exist with the people who already lived here, nor did they want to exist with recently emancipated Black and African American people. Early laws in Oregon made it illegal for a Black or African American person to exist in the area or for free, formerly enslaved people to move to Oregon to settle (Semuels, 2016).

In the last two years, as I have explored my own internalized white supremacy, I had to ask myself, why was I drawn to Portland? I didn't know the history, but I did know it was a predominantly white city. On one level, I disapproved of this fact. I wanted my kids to have more diversity growing up than what we have in our neighborhood. But I have had to come to terms with the fact that on another level, I felt safe in Portland. I felt safe in my white neighborhood. It feels like without the safety and belonging of my own family, deep down in my bones I fell back on what white supremacy culture (Okun, 2022) taught me was a way to be safe, to be with white people. This is a privilege Tom didn't have in our move to Portland. He is often the only Person of Color in the room.

As a relational therapist, when I work with couples, I can see so clearly how people choose their trigger and their savior simultaneously. Certainly, that has been true for Tom and me. One of the things I think drew us together is a sense of nonbelonging and psychological homelessness (Hardy, 2023). My sense of nonbelonging came from being abandoned by my mom and experiencing abuse, poverty, and frequent moves in my early life. I grew up feeling outside my family, left behind in the wake of a high-conflict multiyear divorce and custody battle that defined the first five years of my life. When I left my parents' house to go to college, I knew I could never go back. On paper, I had their financial support and was attending a private college. In my heart and soul, I felt I had no roots and no place to fall. I took summer jobs away and made plans that meant I never stayed at my parents' house more than five days.

Tom was the first in his family to be born in the United States. His parents were part of the first wave of immigration from Asia in the late 1960s following the loosening of anti-Asian immigration laws (Takaki, 1989). Tom's grasp of Thai language and culture was interrupted and fragmented. Despite being conversant in Thai, he always felt self-conscious and childish in his speech. When his family visited Thailand in the summer, he struggled to find his place among his many cousins, aunts, and uncles. Meanwhile, growing up in a town of 10,000 people in Missouri, Tom never felt he knew how to be one of the guys. He didn't enjoy watching or playing football or other sports. His family didn't go to church or know how to celebrate the holidays, which left him feeling like an outsider. We both felt weirdly orphaned from our families for very different reasons and found a sense of belonging together. But we also found in each other our triggers. It would take years and building a family to see clearly the triggers we would become for each other.

After we had kids, our dynamic shifted because I wanted more engagement from him, and he didn't know how to provide that. I was a panicked mother trying not to be panicked and to be perfect without being perfect since I knew intellectually that perfection is an impossible trap. When my demands for his engagement got loud enough, he started working to find a way, but all he had as a tool was trying to be what his parents had taught him to be: perfect, smart, and focused on pleasing others. For a long time, we were both fighting hard to find a sense of adequacy. He would check out to protect himself, and I would push us both harder to try to fix all that I thought was wrong with our relationship. This is the dynamic we have been trying to change for the last few years. It's slow going when the pattern is so ingrained in both our nervous systems since adolescence and underwritten by the culture that wants us both to lose ourselves in not good enough, fear, shame, and thinking.

I was always very verbal and communicative, whereas Tom's family communicates mostly in nonverbal and implicit ways. I have always dominated our communication and demanded that he meet me there. I am quick-thinking and persistent, which makes me a formidable debate opponent. Tom wasn't supported in his family to make a case for his point of view, let alone a decision. But for me, that was something I had learned to do as a survival strategy, to make my case and pursue. I didn't see how that gave me power over him in our discussions. After a childhood of feeling unwanted and invisible, I felt relaxed and able to express myself fully. Unfortunately, I was at times driving right over Tom. And because I was in such a fragmented place, I didn't even recognize the space I took up. All I knew at the time was that for the first time in my life, I felt safe and close to another person. For Tom, it was familiar to orient himself around someone else's needs as he had organized himself around his elders as well as white supremacy culture (Okun, 2022).

Another layer of the power differential in our relationship is that I am a therapist, teacher, and supervisor of relational therapy. To some this may seem like an advantage in a relationship, but in my experience it is hard to say how much that has been an advantage versus a challenge. Being a couples therapist has sometimes meant my thinking is so far ahead of my own heart and body, or ahead of my own personal relational skills, that it creates a wide chasm between what I know and how I actually know how to show up emotionally and relationally. And in that chasm there is fertile ground for shame to grow. At the same time, I always have ideas about our relationship, about Tom, about how we could both be better, do better, and work harder. Sometimes those ideas help us find a next step toward wholeness and connectedness, but sometimes my ideas become an impossible standard that oppresses us both. I have spent a lot of time and energy in a panicky fixing mentality, trying to fix me, him, and us—and my professional knowledge has often been ammunition in that battle.

While I was becoming more aware of power and race in my own relationship, I was also seeing so much more in my work as a therapist and supervisor. It felt scary at times to bring in a racial lens, particularly when my clients or supervisors were white. White culture is assumed, and I had internalized the idea that we aren't supposed to talk about race because it isn't relevant to me or other white people. As I delved into my own racial identity and saw how my race shaped so much of my experience, however, my curiosity about how race impacted my clients and their relationships grew, as did my courage to bring it up. It was clumsy at times, as I tried to find ways to bring a racial lens into my work. Once in a discussion with a colleague, I was sharing my discomfort about bringing up race in therapy, particularly with white clients. She said, "We bring up uncomfortable things all the time. Would you stop asking clients about sex because it might make them uncomfortable?" Her question was a reminder that this is exactly what my job is: to help people face difficult things in their lives even if I have to be clumsy while I learn how to bring it up.

As I talked with more clients and supervisees about race, I saw how these discussions almost always deepened our work together. By working with people to help them own their experience and emotions, my clients and supervisees were emboldened as they unpacked the ways that white colonialist culture wants people to intellectualize, to focus on things and money and not to feel, be vulnerable, or emote.

Working with race and power was particularly transformative in my work with couples, where now I could see that power was always at work in some way. When I began to name it and work with it, my couples' patterns became clearer. As a therapist, I had to embrace my point of view and be willing to use my positional power in the room to give voice to the dynamics at play. I helped my couples see how the force of whiteness moved in their relating, in their blaming, intellectualizing, or perfectionism. Sometimes this became a common enemy my clients could come together to untangle from their connection.

Bringing a racial lens into my supervision and training challenged me to become a leader who prizes equity and connection over being right or sitting in the comfort of my positional power and money. I had to accept challenges and corrections from my trainees and to learn from them. As I got more experienced, I felt it deepened my relationships with my trainees.

These last few years have taught me that without addressing power and identity, we can actually do harm and miss so much of the richness of relationship (Hardy, 2018). Developing my own racial identity transformed my work in every capacity. I became a more informed, humbler, and more accessible therapist to all of my clients. The work will continue, of course, and I will always be in a learning and growing process of knowing my racial self. I am grateful to have had the support and resources to take on this exploration as it has improved my quality of life and enhanced my growth in innumerable ways.

Developing a racial lens has also highlighted an intersection that I come back to again and again. It is the intersection of my trauma and my whiteness. Sometimes I have thought that many of the destructive things that happened in my family are a manifestation of white supremacy culture (Okun, 2022). Our family was shaped by patriarchy and white supremacy, and it imploded dramatically, with a five-year divorce battle, constant moving, poverty, violence, and drug and alcohol use. And after the implosion, we were all required to act like our family hadn't imploded. We were taught to strive for greatness, not feel any emotions, and work hard so we could rise to the top. Not great tools for healing trauma. I didn't want to repeat the mistakes of my parents, but I didn't have any other culture to turn to. Many of the tools I had available were about perfectionism and hierarchy, and they only made it harder for me to be the parent and partner I wanted to be. I spent years in therapy trying to work my way out of these white values, though it was never named this way for me. No one ever reflected on the way whiteness was defining my way of being in ways that were keeping me stuck (Hardy, 2015).

Because I grew up feeling that sense of being orphaned, the culture that filled the vacuum of my family was white culture. Looking back, I can see that it was white culture that was already in me, telling me I had to hurry up and clean up the mess of my childhood so I could go on and have a good life. I spent years trying to get it right as a parent and as a professional, trying to climb a professional ladder to be at the top. I dragged Tom through all kinds of trials and tribulations trying to get our family to be right and good enough. I was driven by my fear, trying to be sure I didn't traumatize my own kids the way I had been traumatized. It didn't occur to me while the kids were growing up that my own racial identity could be a part of the puzzle I was trying to solve.

When I get into conversations about race, often my own trauma is stirred in one way or another. Five or 10 years ago, I don't think I had the capacity to explore how whiteness has entered the precious land of intimate relationship. It would have filled me with shame. But I am accepting more and more that whiteness is inescapable in this culture. Whiteness didn't invade and shape my relationship because I am bad, but because I am alive and live in this culture. There are many other complexities to our relationship that I haven't explored here. But I have spent the bulk of my time reflecting on our dynamics from an emotional or attachment perspective. Right now, though, it actually feels fresh and interesting to me to put all of that aside for a moment and just focus on our racial identities and how that shaped our dynamics.

In the moments when shame or reactivity take center stage, the challenge becomes holding that trauma in my own heart with kindness for my experience so that I can be open and empathic. But I have to do so without centering my trauma in the conversation. I really feel the tension in that intersection as I write this. How do I sort out what is whiteness and what is trauma? Are they different? White culture is a traumatized culture. I don't say this to let myself or other white people off the hook. Rather, I hope it offers a way through to reclaiming our humanity. White people have inherited a culture that traumatized ourselves by oppressing, killing, and dehumanizing others. It seems like grappling with our deepest humanity has to be some part of the reclamation and healing process. How can I hold that I have been the embodiment of whiteness to the people I love most in the world in a way that is humanizing? Because if I get stuck in the shame of that, I can't heal and reclaim my humanity.

This brings me to something I have learned over and over as a relational therapist. Sometimes healing means allowing hurt in and allowing it to hurt deeply while trying to stay open to it all. It is easier in some ways to be the person who is hurt than to be the person who is doing the hurting. For me, it will always be easier to claim my identity as the traumatized partner rather than the white partner who dominates. In my relationship with Tom, I can see that my trauma has gotten more airtime and focus from us both than my whiteness. In my mind's eye, I see a teeter-totter with my trauma on one side and my whiteness on the other. If I don't own my whiteness and look for how it is infiltrating our relationship, the teeter-totter will always be heavy on the side of my trauma, where Tom's needs can easily get lost. Can I bring my privileged self into focus in our interactions and look for the places where I think I am right, where I am acting as though my reality is the only one? Can I open myself to be shown by Tom and others the places where I am doing the hurting and let that hurt into my bones?

One of my mentors from years ago gave me the mantra, "the pain is the path." That phrase has been a touchstone I have come back to again and again. It reminds me that our capacity for pain is also our capacity for joy and other emotions. Running from pain is an understandable human instinct. But when we face pain and tolerate it, our hearts grow and our presence can become more powerful. In healing my trauma, I have held on to this mantra, and it has helped me stay the course of tolerating painful emotions. I am reminding myself right now of this mantra because I know its truth will help me stay honest about my whiteness. The pain is the path to healing and growth. Let it hurt that whiteness is in me. Let it hurt that I have hurt Tom with my whiteness. Let it hurt and let the pain grow me. And if I can do that and then just let it hurt, our relationship can be a catalyst in the lifelong project of untangling whiteness and trauma from my humanity and growing my heart.

CHAPTER 10

Notes From a Diary: Does Jewish Identity Cloud or Clarify an Understanding of Race?

ELANA KATZ, LCSW, LMFT

When I was a newly minted social work practitioner, my first job in the field was at an inpatient neuropsychiatry unit at a major teaching hospital. I remember a patient who couldn't see anything that was even marginally to the side of her field of vision; while her eyes were quite functional, her brain scan revealed lesions that made it impossible to see anything that was just off center of her experience.

◊ ◊ ◊

Decades later, and within weeks of George Floyd's murder in 2020, I was teaching an introductory course in emotionally focused therapy (Johnson, 2019) to a group of therapists who were new to the model, and I received the following email after the close of my first day of the program:

> I attended your course today and I don't understand why you included anything about race, your course sounds just like the news. I came to this training to get a break, I really wanted to have a nice time. I'd like to withdraw from the course and get a refund for the training.

I was upset, exhausted, irritated... and maybe feeling defeated that I hadn't effectively helped her see why race held such a meaningful place in therapy. But to really understand her, and my frustration with her, I had to look at me—and the parts that I didn't really want to see. I wondered if I might have thought anything like this earlier in my career, even if I would never have said it out loud. Could I have been that blind about the critical importance of race?

As I reflect on my own story, I'm white, Jewish, and of Central European descent on both sides of my family. My experience differs markedly from that of those Jews in the United States who identify as Jews of Color (12–15%; Leichtag Foundation, n.d.) and Jews in Israel, where currently the majority identify as Mizrachi Jews (i.e., Jews of Middle Eastern and North African descent) (Mazzig, 2019). While the arrival of my father's family in America is a bit cloudy, my mother's parents arrived in the Midwest in the 1920s thanks to the generosity of my mother's Uncle Harry. He was that proverbial immigrant who arrived at 11 years old with two coins in his pocket, and through hard work and grit made enough money to bring over every relative in my mother's extended family before the Holocaust. And while my mother's family never lived lavishly in this country, they were safe, with enough food and a roof over their heads. My grandfather was set up with a very small grocery store that was his to manage, and their family of five lived in an equally small apartment directly above it. This was something that in the 1920s would have been virtually impossible for a Black family in Chicago to do because of widespread and systemic racial discrimination and racism.

A generation later I grew up in Peoria, Illinois, at the time both the worldwide headquarters of the Caterpillar Tractor Company (Tarter, 2018) and the home of the Bradley Braves (2023), a (then) widely recognized college basketball team. Peoria was often cited as a model American city. "Will it play in Peoria?" was a tagline for asking if something would be received by middle America, in the heartland of the country. We would sometimes come home to find product samples in little plastic bags tied to our doorknobs. I grew up in a modest house and received what was considered a good education—I sang early and often about the "land of the free and the home of the brave" (our national anthem), and I wore red, white, and blue on July Fourth. At some point my brother and I got a small flag that we would rig up outside our front door on national holidays. I was proud to be from the "Land of Lincoln," as our license plates stated, because, as I learned in school, he had freed the slaves. Seemingly we were all here in a great country, and everyone could make it in "the *goldene medina*"—a Yiddish phrase that referenced a golden country of opportunity.

Over time, it became increasingly clear to me that despite all my family's efforts to be American, we didn't really fit in in our small town. I was the only Jew in my class. Classmates—when they saw me—pitied my fate, warning that I would burn in hell for my failure to accept Christ (although one did pray for my soul). My teachers rarely learned to pronounce my name (of Hebrew origin), and they expressed disbelief—year after year—at the number of Jewish holidays for which I missed school (my family observed them all). My brother was convinced that since no one had heard of the holidays we observed that if a truant officer discovered us out of school on a Jewish holiday, we would surely be arrested and put in jail. Since he was (one year) older, I gave him credit for a level of knowledge that exceeded my own, and so holidays became unwittingly braided together with feelings of otherness and fear.

More years didn't alleviate both subtle and less subtle messages about belonging. My fifth grade geography teacher denied that Israel existed. And when civil rights were discussed in our history class later that year, a classmate asked if this would mean that a neighbor who was selling their home could be compelled to sell it to a Jew. I had two teachers in the classroom that year, and I remember that Mr. Preston looked at me and didn't say a word, even as Miss Clark told the student that yes, if the law changed, they would have to sell to a Jew. While my family lived within the school district, I guess the important part of the question was that we were not on or near his block.

As all this was unfolding, what I didn't see was what was happening to Lucinda and Beatrice, the two Black girls in my class; if I received negative attention, I think they received no attention at all. I don't remember anyone talking to them; I didn't say much to them. I was so caught up in wanting to find a way in, or at least get by, that I couldn't afford to see their experience. I never got to know them, only that, to the best of my knowledge, they, like most Black people in town, lived below the hill. Below the hill was both topographically accurate and was an area populated by largely Black and exclusively poor people in our town. The first synagogue in Peoria had been below the hill, but that property was sold and a new, modern structure was built several miles north of the original site by the time I was in first grade. My class was the inaugural year of the gifted children's program in Peoria, and students came from outside the usual catchment area of our school. In another interesting twist, the foreign language we learned was German, so that many of the children could speak to their grandparents in their first language. This, too, had emotional repercussions for me, especially when the class sang the German national anthem, which then included the stanza: "Deutschland über alles" (para. 4), meaning "Germany above all," this being within 20 years of the end of World War II and the incineration of 6 million Jews in the concentration camps. When the two parts of Germany reunited in 1990, these lyrics were dropped due to their association with Nazi Germany (editors of *Encyclopaedia Britannica*, 2024).

I wish I could say that this was an elementary school problem, but of course it was a reflection of our town at that time. I remember we needed our phone line repaired, and the first repair person couldn't fix it; he was Black, and my father said he had to be quite new and without much experience because the phone company had just begun hiring Black people. My mom loved Lena Horne—a Black singer, actress, and later activist—who had come to fame (Biography.com Editors, 2021). My mom quietly said that she was likely gaining acceptance because her skin wasn't very dark. My parents seemed really troubled by these observations, but we didn't speak more about them. And then, like my brother before me, I left town when I was 14 and attended a Jewish high school almost 200 miles away in Chicago. In many ways I was too young to leave, but my parents believed that the social divide was going to become more difficult in high school, leaving me with two bad options: either more discrimination and isolation, or the risk that I would try to bend toward the majority and shed my religious identity. As best I recall, I told no one I was leaving. I imagine Beatrice and Lucinda went to the local high school, and I don't know what happened to them.

In my Jewish high school, I was no longer a minority; my religious identity was centered, all my holidays were not only recognized but celebrated, and I lived in a world where virtually everyone could pronounce my name. While there would be occasional echoes of my former, outsider status (so many of my classmates, and their families, had known each other since kindergarten, if not before), it was rather extraordinary to move into the safety and acceptance that my school provided for me. My memory is that I thrived.

And, in that same context, a different complexity presented itself. In this sizable Jewish community, I also met families who had direct experience of the Holocaust; concentration camp survivors with numbers on their arms, and the unspoken pressures for some of their children—some of my classmates—to compensate for all that had been lost, to somehow fill the cavernous void created by all the family members who never returned from the war.

Indeed, the generation that raised me and many of my white, Jewish classmates were shaped by those who had directly or indirectly seen just how dangerous being Jewish could be. This was not through history, or ancient texts; this generation that survived the invasion of the Nazis across Europe had seen the theft of Jewish homes and businesses, and the evacuation of Jews into ghettos or camps where the "lucky ones" escaped death in the gas chambers and experienced starvation and slave labor; Hitler's explicitly stated goal was to exterminate the Jewish race. This trauma lurked in the shadows even as the privilege of whiteness was extending its increasingly protective arm to the Jews who had immigrated to the United States both pre– and post–World War II.

Thus experiences of opportunity and privilege existed alongside the echoes of the Holocaust. I suspect that any ongoing discrimination in the United States, whether personal or systemic (well into the 20th century there were professions that were inaccessible to Jews, places Jews could not live, and quotas on Jews in higher education) (Anti-Defamation League, n.d.), loomed larger given their close proximity to the assaults of Nazism in Europe. Some Jews in this country chose to go into their own kind of hiding; changing their ethnic-sounding names, sometimes denying their Jewish roots, even using plastic surgery to change ethnic features—wanting so badly to be in at a certain kind of school, neighborhood, job, or club that they erased parts of themselves to get there. Is it a privilege to be able to hide? I feel ill giving voice to this question; that said, it is certainly an option that has never been available to People of Color.

And so this juxtaposition of safety and risk continued—the hushed or not so hushed stories of current discrimination, alongside the promise of safety, opportunity, even prosperity. For me personally, a high school teacher encouraged me to reach, to find and honor my aspirations, and her encouragement brought me to college in New York within a decade of the well-documented student protests in the 1960s against social injustices—poverty, the Vietnam War, and the unfair treatment of Blacks in America.

My initial reactions to any discussions about race and discrimination admittedly fell far short of what was called for—at the time I believed that I understood discrimination from the inside out; some people were against Jews, and others were against Black and Brown people. Wasn't it the same? What I've come to believe is that while there are echoes in these experiences that can offer a gateway to understanding and mutual support, any tendency to collapse the lived experiences into sameness denies both history and current realities in this country, and therefore holds serious potential to divide us from each other. Whatever shared pain and emotions there might be when one is othered and dismissed by virtue of identity, Jews came to the United States voluntarily, in fact eagerly, and largely found the safety and platform to prosper, with experiences of discrimination being the smaller postscript because of their proximity to whiteness; Blacks in the United States are primarily descendants of slavery, kidnapped, ripped apart from their families and social networks, denied the right to honor the traditions they had upheld in safety in their home countries, and brought involuntarily to create wealth for others. Two people may both have a fever, and for one this is a symptom of a virus and for the other it signals a life-threatening illness, and it is important to recognize the differences.

There are certainly examples of a shared understanding. As I was writing this chapter, I found an article that referenced a 1950s study which found that virtually every state had hotels and resorts that barred Jews (McHugh, 2022). At the same time, Black travelers were not only excluded from white spaces, they faced police harassment, physical violence, and lynching. McHugh (2022) noted that

> when Black and Jewish Americans both faced frequent discrimination in accommodations, they sometimes opened their doors to one another. In the early 1950s, Grossinger's [a noted destination for Jewish travelers in upstate New York] invited Jackie Robinson, the

first Black man allowed to play major league baseball, to stay there for the summer. (para. 16)

Grossinger's Hotel had started off as a farm offering relief from anti-Semitism, and it had become an oasis in the Catskill Mountains.

> The Grossinger family extended [this welcome] to a man battling constant discrimination and harassment. "I doubt that she [Jennie Grossinger] knew or could have fully appreciated how important the invitation was to Jack and me in the early Fifties," Robinson's wife, Rachel, wrote in her memoir. (McHugh, 2022, paras. 16–17)

While this story captures an experience of mutual support, to extrapolate that Jewish and Black experiences are the same denies their distinct histories. The above-mentioned laws against Jews that remained on the books well into the 20th century notwithstanding, their impact pales dramatically (pun intended) in the face of the history of Black people in the United States, and the gaps in the history of racism in this country make it easier to inaccurately collapse these differences. It certainly made it easier for me to imagine that our experiences of discrimination had more in common than was true. My own education revealed neither the cruelty with which slavery was inflicted nor the centuries for which it endured. I did not learn about Jim Crow laws, or the disparity between the mortgages available in white and Black neighborhoods that continued into the 1960s. And I was much too far into my adult life before I connected the impact of this history and the threats of overpolicing and mass incarceration with the health disparities between Black and white people. So while I have felt a sense of being othered, I can't equate Jewish and Black experiences in the United States. Even if individuals can reference personal experiences of injustice and the emotions they evoke, the threats and opportunities for Jews and Blacks in this country have been radically different. And yet I'm hopeful that we needn't collapse our experiences into sameness to be willing to see, and support, each other.

Years ago, in writing about inequalities in the family associated with gender, Rachel Hare-Mustin (1987) noted one can err by exaggerating differences between groups of people as well as by ignoring differences that do exist; at the same time she cautioned that "the way the therapist thinks about the world is the most powerful factor in family therapy" (p. 16). History matters. Truth matters. I'm glad not to impose arguments of sameness. And in seeing difference, I now find myself as a therapist revisiting some of the assumptions that have guided my professional work. I'm reconsidering the focus I've placed (as an EFT therapist) on helping clients get out of their left, analytical brain in service of helping them connect more with their emotions, and increasingly wondering if this is a universal starting place or one geared more toward whiteness, work that is needed to undo the emphasis on individualism and competition that separates people from their emotional interior.

And if some of the work developed by white therapists tilts toward addressing the defenses that reflect white culture, what have I missed in addressing what is core to Black clients and attuning to the challenges of their relationships? I increasingly wonder if rather than being cut off from their feelings, or needing help to learn about their emotions, Black clients are struggling with different rules about the display and expression of emotion, especially in white spaces. The actor Sterling K. Brown has spoken about the exhaustion he experiences as a Black man in white spaces, and the need he feels to keep his emotions behind a proverbial mask (Don-El, 2020). He notes that if white men get upset, they are considered passionate, but when he gets upset, he gets the message that he is too much (Don-El, 2020). As painful as this is to digest, Brown's ability to read the room emotionally and know how he is perceived is an important survival strategy. And so I now think more about how I can support Black clients by acknowledging just how hard it can be to keep checking their expression of emotions, rather than assuming that emotional awareness needs to be developed in the way that I work with many white clients.

I'm reminded that for people living in traumatized bodies, including racially traumatized bodies, it's not that feelings are unknown, it's that the safety for sharing vulnerable emotions isn't familiar and doesn't make reflexive sense. With life-threatening consequences for displaying emotions, our Black clients may need us to let them know that we understand how dialing down their emotions makes sense, and at times may save their lives; I think it's on me to honor that it can be a steep climb to revisit patterns that are tied to safety. Additionally, there may be value in acknowledging just how challenging it can be to find a way to leave their proverbial masks at the door if and when these patterns tied to safety unwittingly follow our Black clients home. It can be hard to toggle between the armor needed in the outside world and the intimacy one is trying to create and maintain at home. As a therapist, sometimes my role is to witness and name that truth.

It has also been refreshing for me to experience different ways to begin the therapeutic relationship. I remember the first time a Black couple suggested we get to know each other before we started therapy. I was initially quite surprised, and then I thought—how great, let's do this. Also, Marjorie Nightingale (personal communication, September 2023) has referenced *Black Families in Therapy* (Boyd-Franklin, 2003) and has taught about the use of storytelling in getting to know her Black clients, rather than coming forward with a list of questions to learn their attachment histories. She has found that by inviting clients to tell her their stories, she learns just as much, and in a format that is more welcoming and connected.

I am also beginning to wonder more about my focus on the couple and the nuclear family, as if other relational bonds are not significant. The late Dr. Sue Johnson (2008) was fond of saying that we now ask our partners for the emotional connection and sense of belonging that her grandmother got from her whole village.

My daughter and her family moved to Harlem when their boys were 4 and 8 years old. On moving day, I kept my grandsons with me for much of the day as their parents did the heaviest lifting of moving in. When it was time to bring them to their new home, we took the subway uptown and Milo, then 4 years old, started racing ahead with bursts of excitement. I knew that he knew he was supposed to stop at the corner. He always stopped at the corner. But what if he didn't? What if 4-year-old excitement won out over 4-year-old judgment? Since I couldn't physically catch up to him, I started calling out with some alarm, "MILO! STOP!" And I remember the fear in my body when he wasn't slowing down. And then, a Black man stepped out of a storefront, and he got it—he took in the whole scene—he heard me, he saw Milo, and he stepped forward and he stopped Milo. And not only that, he waited with him until I caught up to them, and he spoke calmly with him: "When your person tells you to stop, Milo, you need to stop." You see, unlike in my mostly white neighborhood where polite people might easily turn away if an adult is yelling in distress at the child or children in their care, this man demonstrated that he cared about all the children, not just his own.

Time moves on, we move on; people and places, too, can change. At a time when the "National Association of Realtors found that home buyers in America were whiter, older and richer than any time in recent years," an article reported that Peoria, Illinois, has become an attractive place for people with historically marginalized identities to buy homes and find community (Kodé, 2023, para. 11). It seems that Caterpillar Tractor, the company that at one time employed one-third of the town, pulled up stakes in 2017, and the loss of the worldwide headquarters allowed something new to flourish (Kodé, 2023). Prices fell, and the opportunity for people to move in and reshape the norms was there. There is a bookstore, Lit on Fire Books, which "focuses on selling works by marginalized authors . . . and . . . it's become a popular place for new Peorians to mingle and make friends" (Kodé, 2023, para. 25). " 'I come from generational poverty. I'm Black and trans. I'm an artist. Owning a house was not top of mind. . . . It feels like I'm ending generational curses,' " reported "Alexander Martin, a 30-year-old founding member of the Peoria Guild of Black Artists" (Kodé, 2023, paras. 48, 45).

And, as it turns out, that phrase I grew up with, "Will it play in Peoria?," had another meaning. It seems that Peoria was known as a city that had both Black and white vaudeville, and "Will it play in Peoria?" was code for "Will it work for all of us?" It seems like it was there all along, always foreshadowing something of great importance.

◊ ◊ ◊

On the last day of my last trip to Peoria, after my mom died and we'd helped my dad relocate a couple of hours north and closer to my brother, I stopped by a house on Moss Avenue, around the corner and just a few blocks down from where I grew up. It was built as a single-family house back in its day, but it had been broken up into apartments long before my time. I introduced myself to the owner and explained that I'd known people who lived in that house years ago, and I'd even been in the house quite a few times, but only after I'd left town had I heard that it had been a stop on the Underground Railroad. I asked if he knew anything about that and indeed, he'd heard that, too. I asked if I could possibly see the room where they'd hidden the enslaved people, and we went to a small, cramped room in the basement with a very low ceiling and no windows, and I imagined the runaway, enslaved people coming off the Illinois River, climbing up from below the hill in the dead of night. The room had been there all along; I just didn't know where to look.

PART III
THERAPEUTIC ISSUES AND APPROACHES

CHAPTER 11

Soul Work: A Pathway to Help Heal Communities of Color

KENNETH V. HARDY, PhD

Historically, the clinical field has devoted minimal attention to the specific therapeutic needs of Clients of Color, although fortunately this has begun to change. Despite gradual increasing interest in these issues, our society's commitment to the romantic myth of color blindness continues to contribute to a massive dearth of knowledge and understanding regarding what is needed to facilitate a healing process for Clients and Communities of Color. Clients of Color undoubtedly grapple with many of the same life stressors as their white counterparts, and they must also contend with the stranglehold of living their daily lives within a vortex of racial oppression. In fact, attempting to overcome the devastating effects of racial oppression is a predictable, normal, and necessary developmental task that must be dealt with across the life cycle for most Families of Color, regardless of gender, class, or sexual orientation. Unfortunately, it is an ongoing endeavor that is neither negotiable nor obviated by other social privileges that People of Color might otherwise possess or enjoy. In this chapter, the terms "People," "Clients," or "Communities of Color" are primarily referring to Black or Brown people, although the approaches presented can be helpful and relevant to other groups.

The racial climate in the United States of America is such that if one is a Black or Brown Person of Color, one is inevitably engulfed in the asphyxiating and soul-crushing dynamics of racial oppression. Regardless of the social outcome measured, whether related to educational achievement, health outcomes, prenatal death rates, home ownership, generational wealth, or a host of other issues, Black and Brown people are typically disproportionately located at the lower end of the negative outcomes. All these disillusioning outcomes are connected to living in a pro-racist society in the firm grip of racial oppression where the impact of the centrality of whiteness is pervasive yet ignored and/or denied.

Throughout the field, scant comprehensive and concentrated attention has been devoted to even attempting to earnestly ascertain what is it that constitutes the centerpiece of a healing process for Communities of Color. Sadly, this issue was never seriously contemplated at any point during my graduate school education in marriage and family therapy or during two postdoctoral training programs I completed in racially diverse cities with large populations of Clients of Color. Once again, the myth of color blindness, and the belief that the process of healing is centered around a universal set of therapeutic common factors, promulgated a one-size-fits-all approach to healing.

Unfortunately, I was heavily indoctrinated into this way of thinking, and it greatly influenced my ideas and beliefs, and how I practiced therapy and approached the process of healing. This was nonetheless the case even when my lived experience as a Black man contradicted the premises and principles of much of what I was taught clinically and academically. In my training, there wasn't much space or freedom to assume a both/and position, which would acknowledge that both common and unique therapeutic factors could and do coexist. The assumption was that all clients were essentially the same regardless of racial background or identity and that healing was healing. There was little to no acknowledgment that the concept of healing and what was necessary to promote it could be powerfully shaped by sociocultural factors such as race, class, gender, sexual orientation, religion, and a myriad of other factors.

On Becoming a Whitened Black Therapist

Regrettably, the formative years of my training were steeped in the belief that clinical efficacy was rooted in understanding the fundamentals of human behavior and how to effectively respond to it therapeutically. At best, this view was somewhere between race-neutral and race-oblivious. In other words, there was no substantive attention devoted to race, racial differences, or how the healing process might be defined or altered by the realities of race. All the theories I was exposed to were advanced by white theoreticians. All my professors, supervisors, and instructors were white, as were my internship and dissertation advisors, and neither their whiteness nor my Blackness was ever acknowledged or discussed. These critical issues were treated as though they were irrelevant. Although race, and especially whiteness, were never, ever overtly discussed, they didn't have to be because they were deeply and indelibly etched into the culture of the training program, often to the oblivion of those entrusted to be trainers. When whiteness is not explicitly named, and white trainers tend to think of themselves as trainers void of any consideration of their racial identities, it is easy to ignore the pervasive and unexamined ways in which who they are racially impacts interactions, policies, and all dimensions of the training experience.

Whenever I or a liberal white classmate amassed enough courage to mention race, the conversation was often brief, lacking in depth and critical inquiry, and often dismissed as my personal agenda to unnecessarily and inappropriately "racialize issues that were not racial." The terse responses to me were never considered racial microaggressions, indicators of racial bias, or inappropriate. Instead, they were considered testimonials asserting and reasserting the purist, Eurocentric view regarding the universality of the human experience. Adherence to this dogmatic view was necessary to graduate and ultimately to be successful in the field, even when it culminated in the "mis-serving" and underserving of Communities of Color. While many of these practices are often challenged in contemporary graduate and training programs, they unfortunately still exist in more sophisticated ways.

After years of training and subsequently entering clinical practice, I quickly and keenly became aware that I was doing so as a well-trained whitened Black clinician, and later as a GEMM, that is, a good effective mainstream minority (Hardy, 2008). I was eventually forced to confront my ineptitude in providing the type of racially relevant care that was so desperately needed within Communities of Color after being challenged by a Youth of Color, Omar. He was perplexed by an incongruity he saw in me that my training had made it difficult for me to discern. In a state of flustered bewilderment, he stated, with a look of painful puzzlement, "Yo Doc, I been tryin' to figure you out and I just can't get a grip on you, man. I mean, I see your complexion, but I don't feel a connection." He went on to say, "To be honest, I feel Blacker than you and I am only half Black. I'm thinking maybe you should check yourself before you wreck yourself. I'm just sayin'."

Like many of my white counterparts, I had been trained to view the slow or minimal treatment progress of a Client of Color as evidence of their resistance to the process or an indication that they were probably not working hard enough. Not once did I consider, or was I ever trained to even hypothesize, that maybe what I was generously offering was grossly misaligned with what they needed. My initial reaction to Omar was to dismiss his difficult—but brutally honest and accurate, I might add—feedback as adolescent resistance, which it could have been. However, it was also an accurate assessment of how I was showing up in our therapeutic relationship. He needed, as he later indicated, to "feel" me, especially as a Black man, who happened to be his therapist. He wanted and needed to know that he could open up and explore issues that were both central and unique to his life as a Person of Color. In a multitude of ways, and especially prior to his confronting me, I was oblivious to all the barriers that I had created in the process for him to receive what he wanted and needed from me. Interestingly, the barriers were neither intentionally nor consciously created. Instead, they were embedded in my approach to therapy and how I had been trained. My indoctrination and subsequent perfection of becoming a GEMM had earned me tremendous respect in the wider field while also deeming me ineffectual in the consulting room with Clients of Color. My distant, slightly emotionally detached, professional psychologically oriented approach to healing was an impediment to the process, rather than the conduit I wished it to be.

It was my work with Omar that inspired me to begin thinking differently about therapy with Clients of Color and how it both parallels and departs from therapy with white clients. My in-depth work with Omar, along with my own experience as a client with a white therapist whom I admired and respected, drastically challenged and changed my approach to therapy and began to enhance my understanding regarding what is needed therapeutically for Clients of Color to heal. While my therapist was empathic, understanding, and insightful, race was always a major barrier in our work. I always had felt that race was a central organizing principle in my life, and I was mystified and chagrined that it was never talked about in therapy unless I raised it. Even then, it was greeted with a polite, superficial, and brief curiosity that lacked traction, authentic interest, or engagement. After a while, I ceased to mention race because it seemed fruitless. I realized how much my experience as a client so closely mirrored what I imagined Omar's early experience was with me as his therapist. It is a major therapeutic dilemma for many Clients of Color when they work with white therapists who avoid mentioning race for fear of saying the wrong thing, and with some Therapists of Color who likewise neglect to mention it in any substantive way because they do not wish to be narrowly defined by their race. Mutism about race in therapy often inadvertently denies Clients of Color the opportunity to participate in a healing process anchored in soul work.

Soul Work as Healing Work

Communities of Color need the same empathic and insightful care that all clients desire and deserve. They also need treatment that is potently racially attuned. The core of the work that so many People of Color need, regardless of the anatomy of the presenting problem, is essentially soul work. It is soul work that begins to stitch, repair, and reconnect all the parts of the human spirit that have been broken, maimed, mutilated, and dispirited by hyperexposure to racial oppression and ultimately racialized trauma. Soul work is a racially focused holistic approach to healing that embraces and weaves together the emotional, psychological, spiritual, and relational dimensions of both the psyche and soul. It is predicated on the belief that full engagement of mind, body, and soul are tantamount to the process of healing.

Whether the presenting problem is centered around enuresis or encopresis, adolescents or adults, death or divorce, the therapist must be committed to engaging in soul work. This racially focused work is not intended to ignore or supplant addressing the pressing presenting issue(s) for which clients are seeking assistance, but instead to augment it. After all, there is no manifestation of pain and suffering experienced among Communities of Color that is completely segregated from the nuances of race.

A Pathway to Helping Communities of Color Heal

To facilitate healing for Communities of Color, critical attention must be devoted to the following: (1) acknowledgment and validation, (2) willingness to engage in authentic race talk openly, (3) addressing invisible racial trauma wounds, and (4) embracing and employing racially relevant healing approaches. It is worth noting here that the effective execution of these therapeutic principles does not de facto constitute soul work, but rather creates and provides the foundation for it to occur.

Acknowledgment and Validation

No matter how ubiquitous race is throughout our lives, our societal impulse is to deny the significance of it. Even when Communities of Color have been openly, directly, and inarguably assaulted by racism and oppression, it is not uncommon for many whites to deny, minimize, or attempt to negate its significance. Unfortunately, the consequence of this common society-wide practice is that many Communities of Color must live concomitantly with the painful realities of racism and the widespread denial that it is a salient issue. The lack of acknowledgment and validation of these experiences is disorienting. It is emotionally and psychologically destabilizing and often leaves individuals drowning in a sea of uncertainty and self-doubt. Many People of Color struggle with recurring and daunting thoughts: "I must be crazy." "Is something wrong with me?" "Is this in my head?" "Am I an imposter?" "Am I being hypersensitive?"

One of the first steps to creating a pathway to healing for Communities of Color centers around the proactive and public proclamation that race is a legitimate and critical issue that is worthy of consideration. When the issue of race is proactively introduced and pursued by the therapist rather than waiting for the client to do so, it conveys the soul liberatory message that "I want you to know that I know that race is an important dynamic for us to consider in our work. It is not the only dynamic; however, it is an important one!" This is one of many ways acknowledgment can be executed and integrated into the therapeutic process. While this might, at first glance, be reasonably construed as a clinical strategy, it is so much more and requires more than a commitment to doing. It requires a commitment to and comfort with being and bearing witness. It is the therapist's emotional availability and presence with the client that provides the groundwork for healing. This is an important task for the therapist to implement even if/when the client is seemingly oblivious to race and its widespread effects.

The healing potential of acknowledgment is fostered by the power and audacity it contains in clearly and directly naming that which is rarely overtly named throughout our society, and particularly in a context where it is neither contentious nor contested. The process of acknowledgment not only names the unnameable, but it also legitimizes (i.e., validates) the process of doing so. It asserts and affirms that the exploration of race is not just permissible but expected and is an essential component of the work to be done. This positioning paves the way for the second critical step toward promoting soul work and a pathway to healing, which involves transitioning from acknowledging race to supporting and encouraging deep, uninhibited conversations that center it.

Race Talk

It is rare that Black and Brown people receive the space and grace to talk openly and uninhibitedly about race, free of threat, reprimand, and/or reprisal. As such, both their voices and the legitimacy of their race-related stories are either managed by suppression, i.e., the willful and deliberate act of holding back, or repression, i.e., an unconscious act of forgetting or denying. Either way, Black and Brown people are coerced to sit in a cesspool of race-based agony with their voices muted, while fiercely fighting off complex feelings ranging from hopelessness to fury and rage.

Creating a safe milieu where People of Color can tell their stories in their own words—without interruption, edit, or censorship—is crucial to soul work and the process of healing. It is imperative that they do so with the understanding that both what is said and how it is said will be graciously and respectfully received with empathy and validation. Paving the way to talk about race enables People of Color to tell and honor the three pivotal stories that are liberatory and constitute the essence of soul work.

These three stories are: (1) stories of suffering (which center what happened to me); (2) stories of struggle (which center my journey to overcome and reclaim myself); and (3) stories of survival (which center how I am overcoming, aspire to overcome, and/or how I overcame). Without sanctioning race talk, expressions of acknowledgment, and validation, these critical stories will remain untold and healing severely thwarted. When the significance of race is acknowledged and talking about it is fully embraced and practiced, it paves the way for the third step of healing, i.e., addressing the invisible wounds of racial trauma.

Addressing the Invisible Wounds of Racial Trauma

It is virtually impossible to be hyperexposed to racial oppression and not be scarred and injured by racial trauma. Unfortunately, even with the nascent trend emphasizing trauma-informed care, the phenomenon of racial trauma is rarely considered. It is typically excluded in the broader discourse about trauma, and it certainly does not exist in our clinical lexicon. It is unnamed, unacknowledged, and therefore deemed nonexistent, even though Communities of Color are vastly affected by it. The deleterious wounds associated with racial trauma are also essentially unnamed and invisible. There are seven intersecting invisible wounds that must be acknowledged, validated, and addressed as a condition for healing. These wounds are: (1) internalized devaluation; (2) the assaulted sense of self (Hardy, 2013); (3) learned voicelessness; (4) psychological homelessness; (5) survival anxiety; (6) complex loss and collective grief; and (7) rage (Hardy, 2023).

In therapy and beyond, tending to these wounds is vital to promoting healing for Communities of Color. When the invisible wounds of racial trauma are acknowledged, validated, and treated as a centerpiece to the healing process, the focal point of the work must be designed to accomplish the following goals:

1. Develop and adopt counternarratives that restore dignity and systematically expunge all internalized race-based toxic messages from the psyche and soul.

2. Actively and assertively promote race-based self-love in all its manifestations—physically, emotionally, psychologically, spiritually, and relationally.

3. Overcome voicelessness and learn how to speak for the liberation of one's soul, rather than for the approval of whites and others.

4. Invest in relationships and relational connectedness.

5. Develop and fortify strategies of survival by investing in the power of community and relationships.

6. Make a deliberate effort to acknowledge and embrace loss and to create emotional, psychological, and relational space for mourning. This process also includes expressing grief for losses associated with one's literal self as well as one's symbolic self (e.g., the members of one's tribe); and

7. Embrace rage and identify ways to rechannel it. During this phase, it is important for Communities of Color to accept that rage is a natural reaction to unnatural and oppressive conditions. Thus, it is critical that they embrace, rather than deny, their rage and understand that doing so is necessary for healing.

These goals are integral to the process of healing but are difficult to achieve if traditional individually oriented talk therapy is the only tool that is used. The type of healing that is desired, needed, and envisioned inevitably requires therapists and aspiring healers to be amenable to using a wide range of racially relevant healing strategies.

Embracing and Employing Racially Relevant Healing Strategies

The healing process needed for Communities of Color requires the acceptance and application of a variety of therapeutic strategies that extend well beyond what has been historically propagated in mainstream mental health services. For example, music, song, poetry, prayer, and spoken word are all powerful culturally based tools that may foster healing. Dance, drama, movement, and somatic embodiment approaches (Menakem, 2017) are important tools for mending and bridging the Eurocentric-imposed fractures that often exist between mind, body, health, and healing. It is not only important that therapy and other sacred places create ample space for the integration of these varied instruments of healing, but also that they are applied with a communal-relational focus. This is not an indictment of individual work but rather a testimonial and affirmation of the healing potential of relationships. The type of relationally based work described here is even fundamentally different from traditional group therapy approaches, which often involve working with a collection of individuals, often without a shared racial experience, background, or history.

When we adopt a relational approach to healing, it becomes easier to call upon and incorporate immediate and extended family members in the process, as well as peers, religious and community healers, and ancestors. In this work, the boundaries of the healing circle are permeable, expansive, and fluid, facilitating the cultivation of a safe and sacred holding space. The space that is cultivated can offer Communities of Color the opportunity to counteract devaluation, mend the assaulted self, promote and model self-love, reignite and reclaim race-related joy that has been stolen or compromised by racism, transform learned voicelessness to voice, allow space for mourning and grief, develop strategies for survival, purposefully direct and rechannel rage, and, perhaps most importantly, create an existential and spiritual home for those of us who are psychologically homeless.

Healing Beyond the Therapy Room

It is widely known within many Communities of Color that the aforementioned approaches to healing are rarely found in traditional psychotherapy settings, at least in a comprehensive and consistent way. For example, in the African American community, healing routinely takes place in the community barber shop, hair salon, fraternities and sororities, and in the Black church, where song, scripture, spoken word, movement, and narratives of suffering, struggle, and survival are acknowledged and validated as a matter of common practice. These are the places where hope is restored and despair defeated, if only momentarily. These community-based resources constitute the epicenter for soul work and healing for many Communities of Color. Yet, more is needed. While these healing centers are vital pillars of the community, many do not offer the depth, continuity, and sustainability to adequately meet the gravity of the need. New and additional pathways for healing Communities of Color are needed. Expanding the conceptualization of therapy by extricating it from the shackles of white supremacist ideology and being more intentional about attending to the impact of racism and other systems of oppression on all our lives would be an important first step. Such a significant change would inevitably challenge our existing preconceived notions about what constitutes healing and what is required to achieve it. Most of all, embedded in this evolving process would be the unapologetic embrace of soul work as a viable pathway to healing that promotes and restores hope and aims to heal the souls of Communities of Color in all the hurt places.

CHAPTER 12

Names: An Effective Approach to Enhancing the Therapeutic Alliance and Addressing Racial Trauma

NIKETA KUMAR, PhD

The origin and history of Western psychotherapy is rooted in white and European thought, and is thus based in the values and cultural norms of these groups (Hwang, 2016). Western psychotherapy tends to position itself, and whiteness, as neutral and objective (Roberts & Mortenson, 2022). Even though the editors, authors, and participants in current psychological science are overwhelmingly white, race as a topic was highlighted in only 5% of publications from the 1970s to the 2010s (Roberts et al., 2020). Findings from mostly white samples are used as the basis for psychotherapy for all people, without acknowledgment of how whiteness may be playing a role. Furthermore, Western psychology is limited in its understanding of how whiteness traumatizes People of Color (POC) on a daily, unrelenting basis (Hardy, 2022). A survey (Horowitz et al., 2019) found that the majority of Blacks, Asians, and Hispanics say they have faced racial discrimination (76%, 76%, and 58%, respectively). The racial oppression that POC face is ill-served by the frameworks put forth in Western psychology, as the significance of race is minimized, and racial issues in therapy are often poorly handled, only further exacerbating harm.

Hardy (2023) has provided a robust conceptual framework for identifying, acknowledging, and ameliorating the impact of racial trauma, which he describes as the "byproduct of persistent hyperexposure to racial oppression . . . an all consuming, crippling, and debilitating condition" (p. 50). He highlights four aspects of racial trauma, two of which I will discuss here. He describes *psychological homelessness*, defining it as "a chronic state of psychoemotional and existential disconnection that assaults and destroys one's sense of safety, connectedness, security, and feelings of belongingness" (p. 208). He also defines an *assaulted sense of self* as

> the culmination of consistent exposure not only to devaluation but to acts of domination that may be physical, psychological, interpersonal, or some combination of these. The acts of domination often involve targeting the core being of People of Color by discounting and denigrating the essence of their racial identity and personhood. (p. 147)

The thoughtful consideration of a client's name(s) in therapy can serve as a culturally sensitive intervention for POC. It can mitigate the impacts of psychological homelessness by grounding an individual in their history, connecting them with groups and identities, and facilitating a sense of belonging. Exploration of how one's name has been related to and treated, which is unfortunately frequently negative and devaluing, can help to identify and address an assaulted sense of self. Devoting clinical time to the consideration of names may also provide benefit in the form of a stronger therapeutic alliance, which is a robust indicator of positive outcomes in psychotherapy (Flückiger et al., 2018).

The Significance of Names and Why They Matter

Personal Identity

For many of us, our name forms the root of our identity. When I think of myself, I think of "Niketa Kumar," which is the name on my birth certificate (though this is in flux—more on that below). When I think, "Who is Niketa, and what is she about?," many associations come to mind: Indian American, Brown, woman, psychologist, grew up in North Carolina, visited

India every year as a child, loves noodles, and so on. Our name is the label that encompasses the vastness of who we are, including identities, facts about our lives, preferences, and values.

I am recently married, and my husband and I both struggled with the decision of whether and how to change our last names, precisely because of the significance and meaning names have. My partner is white and has an anglicized surname that was originally Eastern European. My last name, Kumar, identifies me as Indian to strangers and ties me to my family of origin, both of which I like.

Long before it was a concretely relevant question, I sensed that I wouldn't feel comfortable changing my surname in order to adopt a future spouse's surname. As my relationship with my now-husband deepened and we discussed marriage, I felt even more certain about this, in terms of both resisting patriarchal naming conventions and resisting the systemic oppression of racial erasure via assimilation.

In thinking about whether and how to change our last names, my husband and I decided that we wanted to form a new family unit for us and our future children, and for all of us to have the same last name. We also wanted to select a name that feels representative of us as individuals and as a family, while also honoring where we each come from. For us, this meant that neither of our existing surnames felt right for the other to adopt.

We considered several possibilities. One idea was that both of us change our last name to a hyphenated name that includes both surnames. However, we felt the combination would be a mouthful and also decided against this option when we heard from friends that sometimes the second name in their pair gets dropped in day-to-day use by others.

We also considered various blends of our surnames; ones that incorporate the main phonetic sounds of our two surnames, and ones that incorporate the letters from both names into a new phonetic configuration. We landed on creating a portmanteau that retains the main phonetic sounds of both surnames and combines our surnames into one by dropping one letter of each surname. We involved our parents by sharing our thinking and process with them, as well as sharing different specific name ideas with them and getting their feedback. It was meaningful to feel their support of us and our decision.

This decision entailed a lengthy process of exploration, consideration, and conversation between us. Though it would have been easier (and less expensive) to make the change at the time of our wedding, we weren't ready yet. We filed the paperwork recently to begin the official name-change process and felt good about giving ourselves plenty of time to try out the name we selected before embarking on the legal process.

Though at the time of this writing my surname is still Kumar, it's worth noting that by the time you are reading this, my surname will have changed. I use "Kumar" here because I haven't yet decided how and when I want to update my professional identity with my new surname. This feels like another significant decision and one that I also want to take my time with.

Social Identity

Our names signal information about us to others: in our nuclear family, extended family, tribe, school, neighborhood, religious community, workplace, and ethnic community. Names introduce us and form the foundational building block of connection. Our names prime others' expectations of who we might be—we implicitly and automatically make assumptions about others based on their name.

Names may serve to bind people together, as with family names or naming a child after an ancestor or other important community figure. They can also be used as a tie to the future, as in the example of choosing a new name for a new family unit. Changing one's name may signal a transition, such as immigration, marriage, divorce, gender transition, religious conversion, or spiritual transformation.

Information Encoded in Names

A huge amount of information is contained in personal names. In Western culture, nearly all people have at least one name (i.e., a given name or first name) together with a surname (i.e., a last name or family name). Surnames typically indicate that an individual belongs in a family or other group (tribe, clan). When there are two or more names, typically only the first name is used to refer to the individual in everyday speech (Evason, 2021).

These conventions are by no means global or universal. Cultures differ in the number of names one is given, name ordering, the age at which names are assigned, whether names of ancestors are used or not, what facts are included in the name, and more. In fact, even the concept of having a specific, fixed name to designate someone is not universal: the Machiguenga tribe of the Amazon uses kinship terminology instead of personal names (Johnson, 2003). Someone's name may tell you their gender, nationality, cultural heritage, who their relatives are, what the family profession is, family wishes for the individual, their birth order, what day they were born, if there were special circumstances to their birth, and more.

An Example: Arabic Names

Arabic names follow different traditions based on the specific region. Though there is too much complexity to the naming practices to be comprehensively summarized here, even a broad overview will illustrate their richness.

Arabic names typically have five or more parts to them, including the *ism, kunya, nasab, laqab,* and *nisba* (Notzon & Nesom, 2005). The *ism* is the given name or personal name. It is gendered, given shortly after birth, and typically has a semantic meaning. The *ism* is used to address children but typically not adults, especially not female adults, who are instead called by their *kunya* (Appleton, 2023).

The *kunya* is an honorific name and indicates that someone is the father or mother of a particular person, and would thus be added after the birth of a child (Appleton, 2023; Notzon & Nesom, 2005). A childless person may also be given a *kunya* regarding a trait, such as "father of good deeds" or "Abu el Jamail" (Notzon & Nesom, 2005).

The *nasab* is the name derived from the patriarchal line and can include the names of the father, grandfather, and great-grandfather (Notzon & Nesom, 2005). The *laqab* is a religious or descriptive epithet, such as al-Rashid, which means "the rightly guided" (Appleton, 2023; Notzon & Nesom, 2005). The *nisba* refers to an occupation, geographic location, tribe, or family and can be used as a last name, though this varies regionally (Notzon & Nesom, 2005).

Racial Trauma Triggers Associated With Names

Approximately one in four people in the United States identify racially as something other than white (United States Census Bureau, 2023). Despite this, Anglo names are typically considered normal, while names of other backgrounds are often considered weird or foreign. Injurious treatments of non-Anglo names contribute to the wounds of racial trauma and exacerbate psychological homelessness and an assaulted sense of self. Renaming and nicknaming, mispronunciation, and mocking are three principal and recurring ways in which non-Anglo names are demeaned and devalued, both intentionally and unintentionally.

Renaming and Nicknaming

"That's too hard to remember. Can I call you [Anglo name] instead?" No matter the sphere of life, whether at school, at work, in the public eye, or even in personal relationships, people with non-Anglo names may be asked or pressured to go by an "easier" name, where "easier" is synonymous with white or Western European. When this happens, what may be communicated implicitly is: "My desire for convenience and comfort with your name is more important than respecting your identity, preferences, and personhood" or "the effort it takes to get your name right isn't worth it to me." Or more simply: "You aren't worth the effort."

Anglicizing is directly tied to British and Anglo-American colonization. Beyond the enslavement, theft, and murder of colonization, it is also important to highlight the deleterious impact of cultural colonialism or cultural imperialism, in which the colonizer imposes their culture (including language, traditions, and rituals) to create and maintain inequality and hierarchical ranking of people that dehumanizes and devalues (e.g., white supremacy). Sometimes this process is overt and forceful, as when people of a region are mandated to relinquish existing cultural customs and adopt new ones. My grandfather spent some time in jail for wearing clothes made of homespun *khadi*, instead of those made from imported British textiles.

It can also be more subtle or appear voluntary, as when individuals opt for Anglo markers, as when U.S. immigrants select a new Anglo name (Chao, 2021). Research indicates that names perceived as white American get higher callback rates for job interviews and may be seen more favorably by others (Kang et al., 2016).

However, "whitening" has psychological costs for POC. Zhao and Biernat (2018) found that adoption of an Anglo name by Chinese college students in the United States was negatively associated with self-esteem, mental and physical health, and well-being. The pressure to anglicize one's name sends a powerful implicit message that is at the heart of racial trauma: "I have to change who I am to be safe and accepted. I am not okay as I am."

Some of the most brutal practices of dehumanization involved renaming as an explicit strategy of psychological and cultural domination. Over 15 million people were enslaved in the transatlantic slave trade, and were commonly renamed with the name of their enslaver (United Nations, n.d.). In the late 19th and early 20th centuries, Native people in the United States and Canada were sent to boarding schools and stripped of their given names. Hundreds of children died at these schools, and there was rampant physical, sexual, and emotional abuse (Waxman, 2022). Stripping someone of their name is a way of severing their ties to their history, culture, and even humanity.

Mispronunciation

One of the implicit assaults on POC in the United States is the idea that what is white, English, and Western European is normal, good, and superior to others (Hardy, 2022). White supremacy ideology is present when non-Anglo names are seen as weird or too difficult. In conducting interviews with teachers and students about their K–12 experiences in the United States, Kohli and Solórzano (2012) found that mispronunciation and renaming, and the resulting harms, often begin at a very young age, when children begin to attend school, and have a lasting impact. Specifically, many Children of Color begin to view themselves and their culture as inferior to whites, as white supremacist ideology dictates.

Kohli and Solórzano (2012) share firsthand encounters of students, such as a Latina named Maythee (pronounced "My-TE" with stress on the second syllable), who had repeated negative experiences in school with teachers and the pronunciation of her name:

> Since kindergarten I've had my name anglicized to May-ThE.... In high school [a teacher] spent the whole year calling me Maitai! I just never had the nerve to correct him until the end when a bunch of students told him. I've always known that no one remembers my name so I have to make it a point of repeating it frequently. It's definitely always made me feel like an outsider. Since I come from an immigrant family, it was always yet another way that I knew I was not American. (p. 15)

They shared another respondent's story, who remembered a student of theirs:

> Every teacher she ever had mispronounced her name. She dreaded daily attendance, never raised her hand, and tried to remain inconspicuous and anonymous in the classroom. She graduated from one of Portland's high schools with honors. At the honors ceremony prior to graduation, a vice principal walked to the podium to present the student with a prestigious award. He butchered her name mercilessly, shaking his head and laughing as others laughed along. The student slumped in her seat and hid behind the person seated in front of her. She did not go onstage to receive her award and did not attend graduation the next night. As soon [as] she was able to, the student changed her name to Anita. (Kohli & Solórzano, 2012, p. 13)

Regardless of intent, when educators mispronounce or mishandle a child's name, children often feel anxious, ashamed, disrespected, and devalued. When an individual has repeated experiences of having their name mispronounced, a common outcome is to become resigned to others not getting their name right. This might show up as not correcting the mispronunciation or saying, "You can say it however you want" or "Call me whatever you want" when they do have a preference.

For those who do have a preference around the pronunciation of their name, this acquiescence can reinforce feelings of psychological homelessness, devaluation, and an assaulted sense of self. It can bring up shame in not asserting one's own preferences and going along with what is easier for others. "Your comfort is more important than getting my name right" or "My name is (I am) a burden" might become internalized messages.

I have experienced pain around my name too. Hindi includes phonemes that American-English speakers struggle to accurately hear and recreate. My name has two sounds unfamiliar to American ears: an unaspirated "k" and an unaspirated and dental "t." Hindi's script is phonetic, meaning that it is pronounced as it is written (unlike English, for example). In Hindi, my name looks like this: नकिता.

When we first immigrated to the United States, I hated the way my name was pronounced with an American accent. Soon after, I adopted a shifted pronunciation of my name (ni-KAY-də, rhymes with "cicada") that would be pronounceable (often with some difficulty), and still often badly mispronounced as a more common "Nikita" (ni-KEE-də) by American English speakers. This is still the version I go by, except with other first-generation South Asians with whom I share the Hindi version.

Creating a modified version of my name allowed me to take control of the situation and still be called something I like. Even though I longed for the ease of an Anglo name when I was growing up, I was against adopting a completely different Anglo name (one exception to this was a period of six months spent in England as a teenager when I ended up going by "Niki" because I disliked both pronunciations of "Niketa" there, but reverted back to "Niketa" when I returned to the U.S.). My family and close friends call me a host of nicknames, including "Nik," but that is an earned right—not a shortcut to avoid the discomfort of learning my name.

It has been confusing having two different pronunciations of my name, and it has led to awkwardness for me in situations where people of both groups are interacting. As a child, this would cause shame. Nowadays I accept that it's okay to have two different pronunciations of my name, though I sometimes wonder if one "Niketa" feels more like "me" than the other.

If everyone could pronounce my name with the Hindi phonemes, I would have preferred to have just the one version. However, as this is not the case, I don't offer the Hindi pronunciation to American English speakers because I haven't liked the way my name sounds, even with effort made.

Names originating in an unfamiliar language, particularly those that are phonetically different from one's own, can be challenging to say perfectly. Research indicates that adults are able to improve their ability to recognize novel phonemes with practice, though there is individual variation in how much they are able to improve (Golestani & Zatorre, 2009). It is important to highlight that the complaint among People of Color is rarely about the mispronunciation itself (Adil, 2021). Instead, what hurts is the attitude or behaviors surrounding the mispronunciation: lack of effort, avoidance, dismissiveness, and mocking.

Mocking

In addition to renaming and mispronunciation, those with non-Anglo names may be subjected to mocking of their name. Names that hold value and significance in another culture are treated with outright ridicule, such as "Dong," "Hung," or "Ho."

Bich Nguyen (2021), a Vietnamese woman, writes of her given first name, "I cannot detach the name Bich from my childhood, cannot detach it from the experience of people laughing at me, calling me a bitch, letting me know that I'm the punch line of my own joke, too stupid or afraid to do anything but take it" (para. 6). In describing her contemplation and current use of the first name "Beth," Nguyen (2021) goes on to say:

> Is changing it now strategic, safe, self-care, selling out? . . . What I know is that being Bich, and growing up as Bich in a mostly white town in the eighties, has felt like a test that I was constantly failing. It was a double bind: the people who made me uncomfortable with my given name also thought that I'd be betraying my heritage by changing it. (para. 10)

Nguyen's piece is poignant—the balancing of shame on both sides, the lose-lose she points to as it relates to her name. I understand her choice and affirm her right to be called what she chooses. I also feel deep grief that she must consider the choice at all.

For POC, repeated experiences with renaming and nicknaming, mispronunciation, and mocking are often experienced as hurtful, offensive, and degrading. Since names are used frequently in day-to-day life, the damaging nature of these experiences is constantly reactivated and can aggravate racial trauma over time.

Addressing Names in Therapy

As we understand the particular significance of names for POC—how names impact identity and connections to others—we can also appreciate that having one's names mistreated contributes to racial trauma. Repeated instances of renaming, mispronunciations, and mocking can lead to an assaulted sense of self and psychological homelessness.

Our task as therapists is to validate the importance of these experiences and help clients speak openly about how they have been impacted. Racially sensitive care for Clients of Color means attending to the harmful experiences that are normalized in our white supremacist society. What follows is practical guidance with sample questions to deepen this inquiry.

1. What would you like me to call you?

In the initial session, we as therapists are often conducting an intake assessment or following our client's lead about what brought them to therapy. However, we can still take a few moments to ask about their name and pronouns in a way that sets the tone for later conversations. Taking the time to ask about a client's name and pronouns implicitly emphasizes the relationship and process, versus the task at hand (e.g., treating depression).

We can start with sharing a bit about our own name. I typically share my full name, how I prefer it to be pronounced, and what I like to be called (Niketa or Dr. Kumar), and my pronouns (she/her). I have corrected subsequent mispronunciations of my name—this has felt awkward and uncomfortable at times, but I've found that not doing so is distracting and negative for me. Besides the personal benefit, I believe that by speaking up I am modeling that clients, too, can correct me (or anyone else).

I then ask clients about their name: at a minimum, what it is, how to pronounce it, what they prefer I call them, and their pronouns. Often, clients will share both a full name and a nickname and say I can use either (e.g., "I go by both Priyanka and Priya—you can call me whichever you want"). When someone gives me a choice, I typically ask once about their preference: "I'd love to call you whatever would feel most comfortable. Do you have a sense of which you prefer?" Sometimes a preference is stated, and other times it's not. The aim of these questions is to build the therapeutic alliance and begin to address an assaulted sense of self. At the heart of these questions is a simple and powerful message: "You matter."

2. How do I pronounce it?

As people, and especially as therapists, when we meet someone with an unfamiliar name, we can display respect and cultural humility by taking the time to ask how to pronounce the name and making an effort to remember. This can be done by simply saying, "Could you pronounce your name for me?" If I feel I have enough understanding to try to say it at that point, I do and then immediately check for correction, as in, "Ai-sha. Is that right?" I look for the answer both verbally and nonverbally; I've found it's common to receive a verbal "yeah" but a facial grimace. In this case, I might say, "It looks like I didn't get it. Could you say it for me again?" If I need additional guidance, I might ask by saying, "Could you break it down syllable by syllable for me?" Once I feel I've got it, I write it down and/or create a mnemonic that helps me to say it. If in the future I am again unsure, I will ask again.

There are different ways of approaching a client with a name that one finds challenging that can greatly shift the energy of the encounter and the resulting impact on the overall experience. Staying calm, open, and curious signals to the client that this interaction is okay and normal. It says, "It's important that I say your name how you want it to be said. This is not an inconvenience. We don't need to rush."

Though it's natural to feel uncomfortable or impatient in having difficulty (I certainly have and do), this frustration can be communicated as discomfort or impatience with the client, instead of our own inability. It can lead to giving up on trying to say the name, avoiding the name, continuing to say it incorrectly, or even modifying the name. Even if this isn't the intent, the implicit message then becomes, "It is not worth my time or effort to learn your name."

Most often, it is possible to pronounce someone's name with some effort. There are also cases in which it might not be possible, even after effort. In these cases, the process matters much more than the outcome. As therapists, we can show respect for the other when we hold the difficulty as our own: "I'm sorry that I'm having difficulty saying your name properly" instead of "Your name is too difficult to pronounce." For many clients, to not be blamed or shamed is atypical or new and can be part of the corrective experience of therapy.

Whatever the outcome, there is plenty to process about the interaction itself. "How is it to take some time with this?" "What is it like for you that I am having trouble saying your name? Has this happened before? How does it make you feel?"

3. Tell me about your name.

Asking about names is a way of showing a deeper open-ended curiosity in the individual. It is a way of communicating: "I want to get to know you, all of you."

As therapists, our curiosity about a client's experience may spark their own. Asking about the origin or history of a name may lead an individual to want to learn more about their background or family history, which helps to place them within an interconnected (cultural, familial, ancestral) context, potentially mitigating the harms of psychological homelessness. When we show curiosity, respect, and humility, we invite our clients to see themselves through these lenses and begin to rebuild what has been assaulted.

Prompts for Further Inquiry

Does your name have a meaning?
Who named you?
Do you know why your particular name was chosen for you?
What does your name mean to your parents or whoever named you?
Is there anyone you're named after? If so, what do you know about this person?

4. What does it mean to you?

In addition to learning the history and information in a name, we should also pursue what someone's name means to them. It's one thing to know that my client was named after her mother's mother. It's another to know that her grandmother was the most reliable source of support in the home. A name is often a window to so much more.

Prompts for Further Inquiry

What does your name mean to you?
How have you related to your name over time?
Have you gone by different names over time?
Do you give a different name in any situations (e.g., at a cafe, ordering out, at work, at school, etc.)?
Do you like your name?
Do you wish for a different one?
Did you ever wish for a different one?

5. What's happened?

Since negative experiences with names are common for Clients of Color, it is important to ask about what has happened and the resulting impact. In a racially sensitive model of therapy, trauma history includes racialized trauma that is made invisible in traditional Western psychology and whiteness.

Prompts for Further Inquiry

Tell me about a positive memory that involves your name.
Tell me about a negative memory that involves your name.
Has anyone ever called you something other than the name you gave them when you first met? Did they ask your permission to do so?
Has anyone ever called you something you didn't like, with or without your consent (e.g. a nickname, a different name, etc.)?
If so, how did this make you feel (about yourself, your name, your family, and your culture)?
Have you witnessed someone else being renamed? How did this impact you?
Do different people pronounce your name differently?

Is your name pronounced as you wish it to be by others?

How is it for you to have your name mispronounced by others?

What do you do if someone mispronounces your name?

Have you witnessed someone else's name being mispronounced? How does this feel to you? Did you say or do anything?

Has anyone ever teased or mocked your name?

If so, how did this make you feel (about yourself, your name, your family, and your culture)?

Have you witnessed someone else being mocked for their name? How did this impact you?

Are there situations you avoid because you fear how your name will be handled?

Are there things you do to try and prevent others renaming you, mispronouncing your name, or making fun of your name? These might be so automatic you barely notice them anymore.

6. Meta: How is it to talk about this with me?

Through our inquiry, we strengthen our therapeutic alliance with the client. We can increase the intimacy of this interaction by asking about the meta process, and give the client space to notice how this impacts them on a relational level.

Prompts for Further Inquiry

How is it to talk about this with me?

When we talk about this, do you notice feeling closer, further, or the same distance between us?

What is it like for us to have these [cultural, racial, religious, etc.] similarities? And differences?

What is it like for you to be in relationships with people who have [cultural, racial, religious, etc.] similarities? And differences?

How does it feel to navigate these [cultural, racial, religious, etc.] differences?

Do you notice any desires or impulses, like wanting to check out, give up, avoid, or move closer? Explain; help me understand.

What do you notice in your body right now? [Offer somatic descriptors based on clinical judgment: pulsing, warmth, tightness, heaviness, openness, shut down, etc.

Summary and Conclusion

Traditional Western psychotherapy has a white, Eurocentric bias and has major limitations when it comes to acknowledging and addressing racialized harm faced by POC in our society. Exploring a client's name in therapy is a racially sensitive intervention that can address psychological homelessness and an assaulted sense of self, two invisible wounds of racial trauma. The topic of names allows us to make meaningful contact with our clients and can strengthen the therapeutic alliance.

Names have great significance for our self and social identity. They hold rich tradition and tie us to our family, culture, and history, just to cite a few aspects. We incur racial trauma when our names are changed without our wholehearted consent, when they are mispronounced, and when they are mocked. When we call our clients what they wish to be called and show interest in the stories of their names, we make room for clients to have a positive healing experience in therapy.

CHAPTER 13

Racial Harm in Helping Relationships and an Uncommon Journey Toward Repair

YASMEEN RUBIDGE, MA, AND LANE ARYE, PhD

What This Is About

Yasmeen and Lane

This is our story of a rupture that ended our coaching relationship that was built on a spark of mutual recognition, understanding, years of deep work, and trust. It is written by Yasmeen, a Black and Muslim woman who grew up in segregated Colored townships in South Africa, and Lane, a white Jewish man who grew up in all-white neighborhoods in redlined America. It is unusual in several ways. We write collaboratively, each sharing our experiences of the rupture, its aftermath, and our journey toward repair. It demonstrates the courage we needed to come into authentic relationship across multiple identities and power differentials anew. We grapple with what it takes to bring greater racial awareness, sensitivity, and complexity into helping relationships. Although the context is professional, our writing is deeply personal.

We chronicle what happened when an invitation to write this chapter brought us face-to-face across an abyss. This is a journey into the emotional and relational unknown, discovering what it takes to stay true to ourselves and respect each other, while inhabiting a world where racism seeks to destroy the spiritual truth of our inherent equality. It is our steps forward, pauses, and reversals as we commit to a healing journey and establish new ways of relating across race.

In this piece of decolonial pedagogy, our inner and relational journeys, insights across time and place, and attempts at deconstructing our racialized selves and relationship are the teaching. We hope you will find yourself within these contours.

As we were about to submit our first draft, the bombs had gone off in Israel and Palestine, with thousands of people dead and injured, people rendered homeless again, deeply traumatized, and grief-stricken. Stumbling through emotions to find our words, we do not take lightly the privilege and the poignancy of what it means for us to be writing together in these times. It is not yet usual or safe for those who hold identities like ours to speak and collaborate freely.

How We Came to Meet

Yasmeen

I met Lane at a number of global Worldwork conferences where I enjoyed hearing him speak (IAPOP, n.d.), and learned from his attentive and brave large-group facilitation. I loved his ideas about Unintentional Music (Arye, n.d.). I was young in my vocation. Working in South Africa early in its postapartheid, constitutional democracy, I was seeking methodologies that could hold me in transformational diversity, equity, and inclusion, antiracism, and leadership work. Processwork became a professional home beyond mainstream facilitation ideas and practices. Although there were no Black full-time faculty and few People of the Global Majority at the Process Work Institute (https://www.processwork.edu/), I signed up for the MA in Conflict Facilitation and Organizational Change.[1] I invited Lane to be part of my study committee. A few years postgraduation, I asked him, as a skilled Processwork coach, to support me to refract my experiences through a Processwork lens, so I could hone my craft as coach, facilitator, and change maker with greater awareness, wisdom, and skill.

Lane

I met Yasmeen numerous times in my capacity as Processwork teacher. Having witnessed her in large, international settings where global conflict was processed, I was impressed and moved by how she did not shy away from conflict and directness, yet kept her heart open to whoever was on the other side. I was excited to be on her study committee. When she later asked me to coach her, I felt humbled. How much could I, a white American man with little experience at that time in organizations, and none in South Africa, offer this brilliant Black woman in the context of her facilitation work? Our monthly sessions, which happened online, spanned six years.

The Larger Field

Yasmeen

While the construct of race is a fabrication, it has shaped all of our lives, and racism is most detrimental to Black life. Although Black people contribute enormously to helping professions, historic exclusions and ongoing barriers to access have resulted in white people being predominant in both representation and prestigious positions. This is true even in countries like South Africa, where Black people are a significant majority. As a result, Black people and other structurally marginalized groups often still find ourselves turning to white coaches, therapists, supervisors, and accreditation programmes. Furthermore, most research is still normed on white people from the Global North. And Black people still struggle globally to have our lived experiences and research published and taken seriously in distinguished publications. Thus the experiences, needs, and triumphs of people who fall outside of mainstream research are unlikely to be understood compassionately and in the context of systemic racism. Those actively marginalized by racism, patriarchy, gender oppressions, economic exclusions, and ableism find ourselves having to turn to those who benefit from systemic inequities when we need support. We turn to white professionals even when we hesitate to, and often at our peril.

Where white professionals are not finely attuned to how these power dynamics can lead to dysfunctions in relationships, they are bound to reinscribe systemic inequity at the relationship level. This happens by naming and misnaming the experiences of marginalized peoples; outright -isms; the lack of sensitivity to issues raised; individualizing systemic problems; lack of cultural humility; microaggressions; bias; and blunders and overt power dynamics that communicate that there is no safe place for us, even in relationships entrusted with support.

I have been in such situations many times. When I raised these with a coach, therapist, medical doctor, or faculty, I was usually met with shock, tears, exclusions, and accusations. I walked away many times from places of learning and people of holding, vowing that I would never place myself in harm's way of white professionals again. In this story within stories, I unearth the challenges of trusting white professionals with problems caused by whiteness.

Lane

White practitioners like me in helping professions rarely get adequate training on racial sensitivity or the inner and outer tools that are needed to navigate relationships with People of the Global Majority. Racial conditioning and de facto segregation make it common, in helping relationships between white practitioners and Clients of Color, for racial harm to occur at the same time as help and healing are offered.

Mindell (1995), who defines rank as "the sum of a person's privileges" (p. 28), says, "Rank is a drug. The more you have, the less aware you are of how it [affects] others negatively" (p. 49). The helping relationship invests professionals with power, expertise, and the privilege to frame what is true. This combined with white privilege makes it likely that white practitioners will not see our own potential hurtfulness.

I often hear from People of the Global Majority that years of dealing with white people have made them hesitant and hopeless about being heard if they voice their experience(s) of being harmed. Speaking might actually increase their suffering because white defensiveness makes it likely that white practitioners will not respond from the part of ourselves that is centered, wise, and compassionate. All this makes helping relationships between white practitioners and Clients of Color potentially dangerous for the latter. My complicity sits heavily in my heart as I write.

This story is about whiteness gone wrong or, perhaps, whiteness gone the way it is intended to go. It shines a light on the dangers of white defensiveness and dysregulation. It reveals how I shattered my relationship with Yasmeen with a display of my whiteness. It is my journey toward an ever-increasing awareness of harm, culpability, accountability, and what it means to be more fully human.

Part I: Histories

Ruptures (2020)

Yasmeen

Years into our coaching relationship, I was sharing with Lane in a one-on-one session about difficult experiences I had as a Black woman in a global coaching and leadership development program run by white faculty that took place outside the U.S.

Having completed the initial coursework of this program, I had to practice the method in the presence of the faculty, with me in the role of the "coach" and a colleague, who was a white South African, in the "client" role. He discussed his desire to leave South Africa, because he no longer felt safe there. Although he didn't specifically say so, it was hard not to infer that he meant as a white person in a changing and majority Black South Africa.

As he spoke, memories arose. When I was young, my grandparents, aunt, and uncle had been forcibly removed in South Africa during apartheid state violence. I remember my grandmother's rage, sadness, and eventual capitulation. I remember my father repeating: "They bulldozed our houses. They said we lived in a slum. These were not merely structures, but our homes, communities, the fabric of our lives." These forced human removals flattened communities where people lived together mostly peacefully across color, defying apartheid segregation, to make room for new whites-only communities on stolen lands. Fietas (where my family was pushed out of), Sophiatown (renamed Triomf—yes, Triumph) and District Six, to name a few.

My practice partner was intimating that he was afraid of people like me, yet my family had experienced oppressions like this carried out by people like him. It didn't seem to occur to him that articulating his fear of continuing to live here might impact me as a Black South African. Though he did not know this story, nor was he deliberately seeking to negate my history under apartheid, or diminish me, he seemed unaware of the systemic racisms, injustice, and inequity that formed our respective lives. He seemed oblivious about what it might mean for me to listen to his fears that drove his emigration, while the privileges of choice and access he had in more than one country was clear to me.

I was ripped in two. One part of me, a practice partner in an accreditation course, was giving my fullest attention. I understand the need to be heard. I know what it feels like to long for places of safety and acceptance, an understanding the world from my vantage point, and the need for the deepest inner and outer home. Another part of me, the Black woman, wanted to say, those you are afraid of in South Africa, are Black and Brown people–like me. And because you do not see my likeness to the Black and Brown people here, because you do not see the arc of histories and the trajectory of the futures, except from your own perspective, and because you probably do not see me all, except as instrument of your exploration, you press forward with your plans in my presence and expect me to listen.

Pressure built up inside me. I felt like vomiting. Lengthening my spine, I breathed through my strong desire to stop.

In this method, there was no place to do anything but diligently follow a series of elegant questions. There were no off-ramps for when it became hard for a practitioner or participant to continue, when aspects of our humanity or lived experience felt compromised. There was no built-in process to stop a client who might be saying something disrespectful or harmful. Neither was there space in the training to raise these issues, to interrogate the method or how we hold complex social dynamics as one-to-one practitioners. Embedded in the method was the naive, expedient presumption that we are individuals and equal, as if we exist outside of interrelated, unequal, social hierarchies.

I followed the module script. My practice partner was satisfied with the outcome. I got good faculty feedback. One more module, practice sessions, case studies, and I could be certified.

I felt sullied. In the days that followed I got sick. I had intense body pains. My heart was heavy with the shame of acquiescence. I had betrayed my deepest values and momentarily colluded for the sake of following a method that sacrifices systemic awareness at the altar of individualism and free expression.

How did I go through with that? Why did I not speak?

It took weeks before I could share this experience with the faculty. I hoped to dialogue about the challenges that arise when professional roles and social identity power differentials collide, and how memory and trauma shape such relationships invisibly. It was our professional responsibility to explore how to navigate racialized encounters like these in more nuanced ways than the method made room for.

The practitioner is in a position of power with respect to her client in that relationship. At the same time, complexities can arise when her client, who has greater social power every day, displays that power in a way that is disrespectful or harmful to the practitioner. What happens to the practitioner-client relationship if a client with greater social power says something that is wounding to the practitioner's identity and life experience? How can professionals from marginalized communities care for ourselves within such sessions? How can the training and the method ensure that practitioner and client can express their full humanity, rather than client cast as human and practitioner as machine? I had questions, ideas, and a heart hungry for real exploration.

In meetings following that session, the faculty minimized my experiences and questions. One reduced my questions about how racial and social hierarchies are embedded in helping relations to an issue of my personal discomfort. Another, as evidence of my personal psychology. Another problematized my feelings, caricaturing me as fierce while describing my practice partner as so innocent. They refused to engage on how racial traumas and other oppressive social structures are embedded in and can bilaterally shape helping relationships. They seemed unable to entertain the possibility that they were siding with my practice partner because of their shared identity. Assumed by faulty logic that only privilege bestows; that because the method embraces noble values, then these values are present simply if we follow the method. Floundering in my refusal to accept their facile dismissal of my concerns, one used a loving-kindness prayer as a weapon: "May you live with ease, may you be happy, may you be free from pain" (Seppälä, 2016, para. 8) to quiet me down.

Shortly thereafter, what I thought was a different kind of opportunity to resolve my concerns presented itself. I was invited to a gathering of practitioners who had completed a higher level of accreditation, even though I was only midway through the program. At some point in the meeting, the faculty raised to the whole group the questions I had posed, about how to navigate the tension between professional roles and social identity differentials that may arise in a coaching situation.

I was one of two Black people in the room. When my questions were raised, the faculty repeated the defensive answers, now with an audience. One said that he could not see what the problem was. Another belittled my experience, by saying it was not as if my physical safety was actually at risk. My blood pressure rose—it actually was dangerous to my body. Regardless, were they saying it was okay for Black psyches to be up for private and public assault? Another faculty member pronounced that I was clearly triggered. Another prescribed that I should get supervision. The conclusion drawn by global senior faculty seemed to be that if Black coaches felt upset by or co-opted into racism by their white clients, that was the coaches' problem. Whiteness and their power as faculty gave rise to their freedom to hold a tribunal rather than a dialogue. Having dismissed my concerns, they went on to questions raised by other participants.

I burst, articulating the cost for Black people's bodies and psyches to be in settings like these. Naming my fears of their retaliation, of being discredited beyond the group, I left shaking. For nights thereafter, I did not sleep. To me, it was clear from their questions and responses that they could not address my concerns as a Black professional. They were uncomfortable with not having answers to my questions, not knowing how to integrate into their model what I had brought. As soon as I offered a social analysis, and made race and power differentials explicit, the values that their training promised ceased to be present for me.

I brought all this to Lane, first, to be heard; second, to explore how to engage the faculty so I could complete my accreditation and without further harm. Feeling free with Lane, I was expressing the things I wanted to say to them. I named the shame of self-betrayal and staying silent, and the futility of turning to white people to address the harm white people caused. I needed to get everything out, hear myself, and be received. I was deeply with myself. There was a wild fire inside me, my hands were flames, thrashing rage skyward, waiting to be softened by the rain of Lane's compassion.

All the while, Lane was listening, gently encouraging my thinking and feeling. And then, quite suddenly, he left my side, saying, "You sometimes like to whack white people."

He had now joined them.

Lane

Feeling Yasmeen's distress, I encouraged her to express her legitimate feelings of frustration and fury.

When she said what she wanted to tell the faculty, I felt worried for her. After investing so much in this training, she was nearly certified. She could lose all she had worked for if she told them what she was expressing now. I considered saying this but was scared she would feel shut down by me. I started to unravel, felt dysregulated, searching in vain for the right words. Everything I thought of felt wrong. At some point, she paused. Internally pressured to say something, I grabbed for whichever thought was close at hand.

After Yasmeen's vulnerable and gut-wrenching disclosure, I said, "You sometimes like to whack white people." There was a long, excruciating silence.

My whole body vibrated and flushed hot with shame. *Why did I say that? I hurt and silenced her. How do I come back now? Breathe, Lane. We have developed trust over the years. We can repair this. But what if I just broke her trust irrevocably?*

I had been someone to whom Yasmeen had turned for support, exploration, and when frustrated and threatened by the whiteness all around her. Now I had betrayed her through my unchecked whiteness.

Engulfed by the shame of harming, I was focused on my failure rather than on her. When I tried to focus back on her, I was blank. Then came shame about that. This sucked me further down, away from her.

Breaking the silence, Yasmeen simply said, "I don't resonate with that."

Quickly, scrambling, I said, "I am so sorry. I was projecting because it sometimes feels good to express my anger in a hurtful way when I am hurt."

Yasmeen

I was numb, then became nothing. For some, it is spiritual practice. For me as a Black woman, it is what whiteness always cast me as. My heart, once ablaze, wanting transformation through this conversation, was dead. The fire, gone. I could no longer feel or hear my breath. I stopped fighting. I became silent, again. I cut off my aliveness.

I have no lucid recollection of where our conversation went. Lane must have said something. Surely, I did. But the impact of his words was the loss of memory of my own coherence, and the loss of my heart's desire to keep talking and be witnessed. The bottom fell out. Again. Dropped.

I had naively hoped that Lane could help me sort through how best to respond to the faculty, as a white professional himself. My Black woman guard down, I had not expected that he would become the very white person that I needed to defend myself against. I was left with the unspeakable question that reduced both of us to narrow identities and annihilating assumptions: How could I have trusted a white man with this? Of course, he took their side. To save whiteness, he had to take their side.

A circle of ancestors spoke with sadness and certitude: When whiteness is threatened anywhere, it is threatened everywhere, even here in a place of supposed sanctity. Lane retaliated. Whiteness retaliated through him.

Guiliane Kinouani (2021) says:

> Too often Black people are told directly or indirectly that we must keep quiet when we experience racial injustices—that is if these experiences are recognised as racial injustices. We are told that if we are upset about racist experiences, that is if they are accepted as racist experiences, that there is never anything to be distressed about. If we ever get distressed, we are reminded that we must be more resilient. More robust. More moved on. More mature. Speak not, we are told, but if you must speak, speak gently. Cry not. But if you must cry, cry silently. Write not, but if you must write, write impersonally. Exist not, but if you must exist, be as invisible as you can. Take up as little space as you can take. Let us not see you. Let us not hear you and let us forget you exist because your existence reminds us of who we are. (pp. 14–15)

This is a function of whiteness. To stop us dead. In significant ways. Therapy, coaching, supervision in the hands of whiteness is yet another way to get Black people to *calm the fuck down* and *shut the fuck up*.

Attempted Repair

Lane

I spent a few weeks turning myself inside out, trying to understand and feel what I had done. I spoke with other white people on the path of healing from whiteness. I tried to discern how whiteness had been operating in me and to feel into the potential impacts on Yasmeen. I eventually wrote an email. We had another session scheduled, and I did not want to wait till then to begin an apology.

That next meeting was tense. Gone were the warmth and ease between us. I did my best to repair, saying that I had not validated her experience but instead had contributed to a culture that pathologizes Black rage. When I said that I sometimes like to retaliate when I'm angry, I ignored the huge difference between me getting angry in close relationships and Yasmeen being enraged by a society that systematically puts down and silences the truths of Black voices. Those were the same putdowns and silencing that had sparked her upset with the white faculty. Mentioning my anger had also been an attempt to deflect her attention away from the hurtful thing I had just said. I told her I wished I had owned my racism in that moment and, even more, that I could have held and honored what she had expressed.

When I asked if Yasmeen had feedback for me, or if she wanted to express her upset or say anything about the impact on her, she didn't say much. She expressed appreciation for my growing awareness and apology, but I could tell she was closed. I thought I understood why. I was yet another white person who could not be trusted. Why invest in the relationship?

I did not see a way forward and did not want to burden her with further attempts since I had nothing new to offer. In the coming days, I grieved the harm I had caused and the loss of our coaching relationship and recommitted to developing racial sensitivity.

Surviving and Withdrawing

Yasmeen

I had nothing more to give. Every day, whiteness crashed into me; slanders, threats, accusations, on the street or in professional settings, notwithstanding my education, economic class, or all the work I do on myself. When Lane's email came, I thanked him for his reflections and owning his racism. Even though I wanted to offer something more because of our longstanding connection, deeply exhausted and punctured by the pain of betrayal, I could not.

What followed was my reversal from Lane, without fully saying why. Divorced from feeling in our final session, with the unspoken structured into my question, I asked: could he recommend Black women that I could continue working with?

I was making reversals elsewhere too. I call them my g(race)ful exits. It took me a long time, but years later I asked for a refund on the accreditation course that I had tried to process with Lane. One faculty member responded they would compensate me for the module I had not taken. Attempting to regain control, he asserted that this would conclude our conversation. Compensate? How could he think that a refund for a portion of the program I did [i]not[/i] attend, was a compensation? Did he think this would pay for the many stressors I endured during this process? I had saved for the program to pay for it up front but, as a result of my experiences, I withdrew, foregoing the accreditation I had sought. While a senior faculty member did apologize and acknowledge that his facilitation of my questions in the group meeting made it unsafe for me as a Black professional, ultimately, they failed to deliver. They lacked racially sensitive competence to support me as a Black woman. Harm was done. None was compensated for.

The founder eventually reached out, apologized, told me he had integrated some of my suggestions into their processes and training, and thanked me for setting him on a learning path. His future publication did not reflect any of this learning, and he did not indicate a desire to have further conversation.

It is partially true that some part of me "sometimes like(d) to whack white people." In the context of experiencing and witnessing racism of all forms, it would be unnatural not to feel this way. Wishing to retaliate is internalized oppression turned outward, a trauma repetition. Conscious or unconscious. Everyone who gets put down feels the need to stand up. That is human and requires only compassion. Especially from professionals. As a white man who benefits from racism, it was a poor use of Lane's power to level this accusation at me. I know I could have heard it, had it come on the wings of love, generous understanding, a gentle challenge, and supportive strategies, from a Black coach, who could have contextualized all this and held me in its complexity.

Inner Work

Lane

In the years that followed, I continued to work on my whiteness, particularly the racial defensiveness and dysregulation that causes me to cramp up and blurt out hurtful things. I used trauma resilience tools before and during cross-racial conversations. I also revisited these conversations with other white people to unpack and process my verbal and somatic responses.

Coaching, training, and supervision with Dr. Kenneth V. Hardy helped me get more honest with myself about the myriad ways whiteness is woven through my life and being. His compassionate directness helped me interrogate my thoughts, reactions, actions, inactions, and unconsciousness. It became clear that my core wounds would get activated in racialized situations. He helped me see that my subjugated selves (including the shamed, scared, and beaten children who live inside me) would often take over when I should have been staying fully aware of, and speaking from, my privileged position as a white man.

Working regularly under Black leadership in a Black-led organization helped me notice and pause my impulse to rush in with the answers. When I sat back, trying to not be the white man taking over, I was encouraged to lean in. I learned to bring my contributions while being open to feedback and staying aware of my racial location and potential impact. After living such a racially segregated life, building strong and honest relationships with Black people has been important medicine for me.

More and more, I realized my internalized white supremacy harms not only People of the Global Majority, it harms me. When I walk through the world without seeing the pain I cause, I am cut off from my own humanity. In order to actively or passively contribute to a system that causes harm, I have to harden myself, avert my eyes, and build a wall around my heart.

Nieto et al. (2014), in an exercise they call the Floor Is Not the Floor, invite the reader to imagine a large bustling lobby. At some point in this powerful experience,

> the true substance of the floor [the people] have been walking on is revealed. Suddenly you and they can see that the ground is made of the tops of the heads of people who are forced to stand very tightly together in order to create a surface for their activity. (p. 135)

I have never been able to, nor do I want to, unsee this image. White supremacy has designated white people to walk on the heads of others. Retreating to unconsciousness does not make this reality disappear. Rather, unconsciousness requires that I forfeit my humanity and become a shell of myself.

With this awareness comes incredible grief. When I allow myself to feel this, it tears my heart open. I commit to walking through the world with as much care and as little impact as possible and to helping other white people see this reality so harm is minimized. Despite my best efforts, though, I still sometimes harm, lose awareness, or contract into fear, reactivity, or defensiveness. Then I come back to center, unpeel the next layer, and continue to learn. This work is not about helping People of the Global Majority. It is about healing my own soul.

Part II: Three Years Later

A Request and Questions

Lane

When invited to write a chapter about white defensiveness in helping relationships, I could not get the harmful rupture with Yasmeen out of my head. I knew that, whether or not a chapter would be written, I wanted to finally make a proper repair, or at least ask whether she would grant me permission to try.

I considered the complexities of contacting Yasmeen after being asked to write a chapter. It was likely and understandable that she would not trust me, thinking I was being opportunistic. If the repair did go well, and if she were possibly open to some kind of chapter, this had its own complexities.

Yasmeen agreed to meet. I wanted to be grounded and prepared. I practiced settling my body, mind, and emotions as I revisited the rupture. With the distance of time and self-regulation, I could see the situation and my part with new clarity. I used the lenses of racial trauma and racial sensitivity. I remembered Choudhury's (2015) wise words about working across racial differences: "Self-compassion helps us observe ourselves with curiosity rather than judgment. It is the salve to lessen the painful sting of our mistakes so we do not beat ourselves up. Yet it still holds us accountable" (p. 45). My heart started to open, feeling compassion for Yasmeen and myself, where before had been only shame, remorse, and contraction. I reviewed what I had learned about racial repair, carefully and lovingly considering how to proceed.

Yasmeen

My mind was full of questions. My heart felt marginally open, but I noticed that my body was frozen. The frozen state from the moment of Lane's accusation years ago reappeared. Time had passed, but not for my body.

I knew I had to ask Lane every question I had, for my own integrity and dignity, regardless of what happened. Obscuration or indirectness would serve to coddle whiteness and racism. If it all broke down more, I would live with that. My questions were a source of my power.

Audre Lorde (2007) encouraged us by saying:

We have all been programmed to respond to the human difference between us with fear and loathing and to handle that difference in one of three ways: ignore it, and if that is not possible, copy it if we think it is dominant, or destroy it if we think it is subordinate. But we have no patterns for relating across our human differences as equals. As a result, those differences have been misnamed and misused in the service of separation and confusion. (p. 115)

I had to name my things. There would be no misnaming or misusing. Whatever the outcome, in this moment, in this relationship across difference, making new pathways for equality to emerge between us was my way. So, I asked my questions.

Why was he returning now? Did he want to genuinely repair, whatever that meant in the context of systemic racism, or was this expedient for the purpose of writing his chapter?

Lane

It was true I had not thought of returning to repair until the possibility arose to write a chapter. The chapter, though, was eclipsed by the necessity to repair the harm I had done. I was wide open to forgetting the chapter altogether.

Yasmeen

He wanted my permission to write a chapter on both our experiences? How would this not end up as colonial seeing, where a white man, from the distance of his vantage point, writes both our stories, narrating my experiences through his voice and perspective?

Lane

It did not feel right to leave out her voice by writing my version of what happened. I knew that white people often learn from the pain of Black and other People of the Global Majority, then write about it for profit or acclaim. I did not want to do that.

Yasmeen

On his further offer that he would write the chapter, without my identity being disclosed, ostensibly not to expose me, I felt angry. Why would I want to be protected by the stroke of an invisible-making pen? Context matters. Who tells the story, how the story is told, when the story starts, all matter. Social power matters. How could he possibly write my part of the story?

And then, when he offered that I could write my own experiences, to be woven into his chapter, without having my identity publicized, that felt subservient. Who would get the writing credit?

Lane

It was true that I did not want to expose Yasmeen if she did not want to be named. But I did not want sole authorship of our different experiences and common work. This so often happens to People of the Global Majority, like the many Black songwriters who received neither credit for their songs nor royalties for record sales.

Yasmeen

Finally he offered that we could cowrite it. It was the first time my body softened. A *yes* wanted to emerge, but who would get paid for this? I had too often created conditions for white folks to profit off my contributions, and then been kicked out before the real money was made. Or white people got paid the same or more than me, while expecting me to do double the work.

No, not another bridge called my back (Moraga & Anzaldúa, 1981), where Black women offer our pain, joys, lived experiences, and powers without fair remuneration. I did not come to this meeting expecting, wanting, or needing to write a chapter. But if I was going to, I would not repeat old patterns of being in service of white folks' recognition and financial reward.

Lane

Of course, Yasmeen would get paid; I would not accept sole payment for something we had collaborated on. And Dr. Hardy would never agree to that.

I had only mentioned those halfway, inadequate options because I could not allow myself to hope that Yasmeen would want to write something together, and I did not want to pressure her into more contact with me.

When she started to open to the idea that we could write the chapter together with both our names on it, I felt buoyant. All this could be moot, though. We had not yet discussed the rupture.

Memory and Accountability

Yasmeen

As we began writing, we tried to piece together how that first reconnecting conversation went. I remembered all my questions but very little of what Lane had said. Of emotional memory, I was blank. All I recalled was coming into the call willing to listen, and very cautious.

But Lane remembered. As he started to recount, I wanted to summon up his apology. I felt disappointed that I could not do so clearly. I noticed my own defensiveness. I said I did not want this to be some Hollywood movie arc—where white man says "sorry" to Black woman, she softens, they agree to write a chapter, and then it's happily ever after.

I wanted to find the root of my not remembering. What was right about not remembering? There was something that nonmemory wanted me to know, that might have nothing to do with recollection, but sat, instead, in my body. Images arose of white folks' past attempted repairs. Many experiences, false starts, failures, and being reinjured.

I realized that these failed repairs from white folks live inside me in the same traumatic neural pathway as harm, and sit together frozen. My wounded and weathered Black woman self simply did not trust Lane's reaching out. With so few memories of successful repairs with white folks (other than my husband), my wise body protected me against remembering. Lorde's words soothed me: "Pain is important: how we evade it, how we succumb to it, how we deal with it, how we transcend it" (Hall, 2004, p. 16).

Was my lack of recall a question of science, soul, or conditioned racial survival? Black voices inside me preached: *Don't expect us to remember their good deeds. Why should we?*

I did remember arriving on the call cynical. Was this another white person who wanted to repair simply because he could no longer sit with his own discomfort? Might healing with me be some kind of personal accomplishment? Or was a healing moment simply a pass to a book chapter?

All my years of trusting Lane, on my study committee, then supporting me to develop my process-oriented facilitator practice, were shattered.

Now, I was with and for myself, with the nontrusting part of my Black woman self, let down too many times; the white people who called me "my friend" or "sister" while being unwilling to be intimate with the ways they hurt me, labeled me racist because I named their racism, turned against me when I loved them enough to share with them how their whiteness was showing up, pillaged my work without paying me, shamed me for my vulnerability, blamed me for the rage their harm had constructed, retaliated when I held them accountable, wanted to repair on their terms and maintain control, unwilling to do the real self-interrogating work of repair.

Amid ongoing harm, I feared I had lost my power to discern what is genuine. I came to realize, instead, that my cautiousness is a powerful sentinel.

Lane

I started by describing what I remembered about the hurtful things I had done and said in that session and what I had not done or said.

By inviting Yasmeen to express her deepest feelings, and then not being able to hold them, I had put her into a double bind. By not fully validating her rage at how she had been treated by the faculty, I framed Yasmeen as the problem. My comment that she sometimes "likes to whack white people" was a repetition of the racist trope that Black people are violent or even enjoy violence. I had pathologized her understandable and natural response to being devalued, dismissed, and stifled. I had silenced her, which meant that she was no longer expressing her justifiable rage in what she had thought was a safe space. Instead, in addition to her original problem, she now had to fend off my unfair attack. An active participant in white supremacy, I painted Yasmeen as violent, then silenced her reactions. This silencing, Hardy (2023) says, creates voicelessness, which itself creates rage. Then that rage is used to pathologize Black people, as I had done to Yasmeen, which creates more silencing, more voicelessness, and more rage. I had become the engine behind a familiar vicious and toxic cycle.

I told myself at the time that I was trying to protect her from the white faculty's reaction. I now realized that I was really protecting myself. When

Yasmeen had described what she wanted to say to the faculty, I got scared. One level was fear of saying the wrong thing. More visceral was fear of a woman's rage, even when it wasn't directed at me. And particularly, fear of a Black woman's rage. My racial conditioning about angry Black women seized my body. What if she turned that rage against me?

I told Yasmeen that my role as a coach gave me more structural power in our relationship, adding the weight of authority and expertise to my harmful words. Yasmeen had entrusted me to hold her process with respect, care, professionalism, and racial sensitivity, a trust that had been built over years. My unjust characterization must have cut even deeper because of this betrayal.

Then I left her alone. Focused on my own shame and panic, I fled the scene by retreating into myself, a hit and run.

My heart broke as I said all this to Yasmeen, feeling the depth of my betrayal and the truth of being an integral part of the machine that was designed to deflate, depress, and destroy Black people. I sat with what I had done to Yasmeen and other People of the Global Majority, the times I remembered and many more I had forced myself to forget. I saw their faces: rage, tears, collapse, numbness, disappointment, or turning away. What I felt now was not the shame and panic that had sent me into unconscious disconnection in that damaging session. It was a stabbing, aching soreness. It was a grief and sorrow that came from staying with the reality of inflicting trauma and pain, the reality that the impact of my personal actions was amplified exponentially by similar harms done over lifetimes, generations, centuries, and continents.

Yasmeen

The next day, I wrote to Lane, "Thank you for surrendering to such drenching awareness. That is healing, hopeful, invitational, and begins a journey of rebuilding trust."

This began 10 months of meeting regularly online to work through what had happened, work on our relationship, and write.

Part III: Contours of Complexity

What Writing Together Taught

Yasmeen

We had stepped into a live field.

I got activated at times by what Lane wrote. It brought sediment of racial harm back to the surface. It was hard to turn toward what hurt. Ongoing feedback on each other's writing was weighty and made me edgy. When Lane, well meaning, interrupted my rhythm and style, I felt a white man standing over me. I pushed back. While trying to respect us both, I needed certainty that my perspectives remained salient. We grappled with power between us.

I struggled with the idea of racial repair. Without a commitment to ongoing restoration by strong and tender means, repair is at risk of being a once-off gesture from white folks, a feel-good thing, decoupled from dedication to the toil of deep self-examination. Steeped in ongoing global racial harm, one-to-one relational repair must be seed, not substitute, for all the work required to dismantle systemic racism.

I struggled with Lane's longing for me to write about him more positively. I perceived how hard it was for him to be in constant self-confrontation and felt compassion for him. Yet I was impatient. Whiteness has to rescue itself; that cannot be done by Blackness holding it up, soothing and redeeming it.

I wanted to retreat. Beneath struggles of collaboration, conjoined with hope, lived a chorus of internalized critics. Black radical voices crying, *traitor*; white voices clawing at *the facts*. I had to hold a counterforce to narratives deployed to dehumanize and divide. Multiple histories in my blood, multiple nows in my heart, and multiple futures in my womb, demand the impossible. Those born from inside the cracks must shine the light from below. Remembering my long-ago prayer "to find my voice, release my voice, and facilitate this process for others," I pressed on.

Spring came to me as it does in Johannesburg. Unexpectedly. There are no transitions. One day it is cold. Next, the jasmine is blooming and there is a surprise sweetness in the dusty, dry air. First of September, spring. First draft submitted, spring.

After we hit Send, I went for a walk, at times skipping, up our steep road. I played two songs in my ears: Nina Simone's (1967) "I Wish I Knew How It Would Feel to Be Free," followed by Louis Armstrong's (1967) "What a Wonderful World." At the last bend, something cracked open in me. My knees got weak, I folded over myself, and wailed. Throughout our months of meeting to write together, I had steeled, never cried. While I had witnessed Lane's tears as we wrote, I was not able to trust him with mine. Here, in the last stretch, alone, accompanied by nature and musician ancestors, I surrendered to uncontrollable sobbing.

Lifting my head, I felt gratitude to myself, to Lane, and for writing as a freedom doorway. Lane was willing to be with my anger and destabilizing questions without dictating the terms. On the edge of loss, he was willing to let go of the product for the relationship, and of the relationship—if it would create further harm. When I felt weary, Lane did not do that white "coachy" thing—tell me to *step up* when it is unsafe for Black women's power to emerge—then push me back down because I was "too powerful" or "scary." He did not make me a monster for my strengths. "You are so strong," projected one supervisor, pointing to my strength as something threatening. Nor did he make a weakling of me for my vulnerability. He did not sidestep the harm he caused or rush to put everything quickly behind. One colleague asked, "Why are you still so bitter?"—without looking at her bitterness inside.

I also felt tender toward myself, for having the courage to keep standing for my truth. I did not have to be nice, capitulate, nor take the shape of what oppresses. I burst through shame and soothed my tiredness. I felt an inner stability that racism has not been able to diminish. The knowledge that we were not meant to survive or thrive—yet we do—gives me soft strength, an upright spine and clarity that is without the bewilderment I see in white people's eyes when they first encounter themselves as race-made. I was not merely the person that things happened to, a Black and Muslim woman's body positioned for whiteness's meaning making. I took up my creative agency and roles as storyteller and theory-maker to reauthor. I loved myself for it all. I felt this as a centrifugal force inside me, which I harnessed with purpose.

We had meandered into moments of the blazing inexplicable sacred. Only once we sent our first draft did I realize we had begun to touch this, which rearranged me and strengthened my resolve to keep doing the work to dismantle all racism.

And that is why I sobbed.

Lane

As we wrote early drafts, I sometimes hoped Yasmeen would portray my wholeness. I realized this unfairly burdened her. Letting go of that desire was liberating. I had a visceral sense of how often I had become a child with People of the Global Majority, waiting for them to validate or exonerate me. This had not been good for anyone.

My writing at times sparked feelings and reactions in Yasmeen. In these moments, I might notice a falling sensation in my lower abdomen or tightening in my chest. I would pause and wait. Most of my awareness was on her, listening, trusting her wisdom, trusting that she was feeling and seeing something beyond my momentary perception as a white man. I intentionally kept another part of my awareness with my body, holding its reaction with love without identifying with it, waiting for it to soften. These moments were valuable and helpful to me and, we realized, to our relationship and writing.

I am grateful for the generosity of spirit that led Yasmeen to keep speaking her truth. She could have decided that our relationship was not worth it, too painful. I sensed this as an ever-present possibility, that how I showed up from moment to moment could tip the scale one way or the other. I sat with how to be present in a way that did not harm her or erase myself; how to show up both in my whiteness and my wholeness.

At times it seemed that choosing between Yasmeen's truth or mine was a win-lose situation, until I opened to an unseen path beyond either/or.

It always felt more important to stay with what was emerging between us than to get anywhere in particular in our writing. Being ready to let go of the chapter at any moment brought me a sense of peace and settledness that was unexpected. It reminded me that one norm of white-dominant culture is transactional relating, relating for the purpose of completing a task or transaction (Okun, 2019). Our process felt categorically different;

the relating was the foundation of and nourishment for the writing. Without it, there would be no writing.

Recounting the dysregulation that led to my harmful statement gave me a chance to revisit that moment of rupture and uncover yet another layer. I realized that my racial fear had been superpowered by my own trauma history. A scared little boy had taken over my body and mind. When he saw Yasmeen's rage, his body started to vibrate as it had so many years ago. His mind went blank, scrambling for the right response, like so many years ago. But back then, there was no right response. Knowing that any response would trigger rage and worse, he used to flip a coin and brace for the onslaught. Sitting with the rupture for months helped me understand that I had not been protecting Yasmeen from the white faculty's retaliation. What Hardy (2016) would call my subjugated self—and Fisher (2017) would call one of my fragmented traumatized selves—was protecting himself from Yasmeen's rage, from his mother's rage. In doing so, he was also protecting the white faculty and the whole system of white supremacy. Grown-up Lane, who knew better, was nowhere to be found. The boy was driving the bus and crashed into Yasmeen. I was not a small boy, though. I was a white American man speaking with a Black South African woman, a coach speaking with a client; I should have stayed wide awake to my privilege, power, and potential impact. I had learned this conceptually. Now I could feel it in my bones.

Yasmeen and Lane

Turning around every written word and sentence for precision and emotional truth was grueling and rewarding. One sentence, hours. A paragraph, a week.

Collaboration did not mean consensus. We had to find a way to listen, at times waiting for each other's words to find their place on the page, then in the heart of the other. At times, we laughed. Much later in our journey, rereading and re-feeling each harm—that lived between us but was so much larger than us—we sometimes wept together.

We discovered a deep respect and appreciation for one another as we helped each other midwife and tend to the words that wanted to emerge. Words offered us our way back and our way forward.

Reflections and Offers

Yasmeen

Should Black clients seek support from white professionals? Yes and no.

Yes—only if the helping professional demonstrates a commitment to an ongoing journey of self-interrogation related to racial privilege and can reckon with how they are implicated in Black trauma. There should be a deliberate slowness to use psychological diagnoses, which are incubated in racial inequity and whiteness, without learning how systems of oppression shackle Black well-being. White professionals should use racially sensitive and trauma-informed approaches, ask Black clients what they need to be safe to share experiences unedited, contract early about how clients can give them feedback on how they use their power, and nondefensively integrate such feedback.

No—not when, in response to Black experiences (and in particular related to harm), white professionals assert versions of, "we are all human," "let's not carry our identities into the room," "we are all the same," "you are creating polarization by talking about race," "I don't see color," "don't pull the race card." Aiming these erasures at Black clients means that, at minimum, Black people will be unheard, misinterpreted, have their lived experiences and humanity contested, and their self-knowledge devalued. It also means that Black professionals who may get activated when working with white clients are likely to be judged, blamed, and negatively evaluated when seeking support, as their white colleagues rush to defend whiteness. Constantly having to untangle from the tentacles of racism erodes us and is a waste of our brilliance, life juice, imagination, and time.

We can agree with Coates's (2015) historical analysis that indeed "race is the child of racism, not the father" (p. 7). While the construct of race is fiction and must surely tumble, using well-worn tropes obscures racial identity experiences, indicating that white practitioners are unwilling to engage with how racism shapes us and our relating in helping professions. Such erasure is extremely dangerous to Black folks' physical and psychological well-being, and will not help us flourish. These are costs we must not bear.

The idea that white people can heal from racism, while hopeful, makes it sounds like they have merely been subjected to a kind of malady, isolated from systems of oppression they benefit from. Individual white people working to shift attitudes and habitual oppressive behaviors is a beginning. However, that alone does not change racist systems nor the racial privilege and power they carry. You cannot step gently on someone else's head. But you can keep engaging and challenging yourself and others daily to reduce harm.

Racial assault, neither past nor static, continues to be leveled at Black minds, hearts, and bodies. It rapidly mutates in reaction to every stride and milestone toward equity, justice, and the growth of Black power and brilliance. White professionals must therefore be willing to interrogate the ground they stand on, not assume their PhD gives them competence to work skillfully across race. Understand when they surveil us or try to save us. They must do the hard work of breaking down systems of oppression in helping professions, so that Black people do not have to heal also from the help we receive. For the gift of Black vulnerability, knowledge, and presence, white professionals must learn how racism serves them and subjugates their clients, come to stand naked in whiteness, and face the ways it makes them. Do the work of unraveling in order to come into a reconstituted relationship with their own humanity and dignity—in order to leave ours intact.

As we continue to be confronted by radioactive racial assault, I am not suggesting that Black people dive back into helping relationships where we have been harmed. The late Archbishop Desmond Tutu and Mpho Tutu's (2014) "Prayer Before the Prayer" eloquently describes what the complex and protracted process of forgiveness entails for those harmed by white dominance and oppression.

First we must love and reclaim ourselves. For each, the way is different. An exit from a harm, making clean, unapologetic breaks, cocooning, letting the relationship shrivel into winter, without any expectation of summer. Singing a lullaby, valuing our own voices, dropping our bodies into a cool river, letting our hearts be caressed by our tears and by those we love and trust, making community, dancing, writing our own new stories, tending to our children and gardens, migrating—back to ourselves. We must also study our old healing ways, build networks of well-being to wean ourselves from dependence on white professionals, so we engage them by choice, not by default. This is agency.

Lane

At the core of the harmful rupture was my own white defensiveness. This problem is far too common among white practitioners, even though none of us want to hurt anyone. It often causes white people to withdraw, argue, or explain our good intentions, all of which block us from attending to the other person's experience and pain. White defensiveness often shuts down conversations and makes People of the Global Majority feel unseen, invalidated, dismissed, dropped, and betrayed. It creates distance rather than intimacy and inhibits understanding and authentic communication. The consequences of white defensiveness are incompatible with the goals, objectives, and values of therapy, coaching, training, supervision, and facilitation.

I believe it is crucial for white people in helping and training professions to develop racial resilience. Resilience means that, when impacted by a stressor, we can find our way to recover from it. Racial resilience for white people means being able to tolerate racialized discomfort and stay present with ourselves, which also helps us stay present with People of the Global Majority when stress arises. Practicing restraint, we can pause before speaking, considering the racial implications of our comment and how it might land. Dr. K. V. Hardy (personal communication, January 20, 2018) suggests, "Run it through your heart before it comes out of your mouth." Racial resilience for white people starts with noticing our defensiveness around race, how it shows up in our thoughts, emotions, and especially bodies. Then we can use practices to calm ourselves.

Also essential is working with our own traumas and being wide awake to how they can be co-opted by white supremacy. The combination of trauma responses and white defensiveness can push us off-center and make us say and do things we would never want to say or do. Let us learn to recognize this and return to ourselves and the relationship. The ditch is only a step away. Trust is a precious thing that can take years to build and a moment to destroy.

We can learn to show up in authentic, nonharming ways. Deep and ongoing engagement in fostering our own racial sensitivity is imperative for the well-being of our clients, students, and colleagues who are People of the Global Majority, as well as for our own humanity. All this helps us show up as the wise, compassionate professionals we want to be.

In Conclusion

Yasmeen and Lane

Some will say, "but harm can occur in any professional relationship." True, and racial harm in helping relationships warrants its own distinct analysis. Others might say, "but it was just one sentence!" Yes, one sentence filled with lifetimes of harm.

How many helping or training relationships end in racial harm? How many People of the Global Majority leave their white therapists, coaches, supervisors, or predominantly white training programs without saying why? How many are pathologized as resistant, perpetually unready, unresilient, or unwilling to do the work? How many white practitioners have no idea of the harm they cause? Or, if they are given feedback, do they have the desire, willingness, humility, tenacity, or courage to return and try to make amends?

Moving toward genuine racial repair restores our hearts, minds, and nervous systems. It is an ongoing process of crossing swamplands, entering stagnant, deep waters; not an easy choice. It means we can look again at one another and perhaps enter into new, dynamic, and honest ways of relating, reckoning with unhelpful uses of power. Seeing how we are all shaped by race opens pathways to compassion. Those who caused harm can come to know the pain they have inflicted, be truly humbled by their mistakes, see the full humanity of the other. This returns breath to those who are harmed, a pathway to joy, and an opportunity to rediscover deeper humanity in the other, too. As such, journeys toward relationship repairs across race offer a tiny form of hope and prayer for something bigger in the midst of ongoing polarization. With truth telling, soft hearts, firm boundaries, and clear seeing, we can gather energy and move together toward living in new ways. In more honest partnership, we can continue to dismantle racism and all forms of systemic oppression from our wholeness. Walking through such relationship portals, we can cocreate new ecosystems where we can all thrive. This is also the rigorous soul work of our time.

CHAPTER 14

Getting to the Heart of the Matter: White Therapists Working With White Clients Around Race

VIRGINIA SEEWALDT, PhD

Much has been written about white therapists becoming culturally competent in order to serve their Clients of Color (e.g., Carter, 2004; Kalibatseva & Leong, 2014; Sue, 1998). Wilcox (2023) goes a step further and argues that understanding cultural differences is insufficient, and psychotherapists need to become knowledgeable and proficient at examining the oppressive impact of the structures and systems on Clients of Color. It should go without saying, but perhaps bears repeating, that white therapists should engage in ongoing education in racial literacy, self-reflection, and supervision to understand racism as a form of trauma (Hardy, 2023). White therapists also need to understand how their racial positionality, privilege, and biases impact their relationships with Clients of Color and employ effective skills and racially relevant interventions (Suyemoto et al., 2019; Hardy, 2023).

Very little has been written about the need for white therapists to develop racial literacy, understand whiteness, and how to effectively engage with our white clients about issues of race. The literature suggests (e.g., Stovall, 2019; Malamed, 2021) that white therapists rarely talk about race with white clients. The modus operandi of white people in dyads or groups with no People of Color present is typically silence about issues of race. It is as if a situation or context is only deemed racial when there are People of Color in the room (DiAngelo, 2016). The practice of deeming race irrelevant and the tacit agreement not to talk about it in interactions among white people persists in therapy. In therapy dyads with white clients where the therapist is a Person of Color, the issue of race is likely to be confronted in the relationship. When both the therapist and client are white, there is a high likelihood that race can be avoided or discussed in a way that is superficial and lacking in rigor. Because whiteness is regarded as the norm and most white people do not even consider themselves racialized beings, it follows that within the mental health field, "race" is defined as "non-white," and that racial competence would not encompass an understanding of whiteness. Stovall (2019) asks an important question: "What if whiteness is *the thing*?" (para. 3), as in the thing being avoided, dissociated, and denied, all the while causing the feelings of emptiness, not-enoughness, and self-loathing that belies smiling white people holding shotguns in Christmas cards?

Whiteness and White Supremacist Culture

It has been widely documented that white supremacy culture, that is, "the overt and subliminal socialization processes and practices, power structures, laws, privileges and life experiences that favor the white racial group over all others" (Helms, 2017, p. 718), is not only harmful to People of Color, especially Black people, but also harmful to white people.

I will not go into a long definition or explanation of what white supremacy culture is or its origins. For detailed information, please see *Stamped from the Beginning* (Kendi, 2017); *White Rage* (Anderson, 2016); "What Is White Supremacy Culture?" (Okun, 2023); and *What Does It Mean to Be White?* (DiAngelo, 2016). White culture was founded on and continues to perpetuate and be reinforced by hierarchy, domination and violence, deception, and hypocrisy. White culture reflects the beliefs, values, norms, and standards that uphold a widespread ideology of white skin and European features as "the norm or *standard* for human and people of color as a *deviation* from that norm" (DiAngelo, 2016, p. 148). Whiteness was designed to justify the enslavement of Africans, dissuade whites from aligning with

Africans in protest or rebellion, and mitigate any cognitive dissonance that might cause white people to feel sympathy or compassion for the abhorrent treatment of Africans. This wedge that whiteness was designed to put between Blacks and whites has been maintained and reinforced to the present day. It also works to disconnect and divide all of us from animals, nature, the Earth, and the cosmos and instill an attitude of hierarchy, domination, and conquest over these things. Okun (2023) describes it as a "project of psychic conditioning and toxic belonging" (para. 11) that "colonizes our minds, our bodies, our psyches, our spirits, our emotions" (para. 13). The damage white supremacy culture does to People of Color is overt, violent, and oppressive. The damage it does to white people—by definition—is not equivalent, and is also much less obvious, obscured by the protections and benefits it affords. As much as whiteness tries to convince white people that we are separate and apart from everyone and everything else, our interconnectedness is demonstrated in how, when we bring harm to others, we cannot avoid bringing harm upon ourselves. Because the harm done to white people is embedded into white cultural norms and values as acceptable and is accompanied by the wages (Du Bois, 1935) or privileges (McIntosh, 1988) of whiteness, it can go mostly unnoticed by whites. Jacobs (2014) describes the hegemony of whiteness that affirms white power and dominance as normative, taken for granted by whites, never questioned, and never "problematized" (p. 300). Further, because of the wide reach of white colonization and white culture's tendency to universalize (Ani, 1994), aspects of white supremacy culture that are harmful may be considered by many whites to simply be normal or "human nature." Myers (1993) refers to this phenomenon as *democratic sanity*, a phenomenon whereby a behavior or attitude is deemed sane if most people of the society simply sanction it. However, Wright (1984) asserts that if whiteness were subjected to scientific study, "such inquiry would expose an unthinkable depth of psychopathology" (p. 4).

White supremacy culture is made up of interlocking characteristics that reinforce and are reinforced by this hierarchy of human value (Okun, 2023). Among other characteristics, white culture devalues human embodiment and emotions and hails rational thought, and not even complex thought; whiteness encourages simplistic binary thinking. This culture is upheld by the use of fear.

Menakem (2017) debunks the myth of Europeans coming to America for opportunity. He highlights the dire circumstances such as famine, poverty, plague, persecution, and danger that Europeans were fleeing from. Upon arrival in America, survival demanded assimilation into whiteness, forsaking culture and identity, the relentless pursuit of maintaining one's place in the hierarchy of human value perpetuating an environment of competition and hostility. Thandeka (2001) also describes the process of assimilation of Europeans into whiteness as one of trauma and self-annihilation. Looking further back in the ancestry of whites, Menakem (2017) identifies the trauma Europeans brought with them from the brutal Middle Ages to the so-called Americas. This trauma, unresolved and unhealed, was enacted on Black and Indigenous people. He urges white people to look to our bodies to find and heal our ancestral wounds. He observes that, devoid of context, the collective trauma of a people can resemble culture.

Racial Socialization and White Child Development

Thandeka (2001) defines the racial socialization process into white culture of Euro-American children as psychological child abuse. There is no avoiding this socialization process. What does it mean for one's psyche, heart, and soul when one's culture is predicated on dehumanization of others? When one's culture is in opposition to one's humanity? According to Thandeka (2001), it results in self-annihilation, an "impaired sense of core self," the development of a false self, and "an inability to relate to others with self-integrity" (p. 127).

The process of socialization into whiteness involves instruction on physically, psychologically, and emotionally distancing from groups of people who are not white, Black people in particular, and treating them as subhuman or ignoring and doing nothing about their mistreatment. Consequently, a forced splitting off of the self happens as a result of the white child being confronted with the consequence of rejection and loss of love and approval when they commit a white racial transgression (e.g., bringing home a non-white child to play) or witness another person committing a racial transgression. This process is quickly relegated to the unconscious because it "entails attacks upon one's core sense of self by those who ostensibly love" the child "the most—caretakers, legal defenders and protectors"

(Thandeka, 2001, p. 86). This abuse happens to all white children through simply living in the world; because regardless of any individual child's upbringing, there is very little in the broader white American culture to support a child's emotional development in the direction of resonance and empathy or attitudes of basic humanity toward non-white people, especially Black people. Where in American society would a typical white child get sufficient messaging that Black people are just as valuable as white people? Where would a white child get sufficient support for the idea that Black people are just as competent as white people? Where in white culture does a white child get support for the idea that Black people are just as human as white people? How do even the most well-intended antiracist parents compete with the messages their white child is being bombarded with all day, every day about who has value and who does not? The child learns from media representations as well as their interactions in everyday life as they witness the race of people who disproportionately rise to levels of leadership compared to the race of people who are mostly in service positions. White children may be taught by multiple sources of authority that the police are a source of safety and protection; they may also witness firsthand that this does not hold true for Black people. De facto racial segregation, predominantly Black neighborhoods and schools being labeled by whites as "bad," and most white parents' lack of concern about this racial segregation, also give a message about how white children should value Black people. There is very little in white-dominant culture to support a white child's intrinsic knowledge that Black people are to be regarded as human or that support a white child's natural inclination to connect with other human beings who are Black.

In forming a white identity, white children must disavow the parts of themselves that notice racial injustice, have empathy for Black people, have curiosity about Black people, and want to have close relationships or community with Black people. During this socialization process, a white child experiences attacks until the child "learns to be white." The white child discovers that their fundamental humanity is an unlovable part of themselves. Because humans are not born racist and the child has no choice but to conform, this socialization process entails a splitting of the psyche. "The Euro-American child is socialized into a system of values that hold in contempt differences from the white community's ideals" (Thandeka, 2001,

p. 17). Therefore, the socialization process into whiteness is an "injury to one's core sense of self" (p. 17). Thandeka (2001) highlights the resulting self-alienation that leaves the white child with "a sense of emptiness, futility or homelessness" (p. 19), drawing parallels to narcissistic psychological abuse first described by Miller (1979) and characterized as a type of soul murder.

Parker (2019) conducted interviews with white adults about their childhood experiences learning about slavery and found that as children they felt confused and entirely alone with their confusion and sense that something was wrong. Most reported that there was no one with whom to talk about it. As a result of this socialization, white children are forced to disconnect—to stop thinking, to stop noticing, to stop linking reality and history, and to turn off their empathic curiosity and care toward people who are not white, and Black people in particular. What results is a splitting of mind, body, and soul and "closing door after door until one's mind and heart and conscience are blocked off from each other and from reality" (Smith, 1994, p. 29).

Menakem (2017) addresses white children, during the Jim Crow era, being brought to white lynching "parties" and the inevitable layers of trauma caused by the juxtaposition of violence, horror, and celebration by one's family and community. Whiteness teaches white children that some humans are disposable, which implies that they too could be disposed of if they do not conform to the cultural norms. And because no child can afford to lose the safety that comes from a feeling of belonging to one's culture, all white children are socialized into whiteness. White children are forced into this bargain of suppressing their humanity in exchange for their very survival in their own culture. Thandeka (2018) describes the aim of the acculturation process to dull the emotional lives of white people so that "they could not see and feel what they had in common with blacks: feelings of loss, fear, sorrow and remorse, feelings of being at risk, and anger and rage at being taken advantage of" (p. 38).

White Identity Development and Therapy

If one looks at the diagnostic criteria for narcissistic personality disorder (American Psychiatric Association, 2022) and applies it to the group behavior of whites toward non-whites, as a collective we easily meet the criteria. Miller and Josephs (2009) also describe whiteness as a pathological narcissism, as does Anen (2022). Parker (2019), Helms (2008), and Yancy (2012) explain the psychic splits and distortions of whiteness.

Wright (1984) takes the cultural diagnosis a step further and describes the psychopathic nature of whiteness, citing historic and ongoing atrocities devoid of empathy, remorse, or accountability and the mental manipulation known in the literature pertaining to abusive relationships as DARVO (Deny, Attack, and Reverse Victim and Offender) used by white culture that attempts to position whites as the victims and Black people as offenders. Similarly, Parker (2019) suggests that white people have developed an identification with the original aggressor (enslavers) alongside a powerful disavowal. The cultural anthropologist Marimba Ani (1994) offers that white culture is one of hypocrisy and deception.

Considering all of this, it's understandable that for white people, examining and coming to terms with one's racial identity can be "uncomfortable, even frightening" (Tatum, 1997, p. 113) and as therapists, we can be there to support our clients through this painful exploration.

Although race, and especially whiteness, has not typically been considered a topic for psychotherapy, and most clinicians have received no training in how to talk with white people about this weighty and fraught topic, more and more clients may want to talk about race. Since the murder of George Floyd and the multiracial coalitions of protest across the country, more white people have become interested in understanding their whiteness. For the first time in my career, I have had white clients who were referred to me by white colleagues specifically looking for someone they could explore their own whiteness with or clients who have mentioned during our first conversation that they were curious about exploring race and whiteness. I have two white women friends who have complained about the lack of white racial literacy among white therapists. One complained that she cannot find a new white therapist that has any understanding of whiteness, and the other described how, when she brings up the topic of race, her white therapist changes the subject and redirects her. Racial awareness in psychotherapy should not be considered an area of specialty; it is something that impacts all of us, whether we choose to recognize it or not.

Despite the scholarship on the harms of whiteness to white people, there is no widely held tenet of mainstream psychotherapy that acknowledges the clinical significance of white therapists talking to white clients about the experience of being socialized from birth into a racial culture that accepts, as normal, the forceful domination of non-white people. Miller and Josephs (2009) described the dyad of white therapists and white clients as "white mutual admiration societies" where "whiteness remains invisible while being unconsciously mirrored" (p. 108). Malamed (2021) demonstrates the stark contrast between therapy with Clients of Color and white clients: "instead of the liberatory work that those with minoritized identities more typically engage in (successful) therapy, folks with privileged identities often end up unwittingly re-committing to various states of imprisonment" (p. 6).

The force of whiteness and white solidarity's insistence on silencing discussions on race has led scholars to spend considerable energy preemptively defending the ethics of bringing race into the room with white clients as if it could be condemned as a potentially serious ethical breach or harm to white clients (Drustrup, 2020, 2021; Malamed, 2021). The looming white institution of the punishing ethics board represents the unconscious fear tactics (Okun, 2023) always operating on the minds of white people to deter us from addressing race in all contexts.

White clients need a place to talk about their interactions with People of Color, areas of confusion, and shameful, persistent biases. Without a racial lens with which to examine cross-racial interactions, as white therapists we run the risk of merely reassuring our white clients that they are "not racist," or that it was not "their intention" to do harm. We too often forfeit the opportunity to help them gain clarity around their potential perpetration of microaggressions or the deeply embedded harmful racial biases and beliefs that they might be acting out in their cross-racial relationships. Many People of Color are harmed by our clients; our clients' cross-racial relationships are suffering and possibly being destroyed, and our clients have nowhere to turn for help in understanding what is happening and their role in it. Through this lens, it feels unethical not to explore a client's racism, whiteness, and the impact of living as a member of the only racial group safe from race-related harm within a system of violent domination.

Drustrup (2021) describes a clinical model of working with white clients that begins with therapists engaging in a lifelong journey of racial literacy and consciousness, followed by listening, empathizing, and validation, then exploring the client's racial consciousness, connecting race to their current concerns, psychoeducation, and encouraging clients to engage in new experiences. In Chapter 2 of this book, Kenneth V. Hardy offers a list of concrete strategies that white therapists can employ to facilitate efforts to become racially sensitive therapists.

The therapist's development of racial awareness and literacy is a crucial step in working with white clients around race. This includes an understanding of our own "racial identity status" (Helms & Cook, 1999, p. 91). If we do not understand what it means to be white in our own lived experience, we will very likely be lost, unable to help, and worse, very likely misguiding our clients and causing them harm.

Race, Whiteness, and Countertransference Reactions

Miller and Josephs (2009) observed that "it seems to be virtually impossible to raise the issue of white racial identity without raising persecutory anxiety about being perceived as racist" (p. 101). White therapists may feel unprepared to rub up against this shame and the rage that can follow. Because during conversations about race,

> the capacity to think can collapse, the brain's stress response system gets turned on, heart rates go up, and deep fears about loss of love and rejection are stirred. A sense of badness threatens to consume and staying in touch with one's own and another's basic humanity can be difficult. (Parker, 2019, pp. 3–4)

The transference-countertransference matrix during these discussions may elicit extreme and polarizing reactions in therapist and client that may have never arisen before and may have never arisen but for the topic of race. The good/bad binary of whiteness is also at risk for manifesting in the transference when engaging in the topic of race. Because of power dynamics, and clients' tendency to idealize their therapist, there is a risk of the client (and the therapist) seeing the therapist as the "good" nonracist and seeing the client as the "bad" racist. This can possibly be mitigated by the therapist's transparency around their own white socialization process, biases, and other racially internalized beliefs. This transparency can serve to discourage binary thinking and idealization of the therapist as a "good white person" from whom the client needs to hide or minimize their racism. It's also possible that the label of "bad white person" might get tossed around like a hot potato between white therapist and client. The shame, rage, and self-loathing white people feel about our own racialized "badness" is at risk of being acted out on our clients, leading to a need to locate the "bad" racist in the client. We may find ourselves shocked by severe judgmental feelings toward a client that we've never experienced before when they say something racist. One strategy we can engage in is (nonjudgmentally) noticing these feelings and asking ourselves: How far away am I from these beliefs? Was there a time I felt this way / thought this way / held these attitudes? Does my client remind me of a white person in my life with whom I am struggling around issues of race? Is this self-righteousness or superiority I'm feeling? Am I feeling indignant toward my client? Is this feeling endorsing a sense of myself as a "better white person"? Engaging in honest self-reflection around these questions can illuminate a desire to distance from our own whiteness that could interfere with empathy and compassion for our white clients.

Therapeutic Challenges

We need to be able to discern between "coddling" by giving in to clients' conscious or unconscious demands for comfort, and compassionately helping clients develop an increased capacity to tolerate all the difficult feelings and sensations that arise around the topic of race. Therapist self-disclosure and joining without endorsing racism are encouraged, as is modeling nondefensiveness (Helms & Cook, 1999). This is uncharted territory, and it is crucial that we have this same attitude of compassion toward ourselves. Our work with white clients will be far from perfect (and if that is our expectation, we can interrogate the roots of white supremacy culture embedded in that belief). We may look back on a session and recognize how we neglected to hold the client accountable for a racist action. We can show compassion for ourselves and hold ourselves accountable for developing emotional muscles of intensity, intimacy, transparency, congruency, authenticity, and complexity (Hardy, 2023).

A sense of urgency may emerge as we work with white clients, an overwhelming feeling that we must solve the problem of racism, and the work with our clients is too slow. We can notice that sense of urgency and recognize it as both real (the problem of racism demands urgent attention) and a product of white supremacy thinking. Racism and white supremacy in its current form started centuries ago; it is not likely to be solved in our lifetime. Patience and an appreciation for the degree to which racism and white supremacy culture have been embedded and normalized in the psyches of all white people will serve us well in this work.

Our desire to see ourselves as the "good white person" might impact our ability to have empathy when engaging with our clients' racial blind spots. I don't want to put myself in my client's shoes—I just finally got those shameful shoes off! We can notice when we are trying to distance from our clients' experience and instead join them in their pain and sadness at having been robbed of their humanity.

Therapeutic Techniques and Strategies of Engagement

Helping Clients Build Increased Emotional Capacity: Developing a Thicker Skin

We can use whatever techniques we already use for building emotional capacity and apply them to build increased emotional capacity for addressing the topic of race. Body-based therapies are particularly suited for this work, particularly by increasing clients' tolerance for the somatic experience of guilt and shame that arises frequently in relation to race. Jacobs (2014) suggests that we contextualize and normalize guilt and shame as inevitable aspects of confronting whiteness to prevent a vicious shame spiral. Shame is an appropriate feeling when coming to terms with internalized whiteness. The process demands an answer to the questions, "Who am I and where do I come from?" "What happened to me and what has that done to me?" Whiteness work is trauma work, and developing an increased capacity to feel and move through shame can keep it from overwhelming and derailing the process. An increased capacity to tolerate race-related shame can also aid clients as well. For example, while engaged in cross-racial discussions about race, especially when confronting a racial misstep or the perpetration of a microaggression that they may have committed, being able to manage shame will help clients to avoid centering themselves in racial discussions, be open to feedback about their behavior, and engage in relational repair, rather than avoidance, defensive, or aggressive reactions that allow them to escape their feelings of shame.

Pulling Back the Lens

Framing a white client's symptoms in the context of white culture can be particularly helpful to white clients who already feel a sense of alienation from others and American culture at large. Having a sense of collective trauma that intersects with and informs individual trauma can reduce feelings of isolation and aloneness. Many white people subscribe to the idea that there are high-value people (winners) and low-value people (losers). Interrogating this belief, where it comes from, whom or what it serves, whom it harms, and how it does harm to themselves and others, especially as it relates to race, can be an enlightening and enlivening process, particularly for clients experiencing a deadness or emptiness. Helping clients explore the impact of existing in a culture predicated on a hierarchy of human worth and value can shift feelings of self-recrimination and loathing, redirecting these feelings to the true source of the problem, a toxic culture. The result can be a sense of clarity, a feeling of deep relief, a desire to find an antiracist community and engage in antiracist action.

Racially contextualizing a client's struggles with depression, anxiety, or other diagnoses can alleviate the shame and stigma of mental illness. Helping white clients become curious about how living in a violent racial hierarchy that is never named as such has been impacting them might aid in normalizing a wide array of symptoms. If a client had parents that were abusive or sadistic, we can make parallels to the abusive and sadistic nature of whiteness that may have been, while still holding a client's parents accountable for their behavior and putting some of this behavior in a larger cultural context, which potentially allows for more compassion and perhaps even forgiveness.

Exploring White Racial Identity Development

Helms (2008, 2017) and Helms and Cook (1999) discuss white people in terms of white racial identity development, and this can be a useful frame within which to understand how to work with white people around issues of race. Having an understanding of white racial identity development is important for knowing best how to approach our white clients. An understanding that intense racist attitudes and behaviors, for example, might be the result of having been overwhelmed by horrific truths and a lack of capacity and/or social support to hold these truths in conscious awareness can make room for compassion and curiosity about our client's racial history. Knowing a client's primary white racial identity development status and/or the status toward which a client is heading (whether moving forward to a more advanced status or regressing) can help us shape our interventions to increase the likelihood of their moving forward to a healthier and more realistic sense of themselves as a white person with a healthier and more realistic sense of non-white people, and reduce the risk of their retreating into oblivion or disengagement.

Rethinking the Rules

It seems like many rules may need to be broken when working with white clients around the issue of race and white supremacy. Much of what is needed in holding white clients as they do this difficult work (intimacy, vulnerability, transparency, and self-disclosure on the part of the therapist) may be considered to be outside the frame of how one is supposed to conduct traditional psychotherapy. Considering that "white cultural dynamics are the central themes in counseling and psychotherapy theories, models, and measures" (Helms & Cook, 1999, p. 109), this frame arguably upholds white supremacy, and a different frame is needed. We as therapists can lead by example, breaking the conventional frame and sharing our own experiences, growth, and hope.

As white therapists, we need to develop an ability to listen with a racially-attuned "third ear," that is, an ear for issues around race and white supremacy. Keep in mind that white supremacy culture is harming white people, regardless of the degree of our contact with People of Color. When clients talk about perfectionism or exhibit binary thinking or other aspects of white supremacy culture, we can point these out and explore where these attitudes come from and how they are in service to white supremacy culture and generally not in our client's best interests.

It might be easier for white people who grew up with explicitly racist parents to identify how and when they began internalizing and/or experiencing conflict regarding messages about race. For these children, racism was injected with a needle, and the site of the injection is still visible. For those who grew up in liberal homes, the socialization process was likely much more subtle and insidious, entering the unconscious like a poisonous gas. With these clients, racism may present in more subtle ways and be harder to identify and interrogate. There may be more dissonance, shame, and pain involved in coming to a more sophisticated awareness of racism.

As white therapists, we must also be well versed in our understanding of the stages of white identity development (Helms & Cook, 1999) to help inform our interventions. Thus, our interventions will differ from client to client, depending on their stage of racial identity development. Clients in the beginning stages of their racial identity development will require a different kind of intervention than would be the case for one in the more advanced stages of understanding and critiquing their whiteness. For these clients, a gentler probing inquiry regarding race may be necessary. On the other hand, a client in the later stages of the racial self-interrogation process can be confronted about race more directly and will tend to have a greater emotional capacity and ability to be self-reflective without risk of spiraling into shame, confusion, and defensiveness.

Demonstrate Diligence About Leaning Into Race Talk

Therapists of all races, and especially those who are white, often ponder about when to bring up race in therapy. The simplest response is early or, at the very least, whenever we encounter a "window of availability." When a client says, "I don't want you to think I'm racist but . . . " and then describes a racial interchange, thought, or feeling, this is an opportune time to explore the client's thoughts and feelings about race. It is important for white therapists to remember that race is relevant in our clients' lives even when they are not directly involved with People of Color. Some discussions about race may be designed to cultivate curiosity about white cultural norms and may not necessarily require the direct naming of race. For example, "What did you learn about perfectionism?" "When were you encouraged to think of issues as an either/or?" "When were you encouraged to think of issues as a both/and?"

Self-Examination

White therapists are encouraged to regularly examine the sources of our own resistance to bringing up the issue of race with white clients. It is not typically a white client's expectation that their white therapist will bring up the topic of race; therefore doing so might be met with a range of reactions, from a casual dismissiveness to strong negative emotions and a refusal to engage. It can be difficult to initiate and engage in difficult conversations about race that have the potential to strain the relationship, especially when we are socialized to avoid talking about it. When it is a topic area that is not widely acknowledged as necessary by the mental health community, it is even more difficult to enter these conversations. However, like any other topic in therapy, the more we raise it, the more normalized it will become to discuss, both with our clients and in the community at large. Consulting with other white therapists also attempting to find ways to talk about race with white clients can be of great value. In these settings, we can openly discuss the obstacles we encounter, especially our own resistances.

It is critical for white therapists to be perpetually curious about race and to constantly ask oneself: How do racism and whiteness fit here? Whiteness can probably be connected to many more of our clients' concerns than we might even be aware of. The problem often is: How much psychoeducation are we going to have to do to link our white client's presenting problem to the larger societal ill of white supremacy culture? For example, how do we explore the racial dynamics between a white client and their Black housekeeper when they are consumed with grief over the death of their spouse? When a client comes into the session bringing in the here-and-now problems of their life, it is easy to get absorbed in their world, their problems of living, their white bubble. We can delve into the dynamics of their family history to explore how the past impacts the present, but it is more difficult to bring race into the room when the client is not talking about it.

Clinical Examples

Why Are You Not Enraged?

In 2020, during the height of the protests in response to the murder of George Floyd and Breonna Taylor, a client was talking about an asthma attack and using words and phrases about their experience that provoked thoughts and associations about the Black Lives Matter movement ("It's oppressive; I feel like I'm in prison; I can't breathe"). We had been working together for over 10 years and had a solid therapeutic alliance, so I shared with them my associations. They paused, nodded, and said, "If I were a Black person in this country right now, I'd be enraged." I saw in their response an opportunity to explore the empathy gap and said, "Yeah, I really get that. I'm curious about something, though. Why is it that as a *white* person in this country right now, you're *not* enraged?" This question caused them to take a much longer pause, and they responded with, "That's a *really* good question." This opened the door for some further exploration and psychoeducation around the disturbing truth that a deficiency of empathy is frequently the experience of white people vis-à-vis Black people.

Don't Think I'm a Racist, But . . .

A patient began to describe a racial interaction by saying, "I don't want you to think I'm racist, but . . . " This was much earlier in my own racial literacy development and, excited by the then-rare opportunity to engage around race, I blurted, "All white people are racist." My clumsy response gave him pause, and he asked me what I meant. I engaged in some psychoeducation about the socialization of white people in the United States and the inevitability of having racist attitudes and beliefs. Toward the end of the session, he expressed an interest in diving deeper, and I referred him to an Undoing Racism Workshop with the People's Institute for Survival and Beyond (PISAB). He returned from that workshop with more questions than answers and a bit disturbed by some things in his ancestry that he was now trying to reconcile. As it was earlier in my own racial literacy, while I was superficially familiar, I was not at all mindful of Helms's (2008) statuses of white identity development. Had I been holding these in mind, I would have been acutely aware that our conversation and his weekend at the training had catapulted him into a painful and disorienting place. I would have shown much more empathy for the pain he was experiencing around his complicated family history. Instead, I read his defensiveness as fragility, and in my urgency to move him along in his racial awareness, I fell short on validating his experience. My own unexamined whiteness was expressed through binary thinking that I could only be empathic either for him or for the People of Color connected to his family history, which led to a breakdown in my empathy toward his pain. I was also not aware that my less-than-empathic response to his emotional distress put him at risk emotionally, which began to manifest in defensiveness. He ultimately expressed anger toward me for being more concerned about racism than about the issues he wanted to talk about in therapy, and he wasn't wrong. I had lost my focus and was not framing my work with him through the lens of the harm white supremacy had been causing him. I listened, acknowledged, and affirmed his observations and validated his feelings and apologized. But I also felt at a loss. I knew that ultimately it would be psychologically and emotionally healthier for him to stay on an antiracism course, but I minimized how excruciatingly painful this process can be before there are even any glimmers of liberation.

Sounds Like White Supremacist Culture

A 53-year-old white male client from New England with a history of severe suicidality was describing a childhood where he wanted to be an archaeologist and the idea was scoffed at by his parents. "No one I knew was an archaeologist. 'People' didn't do that sort of thing." By "people" it was implied that wealthy, white, Anglo Saxon, Protestant men don't become archaeologists. Instead, he went into finance, where he always felt like an outsider. As he described a childhood of loneliness and pressure to conform and suppress his immense curiosity, creativity, and love of learning for the sake of learning, I blurted out, "This sounds exactly like white supremacy culture!" and he looked at me with confusion and even some concern. I attempted to engage in some psychoeducation but ultimately became overwhelmed with where and how to even begin to connect these dots. Coming to appreciate his authentic desires has been immensely helpful to his well-being; however, linking whiteness to the harm done to him as a child has been more challenging.

Being embedded in this process as white people ourselves, we are swirling in our own whiteness and biases, all the while trying to help our clients sort through theirs. We have to hold on to our awareness, gleaned from our own experience of harm, that white supremacy culture has done, and continues to do, real damage to our clients, despite the fact that there is nothing about it in most books that cover the treatment of trauma, with the notable exception of *My Grandmother's Hands* (Menakem, 2017). We did not learn in graduate school about the harm white supremacy culture does to white people, and it is not listed anywhere in any diagnostic or clinical manuals. To hold on to this knowledge for our clients, we are forced constantly to be face to face with the damage white supremacy culture has done and continues to do to us. This is no easy task. It's humbling. I am not only a therapist on this journey with my clients, I'm also a fellow traveler. I am perhaps a little bit further ahead on the journey in some areas, but possibly further behind with more blind spots in others. The prospect is daunting. Here are some critical steps that can be helpful to us as white practitioners:

1. **Be aware of the "white vortex."** As white therapists, we are so entrenched in white supremacy culture in many respects. As much as we may consciously reject it, unconsciously it is, was, and has been our "normal" for most of us for many more decades than it has not. I frequently find myself falling into massive denial about the harm that whiteness does to myself and other white people. The visibility of whiteness and its toxic effects on white people are so well hidden that connecting the dots for clients is an endeavor requiring exquisite patience. Most white people do not even know

or have models for a better way to live racially, or that there is more humanity to be had, and a deeper connection to be had to self, others, and the Earth.

2. **Ask about racial history at intake.** Including rudimentary questions about race, and more specifically whiteness and/or white identity, in the intake process would skillfully introduce the topic into the therapeutic process from the outset. It would eliminate or minimize the usual awkwardness related to when is the right time or the best way to address race. During the process of therapy, white therapists can ask white clients important self-reflective questions, such as: When did you first learn that you were white? What is your first memory of learning something about race from your parent(s) or caregiver(s)? Do you feel that you are a valuable human being? Why or why not? Where do you get your sense of value or worth from? What role did your race as a white person play in your development? Have you ever wondered about the impact that living as a white person in this society has had on you?

3. **Embrace white affinity.** Healing from the internalization of whiteness is probably best done in community because it enhances opportunity for self-reflection and accountability. For white therapists, participating in group experiences with other whites where whiteness can be named, explored, and deconstructed in thoughtful and deliberate ways can be quite valuable and transformative. There exists scant support for white therapists who wish to engage their white clients around race. Peer supervision groups of white therapists talking to white clients about race can be immensely helpful to us as we do this work.

After all is said and done, white clients may choose to embrace their white privilege and all aspects of white supremacy culture and choose to change nothing about their relationship to race. And just as we would with a client whose substance use concerns us but who has no desire to address it, we can continue to bring up the topic of race and connect the dots we see between whiteness and what plagues them so that they are making the most informed and conscious decisions possible. As white clients understand more about their socialization into whiteness, we as therapists are bearing witness to "the grief of a person who was not allowed to develop into a full human being" (Lateiner, 2016).

Conclusion

The ongoing socialization process into whiteness is a trauma. As therapists, we are here to bear witness to the damage done to psyches, hearts, and souls. Addressing with our white clients the traumatizing impact of socialization into whiteness is in direct alignment with the goals and objectives of good clinical practice. Failing to address whiteness perpetuates ignorance of all the potential harm that whiteness has done, is doing, and, if not addressed, will continue to do. Addressing whiteness is "Homecoming" work; coming back to one's true self in full humanity. Because whiteness as trauma is not an ideology that is supported by the larger culture, or even the therapy community, it may be difficult to hold this in mind. On a personal note, the community I have found among committed antiracist people is more precious and sacred than any other I have been a part of. The community of antiracist white people, specifically, is a courageous one of which I am proud to be part. We are a group of people who are working on reclaiming our humanity, learning to love ourselves and others more fully, and engaging in mutual support as we engage in antiracism in our own spheres of influence. This is the kind of experience of self and other we can invite our clients to be curious about.

CHAPTER 15

Race and the Need for Racial Reckoning in Clinical and Educational Training

VANESSA M. BING, PhD

This chapter is dedicated to Roxsian Sharpe, a young Black woman in graduate training who so generously shared her stories of her training and struggle, and her hopes and dreams of the profession. While her life ended far too soon, well before she could contribute to the clinical profession, her community, and the young Children of Color she had hoped to serve, her impact will never be forgotten, nor will her powerful words, some of which are reflected in this call to action.

Racial Reckoning in the COVID and George Floyd Years

The summer of 2020 was difficult for most people in the United States and across the globe. The world was dealing with a deadly pandemic that had taken away millions of lives, and the United States was dealing with the twin pandemics of COVID-19 and violence perpetrated against People of Color in general, and Black people in particular. In one calendar year we heard the stories of Communities of Color having a disparate response to COVID, where exposure to the virus, illnesses, and related deaths were significantly higher than in white communities. Moreover, these same communities were reeling from the assaults on Black bodies. The violence perpetrated against individuals and Communities of Color made national and international headlines. U.S. citizens were protesting police violence against Black bodies, and countries across the globe were chanting "Black Lives Matter." Seemingly, the world was in the midst of a racial reckoning, and the mental health profession also responded to the violence and ills of the world that were fueled by the viruses of COVID-19 and of racism.

The Helping Professions' Response

Fortunately, the mental health profession was not immune from the racial reckoning. In October 2021, the American Psychological Association (APA), one of the largest organizations in North America that represents practicing and research psychologists, issued a formal apology to People of Color for the organization's role in promoting and perpetuating racism and racial discrimination in the profession. The apology reads in part:

> The American Psychological Association failed in its role leading the discipline of psychology, was complicit in contributing to systemic inequities, and hurt many through racism, racial discrimination, and denigration of people of color, thereby falling short on its mission to benefit society and improve lives. APA is profoundly sorry, accepts responsibility for, and owns the actions and inactions of APA itself, the discipline of psychology, and individual psychologists who stood as leaders for the organization and field. (APA, 2021, para. 1)

In a similar vein, the National Association of Social Workers (NASW, 2020) issued a statement in August 2020 and expressed very clearly how the history of social work has been fraught with racist ideology and practices: "Racism and white supremacy are ingrained within American institutions and systems and have therefore affected social work ideology and practice for generations" (para. 1). This statement speaks pointedly to how social workers have been complicit in perpetuating harmful social systems that have been especially punitive toward Black, Brown, and Indigenous families. However, it notes that these very individuals play a critical role in the creation of an antiracist society.

Indeed, the social work profession, which originated in the late 19th century, was born out of a response to poverty and social disruption in the United States and Europe. The guiding principle of the profession effectively pointed to the "moral failings" of individuals, and the belief that "charitable efforts" given to those who were deserving would help to rehabilitate them. This reflected an ideology based on white, middle-class norms, values, and behaviors, and an approach that was biased, oppressive, and reflective of a caste system (NASW, n.d.).

Like the social work and psychology professions, marriage and family therapists too have taken a position against racism. The American Association for Marriage and Family Therapy (AAMFT, 2020) stated:

> Marriage and family therapists have a direct responsibility to counter racism. We are uniquely positioned to understand and recognize the systemic effect that oppression, inequity, and overt and covert racism have on individuals in marginalized communities and have a role in fostering healing and growth. (para. 3)

While all of these national organizations have issued statements in support of antiracist practices and have decried racism and racist practices or apologized for their own complicity in promoting racism within these professions, we still remain challenged in actually advancing antiracist work. We continue to lag in cultivating teaching and training environments that provide instruction in antiracist practices, promote inclusivity, fully represent diverse populations, and provide equitable opportunities for successful development of Trainees of Color.

Even before the APA (2021) issued its apology, one of its divisions issued a report that recounted the history of psychology's colonial practices and harms done to BIPOC individuals; this report was used in part to frame APA's equity, diversity, and inclusion (EDI) framework (Akbar & Parker, 2021). It acknowledges that "mainstream psychology in the U.S. has at its foundation a White Eurocentric perspective" (Akbar & Parker, 2021, para. 6). It also acknowledges how BIPOC scientists have produced research that can enhance our understanding, yet these writings have been "systemically discounted by the field of psychology, academic institutions, and the publication process in ways that diminish representation and impact the field"

(Akbar & Parker, 2021, para. 6). In summer 2022, the APA issued a Racial Equity Action Plan (Akbar et al., 2022), and has since provided updates. These efforts, while seemingly aligned with goals of inclusion and full representation, seem to beg the question of why so much effort must be made in a profession seemingly dedicated to the advancement of people.

Eurocentric Entrenchment: My Training in Clinical Psychology

After attending a predominantly white institution for my undergraduate training in psychology, I attended a public university in a major city in the northeast. At the time, I believed or assumed that, because the institution was situationally located in a racially and ethnically diverse, poor, working-class community, my training would address the concerns of this population; that it would prepare me to work with all groups of people, with a specialized focus on individuals residing in marginalized communities. The setting of my graduate training, and the psychological center that was a core part of my practicum training, would be the foundation of my clinical training. However, in very short order, I would quickly learn that many of the largely white faculty members were steeped in Eurocentric models of training and used readings that made up the canon of psychodynamic theory (which excluded writings by racially diverse scholars). It was clear that many of these models could not adequately speak to the experiences of People of Color who had been oppressed by systemic and structural racism.

At the time, I did not have the words to express the white centeredness of the works that I read, nor could I speak to my own discomfort in barely hearing clinical case presentations that spoke to the struggles of People of Color as a direct result of systemic racism. The unrelenting exposure to color-blind approaches to treatment that sought to address the universal human experience—one which negated the onslaught of persistent and recurring trauma of People of Color that was the direct result of racism—was not addressed. Rather, I was forced to apply psychodynamic principles and attempt to explain the challenging behavior of people abused by systemic structures and the pervasiveness of whiteness. I had to use terminology that would reveal my understanding of intrapsychic defensive maneuvers—attempts to address anxiety states. I had to speak using terms like regression, repression, denial, reaction formation, and other defensive maneuvers when addressing a person's struggles with finding and maintaining employment, as well as their sense of being abused by a system that was against them. There was little discussion of systemic issues that crushed a person's spirit and that kept them in marginalized states. We had to focus on the psychological theories and models, not the very real structural assaults on people.

While it was rare that People of Color would be included or discussed in clinical material, I readily recall one faculty member's persistent assault on African American men with his repeated presentation of an "impotent Black man." It was my sense at the time that this presentation reflected the professor's effort to provide a racially diverse clinical example. I frequently wondered whether this was his lone Black patient, or was he the only one that was worthy of presenting? If so, why? Is it because he defied the stereotype of the physically endowed Black male who represented sexual potency? While a myriad of questions entered my mind, as a student/trainee, I merely had to experience the assault on my sense of self as a Black person and ingest a case presentation that focused on the powerless, impotent Black man. Was this faculty member even aware of the microaggression that he brought into the classroom that was delicately cloaked as a clinical case study? Was he fully aware of his own countertransference as it related to his impotent Black male patient? In my recollection of the presentation of this projection, there was no explicit mention or discussion about the professor's racialized conception of this Black man and how it was related to his clinical conceptualization. Was my professor projecting his own wishes or fantasies about Black men?

Psychiatrist Beverly Stoute (2023) speaks to how unconscious racism, in the form of derogatory racial fantasies about Blackness, restricts clinicians' views and feeds into judgments made by clinicians about a client's readiness for treatment, level of psychopathology, and types of diagnoses. For individuals trained to work psychodynamically, issues of transference and countertransference are seen as integral to the work. Yet, if clinicians fail to consider issues of race and operate from a lens of color blindness, they will fail to see how their countertransference may be related to their own unconscious racial biases. To this end, Stoute (2023) notes the importance of clinical education and training that addresses cultural sensitivity and cultural values. She reminds us that potentially learned mistrust can significantly impact treatment. She posits that "understanding how the psychodynamics of race, racism and discrimination are encoded in the derogatory unconscious fantasies held about Black people in our culture can open a multiplicity of rich entry points for interpreting transference and countertransference" (Stoute, 2023, p. 9).

The Struggle for Students of Color in Academe

The classroom is a place for clinicians in training to learn not only the tools and techniques of the practice of therapy, but also how they bring themselves into the therapeutic process and learn how to manage their feelings. For Trainees of Color, this process can be more complicated.

It is not uncommon for Students of Color to feel that they are lacking and do not possess the experience and insights of many of their white peers in training. Hardy (2022) recounts his experience as a Black man training to become a therapist. He describes moving through white spaces and experiencing devaluation—an experience that he views as being a central force in the experience of Blackness. Devaluation is defined as a process by which an individual or marginalized group of people are "stripped of the essentials of their humanity" (Hardy, 2023, p. 130). It is seen as akin to an untreated cancer that perniciously attacks us at our core, slowly eating away at our sense of self (Hardy & Laszloffy, 2005). Hardy (2022) describes forging relationships with peers "where race was always the unspoken and unacknowledged dimension of these relationships" (p. 453). Moreover, he describes the experience of the therapist in training confronted with learning mastery of two curricula—one explicit, one implicit, the latter being for minoritized people only. This specialized curriculum for People of Color involves learning how to deal with racially charged issues on a regular basis. One has to be ready to confront these issues without ever being able to actually raise the question of race in one's training. If issues are raised that cause discomfort, one would simply manage the discomfort and engage in emotional self-regulation—essentially, never reacting, never showing anger, never letting your white faculty and peers "see you sweat."

When I think about the numerous differences shared between me and my classmates, I recall that many of them had parents who were psychologists, analysts, or other trained therapists. Many of them had a singular focus on carving out a future in private practice and seamlessly moving from graduate school to professional practice. Many of them had ample time to engage in readings and to immerse themselves in research opportunities that seemed to fly over the radar of many Students of Color. Many students had a certain personal familiarity with faculty and could be seen leaving campus to play tennis with a senior faculty member. How exactly was that relationship cultivated? For me, there was a mystique in this process of developing deep relationships with faculty. One had to become adept at forging cordial relationships to ensure that one could demonstrate a good fit. Many of the Students of Color had heard the stories of other BIPOC students who never finished their degree and left the training programs with the status of "ABD" (completed all but dissertation) rather than with their PhDs. One had to make sure that one would not be one of those students who would be marked by the shame of being unable to complete training. This stereotyped threat may have ushered many of us through but surely did not allow for a positive and congenial experience during the course of our study.

My recollections of graduate school mirrored many of the comments that I heard from a group of graduate students I met with in the summer of 2022. This group was invited to share their stories and experiences with an interracial and intercultural group of clinicians known as Join the Reckoning (JTR), who are working collectively to take direct action to eliminate racism in the mental health field.[1] These graduate students spoke of not having access to experiences, being unable to cultivate intimate relationships with faculty, constantly wondering if they were good enough, and questioning whether they should remain in their training programs. These feelings and questions can easily arise when training programs are not cognizant of the fact that they are steeped in white supremacy.

BlackDeer and Ocampo (2022) offer a perspective in examining social work training programs. They suggest that despite the profession's stated dedication to achieving social justice, social work has perpetuated settler colonialism and white supremacy. Likewise, Mackey et al. (2022) contend that doctoral social work education upholds white supremacy in a variety of ways through policy, practice, and discourse. By failing to take explicit steps that are antiracist in nature, the training model becomes complicit in harming the communities that they serve and perpetuates structural and systemic racism. BlackDeer and Ocampo (2022) speak directly about how colonization exists in the classroom when educators place an emphasis on utilizing Eurocentric models and negate the knowledge of Indigenous peoples and other non-white populations.

The fact that other models and techniques of practice are never introduced is what sustains white supremacy in clinical training. As Rev. David Billings (2016) of the People's Institute for Survival and Beyond (a national, multiracial, antiracist organization dedicated to ending racism and other forms of oppression through collective action) suggests, most educators "obtain degrees, publish and teach with little understanding of how white supremacy affects our lives and work" (p. 91). He further goes on to state that "those of us who are white, while understanding vague notions of white privilege, rarely delve deeply into the impact of centuries of white supremacy on our current lives" (Billings, 2016, p. 91). The consequence of this is internalized racial superiority. When this occurs, training institutions build their pedagogical foundation, utilizing the tools and training materials that have been used for decades, and come to believe that these tools are in fact the quintessential training materials that all students need to become competent clinicians. This typically goes unquestioned and unchallenged.

White-Centered Scholarship: Is There Another Way?

Discussions of the existence of white supremacy and the singular use of white-centered scholarship rarely occurs in graduate study. If it is raised as a point of concern, as I and many of my Colleagues of Color did decades ago, one could expect a level of ostracism from faculty who will view you as a troublemaker. Alternatively, one can be told (as I and my classmates were) that academic freedom preempts students from demanding faculty teach in a certain way. This academic freedom shield disrupts any possibility for any serious dialogue and true understanding of why it remains important to talk about race and, concomitantly, white supremacy.

In my experience, when any discussion that is centered on race is highlighted, it is usually centered around discussions of white privilege. With a growing body of literature explicitly addressing white privilege and its accompanying characteristics of white fragility (e.g., McIntosh, 2002; Rothenberg, 2016; Wise, 2016; DiAngelo, 2006, 2018, 2021), educators may have some willingness to address issues of privilege, while still revealing an apprehension about addressing white supremacy explicitly.

Leonardo (2004, p. 137) argues that a critical look at white privilege must be joined with an equally rigorous examination of white supremacy or the analysis of white racial domination. He posits that it is white supremacy that allows for the possibility of what we understand as white privilege. Leonardo (2004) challenges educators to examine how surface discussion of privilege obscures the concept of domination and how there must be an active agent involved. In other words, white privilege does not occur passively; it doesn't just happen. Rather, it is through the action of agents (institutions, people, structures) that white privilege exists and persists.

When Students and Trainees of Color are required to integrate white, Western, European teachings into the way they practice clinically, they may experience internal discomfort with such models. Yet they likely fail to question it or challenge their professors on the narrow scope of their training. Without demanding a broader discussion of clinical practice models against the context of race, racism, and white supremacy, it is unlikely that practice strategies will ever meet the needs of a diverse clinical population. As Almeida (2019) offers, "the naming of operations of white supremacy creates a space that anyone can participate in and advocate for intersectional analyses toward decolonizing practices" (p. 34). Essentially, when we can name it, we can begin to dismantle it and work to decolonize the practice of therapy.

And while it is certainly true that there are varying perspectives on clinical models, few, if any, of these models speak directly to practices of Indigenous and non-white people. Similarly, in discussions of why People of Color tend to underutilize psychological services, there may be a tendency in traditional psychological literature to blame the victim. Indeed, early literature described People of Color as evidencing a level of cultural paranoia when seeking help from a medical or mental health professional. This paranoia stands in the way of acceptance of treatment. This perspective places the onus on Black folks and other People of Color in failing to seek out treatment and does not offer the alternate possibility that the types of treatment approaches utilized in traditional settings fail to reach Indigenous and non-white people in ways that are beneficial to them.

The Persistence of White-Centered Teaching and Training: Impact and Unintended Consequences

The challenge for People of Color seeking to train in the clinical professions is just beginning to be understood. In a report examining the lack of diversity in the field of psychology, Huff (2021) claims that psychology's educators must step up and provide increased support for Students of Color and "break the bottleneck of obstacles the profession has created" (line 2). Citing data from the APA's Center for Workforce Studies, Huff (2021) notes that "83% of psychology's workforce self-identified as White" (para. 5) compared to just 7% Hispanic, 4% Asian, and 3% Black. This is explained in part by the lack of diverse students entering graduate training because of multiple roadblocks and obstacles placed before them. The pathways that have been established to enter these hallowed halls have been set up by the psychology community itself: " 'It's a bottleneck that we've created where only the most prepared, the most organized, those who have the most knowledge and the most resources are the ones who get through the bottleneck' " (Huff, 2021, para. 7). Students are expected to leave their undergraduate studies having acquired research experience, authored or coauthored scientific articles, presented at conferences, and given poster presentations, just to name a few. For the undergraduate student, this requires finding a mentor who will bring you into their research team and guide you in the process of doing research and publishing.

One British study (Bawa et al., 2019) highlights the multiple barriers that prevent minoritized individuals (what they refer to as BME, Black, minority ethnic individuals) from even entering the field of psychology at the doctoral level. They note that systemic barriers are largely responsible for keeping them out of programs (being rejected at the short-list phase for not meeting "academic requirements" and less likely to gain a training place). They also note that poverty, limited family resources, and lack of role models contribute to a sense of not belonging, and institutional racism negatively impacts attainment (Bawa et al., 2019, p. 4).

As I reflect on my early years in practice that I (and other Colleagues of Color) experienced, I am reminded of the persistent sense of feeling outside of several systems. The consequence of this is questioning one's own value and sense of belonging. Even after completing many years of graduate study and entering the profession, one may be faced with a different kind of hostility, however benign it may appear to be. When a Person of Color is hired to work as a doctoral-level psychologist, they are often faced with a devaluation and lack of recognition. Often not being referred to as "Dr." is one of the many microassaults that a Person of Color may confront. This can lead to a sense of being a fraud, having the sense that one is an imposter, so to speak. This can be omnipresent. The question of whether one belongs is ever-present. The multitude of questions concerning how to begin a private practice may be without an audience. Whom do I speak with about this? Why have my white peers from graduate training found a way to begin a clinical practice? What is the magic formula?

As Trainees and early career Psychologists of Color come into professional settings, some may experience internalized devaluation—a process that occurs when one has incorporated the many negative messages around racial valuation that have surrounded most People of Color throughout their lives. It assaults a person's sense of dignity and how they are perceived (Hardy, 2013, 2023).

When one experiences this sense of devaluation, one may embark on a never-ending quest to gain the respect of those in power. This may take the form of trying to curry favor with the white supervisor; trying to do everything that one is told or taught, unquestioningly; going against one's gut when making clinical decisions that would not be approved of by a white supervisor. In effect, Trainees of Color, whether they be in psychology, social work, counseling, or marriage and family therapy, must strive to be what Hardy (2008) calls a GEMM therapist. GEMM is an acronym for a good, effective, mainstream, minority therapist. Hardy (2008) advises that "because people of color have very little influence in shaping the culture of most predominantly white institutions, becoming a GEMM is essential for survival in virtually all major institutions in our society" (p. 463). This is tantamount to adding insult to injury. Not only does one have to do all the work that is required to meet the basic requirements of one's training program and never raise issues of race (or challenge the status quo or align yourself with people who start trouble), one must also be prepared to become "GEMMified." This process can occur during your academic training as well as upon entering the workforce. Hardy (2008) outlines multiple ways in which one moves toward becoming a GEMM. He provides 15 strategies that clinical trainees may employ to function in training settings that often demand homogeneity despite providing lip service to the notion of diversity. I highlight the following 10 (Hardy, 2008): "1. Never discuss race; 2. Accept that the field is color blind; 3. Smile!; 4. Become comfortable with invisibility; 5. Keep the faith" (p. 464), and never speak of racial unfairness; "6. Become comfortable with cultural schizophrenia" (p. 465)—in other words, learn how to function in your culture of origin while operating in a world that ideologically is committed to diversity but is "experientially allergic to it" (p. 465); "7. Embrace the sameness-differentness dilemma," or "learn to live with the implicit contradictory messages of our field that encourage differences but reward sameness; 8. Support the profession" (pp. 465–466); 9. "Work harder, be smarter, and focus on abolishing *your* racial hang-ups" (p. 467); 10. "Develop comfort with being judged by others' standards" (p. 468).

As one begins to adopt these techniques and maneuvers to be accepted, it paradoxically creates a sense of self-doubt and diminishes our capacity to speak to issues that once mattered. Hardy (2023) refers to this as a sense of voicelessness. One can begin to lose the capacity to speak in any meaningful way. One becomes afraid of saying anything that will rock the boat or that might call attention to you. Voicelessness strips personal power, agency, and the ability to advocate for oneself. This is especially true if you are the only Person (or one of few) of Color in a workplace or academic setting.

Personal Reflections

As a Black psychologist who has traversed graduate studies and postdoctoral training in a range of settings, it is easy to pull on the multiple strands of inequity and devaluation that I experienced over the years. From training in my PhD program to the halls of postdoctoral training, I was frequently swimming in a sea of whiteness where I had to fight for my voice to be heard. When one starts out as an early career psychologist, whether pursuing research, a teaching track, or that of a practitioner, it becomes important to perform well and be accepted by our peers. Certainly, this is no different for a psychologist of any race, but it becomes more pronounced for the Trainee of Color who is the only one or one of very few. If one is lucky to make connections with another Person of Color or find an ally in a white colleague, this can help the transition, and to navigate what sometimes can feel like unwelcome spaces.

I, like many before me and those after me, learned to play the role of the good Clinician of Color who learned not to make waves; who learned to silence themselves to be seen as a team player. It has only been in the last decade or so that I have begun to reclaim my soul and spirit, find my voice, and literally name how white supremacy has suffocated me. While I may have internalized the pain of being mistaken for the cleaning lady when engaged in a postdoctoral professional training simply because I was the only Black person (other than support and custodial staff) in the conference center, I am now better equipped to confront my aggressor and ask that they reflect on why they might have confused me with the cleaning staff. What was it about my look or appearance that allowed them to immediately associate a Black woman with someone perceived to be in a subordinate role and ready to serve them and to meet their needs? While I can recall the pain of not calling out a racist predoctoral supervisor who transgressed upon me by denying my need to reschedule our supervision session because a family member was being appointed to the judiciary at the state level (a moment of great pride for my family), I can now name the pain and discomfort that I experienced.

Lest we forget, the professions of psychology and psychiatry have had shameful histories. Not only were they instrumental in introducing deficit theories and models to describe Black people's behaviors, formalizing intelligence testing that was based on inadequate research, and creating diagnostic labels for enslaved people who ran away as suffering from a form of lunacy (*"drapetomania"*; Dimuro, 2018), but they also relied on and promoted research that routinely centered white people. Lest we forget, there has been evidence of medical apartheid and government-sponsored research and testing that has caused direct harm to Black people (e.g., Tuskegee Syphilis Study; surgical experiments performed without anesthesia by Dr. J. Marion Sims on enslaved women to advance gynecology), all occurring under the guise of medical advancement that was built upon notions of White superiority.

Reclaiming My Soul

Reclaiming my soul has been a journey of facing painful truths, including the fact that the field of psychology was built on racial tenets that denigrated and subordinated people who looked like me. In my more than 25-year journey as a practicing psychologist, it has only been in last 10 years that I have felt a rebirth. This process has been born out of working through the pain of being required to internalize modes of learning that negated my race and culture, espoused an idea that color and race should be blind, and that clinical approaches should be objective and neutral. All this meant that I had to reject the parts of my personhood that were to be left out of the consulting room.

As I began to cultivate a deeper understanding of the insidious nature of white supremacy and how it infiltrates a helping profession, harming the very people it is intended to serve, I have been able to give language to my many moments of discomfort and sense of exclusion.

As I pursued postdoctoral study and struggled to integrate newer ideas that were intended to deepen my knowledge, I was often distracted and disappointed by the physical surroundings of the lecture halls. The inundation of images of white men who represented the founding fathers of the profession, libraries that contained texts by white theorists and rarely, if ever, Theorists of Color, teachers who never looked like me, and ideas that rejected the souls and spirit of People of Color, often left me feeling overwhelmed. I began to understand my anger and disappointment and what Hardy (2023) describes as my sense of psychological homelessness. My inability to forge the most intimate of relationships with teachers and supervisors was because they failed to show an interest in my racialized experiences and those of the Black and Brown clients I saw.

The mandates and dictates of the profession failed to understand the unique needs and experiences of Indigenous and non-white groups, and the different approaches that might prove invaluable to working with this population, approaches which sought deeper connections and disclosures that would allow for the development of more authentic relationships that would constitute the therapeutic alliance.

It is imperative that the People of Color in training not be the "one and only" or represent just a handful of that which makes up the diversity of the training class. It is essential that supervisors and supervisory processes integrate discussion of race and white supremacy into supervision. Doing so would help acknowledge the experiences of Trainees of Color, as well as invite proactive conversations about race throughout the training process, including critiques of the racist and white supremacy ideologies that have been endemic to the profession.

Recommendations

If the mental health profession, like other societal systems, is committed to re-visioning, achieving, and promoting racial equity, broad sweeping structural changes are needed. These changes must note how services are delivered, who the service deliverers are, and most importantly, how the next generation and future generations of clinicians are trained.

Moreover, we cannot wait until civil and social unrest occurs before we engage in direct action to affect broad change. We must be actively attuned to the needs of trainees as well as consumers of mental health care, and must recognize that a paradigm shift is warranted precisely because many clinicians have been trained in and utilize approaches that have been steeped in white supremacy ideology. This is unacceptable and a change is needed. There must be an abiding commitment to training racially sensitive therapists. To act on this commitment, programs must take decisive actions to ensure that racial dialogues are occurring in the classroom and within supervision. Additionally, trainees must be encouraged to engage in Self of the Therapist work that promotes racial self-interrogation. And finally, student bodies must be diverse and representative of multiple identities and social locations.

There is a unique burden that must be placed on training programs and institutions to mitigate the pervasiveness of white supremacy and to train racially sensitive therapists. Many scholars (e.g., Bawa et al., 2019; Carten et al., 2016; Comas-Díaz, 2020; Castañeda-Sound et al., 2020; Holmes, 2016,

2017; Hardy & McGoldrick, 2008) have offered recommendations in working toward this objective. Here are some recommendations for changes:

1. **Hire diverse faculty:** Students of Color and other underrepresented groups must be able to see themselves in the classroom and in the research being performed, and hear the language of diversity of experiences that is not relegated to a singular course named Cultural Competence or Multicultural Issues in Counseling.

2. **Promote racial conversations:** Racialized dialogue must occur in the classroom where the centrality of whiteness is named, explored, and critiqued. Faculty and students must be introduced to concepts of internalized racial superiority and internalized racial devaluation. Additionally, students and trainees must develop the various muscles (intensity, intimacy, transparency, authenticity, congruency, and complexity) that increase their capacity to stay in the (racial) conversation and in effect become racially lingual (Hardy, 2020, 2023).

3. **Mandate racially focused Self of the Therapist work:** Self of the Therapist work must be a core part of the training model, where faculty and students engage in self-examination of their racial backgrounds, personal history, and how aspects of the self are presented in therapeutic encounters. Watts-Jones (2010) offers clear guidance on how implementation of the Self of the Therapist model can be tremendously beneficial in clinical practice.

4. **Be intentional about promoting belongingness:** BIPOC students must be welcomed by faculty and provided with a mentor or someone who will help guide their journey. The faculty mentor, regardless of race, must demonstrate an openness to discussing and learning of the interests and experience of Trainees of Color and send the powerful message that "you belong here" and "we value your presence."

5. **Increase access to racially informed research and funding:** To increase the interest and opportunities of potential graduate Stu-

dents of Color, there must be greater interest in research that addresses diverse communities and funding earmarked to support such research. Relatedly, there must be faculty engaged in such research or supportive of such research to encourage BIPOC students to add to the growing scholarship.

6. **Increase funding to support graduate Students of Color in training:** As exciting as it is to gain admission into a graduate training program, financing can be a huge obstacle. This is equally true at the postdoctoral level. It should come as no surprise that many graduate Students of Color struggle financially and have to take out student loans. The idea of leaving graduate school with huge debts can make the thought of entering training seem unrealistic. For students attending graduate training in urban areas, there may be additional costs related to traveling to supervision, whether that be to areas that are local or training sites that require additional travel on suburban commuter railroads that are very costly. Maintaining a physical residence in an apartment is an essential need that most graduate training does not account for. When students have to take up ancillary employment to finance their daily living needs (food, housing, local transportation), this too can greatly impact one's ability to attend graduate training or to be fully present in the program.

7. **Integrate alternative (Indigenous) approaches to mental health care:** Clinical training must expand its approaches to training and consider offering readings and courses that address Indigenous and other non–Western European approaches. By moving away from practices that only perpetuate models of treatment steeped in whiteness, we can demonstrate an openness to valuing cultural approaches that have existed for many years that have been discounted or devalued by the academy.

8. **Implement diversity, equity, inclusion, and belonging (DEIB) training for faculty and enrolled students:** Because no one is immune to the impact of white supremacy that is endemic to our culture, clinical training programs must own the fact that those who make up

these institutions may need to be reminded of the pervasiveness of white supremacy ideology. There is value in contracting with DEIB consultants to engage faculty, staff, and trainees in racial awareness experiential training to mitigate the effects of unconscious bias, unintended microaggressions, and the range of transgressions that are routinely part of the training experience.

9. **Adopt decolonizing psychology and clinical fields of study as a paradigm shift:** Rivera and Comas-Díaz (2020) as well as others (e.g., Bhatia, 2018; Duran, 2019) have suggested liberatory approaches to psychology that seek to decolonize the Euro-American approaches of the field. Liberation psychology has as its goal to understand and address oppression among individuals and groups, and psychologists who utilize this approach understand oppression as "the interaction of intrapsychic factors with systemic factors, such as sociopolitical injustice" (Rivera & Comas-Díaz, 2020, p. 3). Similarly, Bhatia's (2018) writing seeks to encourage the imagination and creation of an alternative psychology that departs from Euro-American hegemonic structures—structures that are "mechanistic, universalizing, essentializing and ethnocentric" (p. xx). Bhatia (2018) argues that the Euro-American approach is the dominant one that attempts to speak for all of humanity and limits and marginalizes other perspectives that fall out of its canon.

    Scholars and educators alike must seek to decolonize the field, and clinical practitioners must seek out approaches that are more inclusive and speak to healing practices that are outside of the Western canon. As an example, Duran (2019) introduces his readers to the *soul wound*, a Native American concept that speaks of historical trauma that is best addressed through the understanding of historical context and application of approaches sensitive to the experiences of Original Peoples. Duran's (2019) writings attempt to bridge Western worldviews with traditional concepts espoused by Native and Indigenous people. He speaks of "shifting the modern pathological diagnoses to an understanding that is harmonious with the natural world as perceived by some Indigenous cultures" (Duran, 2019, p. 8).

By taking some of these steps, we can hopefully move closer to creating training opportunities in all clinical disciplines that encourage an "inward looking" of all therapists, where race, racism, and white supremacy are named and discussed. Clinical supervisors must engage in Self of the Therapist work and connect with their own sense of subjugation and privilege in order that they may better address issues of race, culture, and white supremacy that blind the helping profession. And scholars and practitioners must be open to examining healing models that depart from westernized approaches to treatment. By offering trainees opportunities to examine a broader view and conception of illness, health, and healing, we invite disparate views to the table and embrace traditional approaches that hold relevance today.

Conclusion

As we move through a period in the history of the United States and the aftermath of a worldwide pandemic that shone a light on racial disparities and state-sanctioned aggression against People of Color, we must be prepared to address the growing pain, suffering, and trauma that accompany these experiences. If we don't adequately prepare our profession to embrace the growing diversity of the world and instead continue to rely on antiquated methods that center white research, white theorists, and white practices, we cannot advance the field. We cannot afford to continue to ignore practices advanced by People of Color and Indigenous folks who have been steeped in the business of healing for centuries. If we maintain what has become the standard approach to training, we will fail to make the helping profession anything more than just another oppressive force that maintains the status quo. Moreover, it will also serve as a potent reminder that we will have failed miserably in our quest to prepare and produce a generation of racially sensitive clinicians and practitioners.

Notes

Chapter 4

1 A helper, for the purpose of this discussion, is someone who has attended the training before and is supporting the trainees, such as by helping with role-plays. Many of the same dynamics being explored here could also apply to teaching assistants.

2 Many therapists volunteer their time to support trainings as helpers in professional trainings. When supervisors and helpers are not paid or are underpaid, this ensures that only people with means will be able to be helpers and supervisors in trainings. Helping in a training is an important way that therapists get exposure to the model to deepen their learning or to practice their supervision skills with support present. Being a helper in a training also increases a therapist's recognition in the community as a dedicated practitioner, sometimes also increasing referrals. If, however, only people with means can participate in trainings, this situation creates a powerful bias against a diverse training support team.

Chapter 13

1 The term People of the Global Majority, coined by Rosemary M. Campbell-Stephens (2021), speaks to the truth that the majority of people on this planet are racialized. It is an active and powerful assertion that groups made marginal are actually in the majority. We use this term rather than the U.S.-centric People of Color or BIPOC. For ease of reading, we may say Clients of Color.

Chapter 15

1 Join the Reckoning (JTR) is a collective of People of Color and white therapists, activists, and trainees invested in using direct action to eliminate racism in the mental health field and repair the harm that the mental health field has caused.

References

Preface

Boyd-Franklin, N. (2003). *Black families in therapy: Understanding the African American experience* (2nd ed.). Guilford.

DeGruy Leary, J. (2005). *Post traumatic slave syndrome.* Uptone Press.

Guthrie, R. V. (1997). *Even the rat was white: A historical view of psychology.* Allyn and Bacon.

Hardy, K. V. (1989). The theoretical myth of sameness: A critical issue in family therapy training and treatment. *Journal of Psychotherapy and the Family, 6*(1–2), 17–33.

Hardy, K. V. (Ed.). (2022). *The enduring, invisible, and ubiquitous centrality of whiteness.* W. W. Norton.

McGoldrick, M., Giordano, J., & Garcia-Preto, N. (Eds.). (2005). *Ethnicity and family therapy.* (3rd ed.). Guilford.

McGoldrick, M., & Hardy, K. V. (Eds.) (2019). *Re-visioning family therapy: Addressing diversity in clinical practice* (3rd ed.). Guilford.

Menakem, R. (2017). *My grandmother's hands: Racialized trauma and the pathway to mending our hearts and bodies.* Central Recovery Press.

Nealy, E. C. (2017). *Transgender children and youth: Cultivating pride and joy with families in transition.* W. W. Norton.

Chapter 1

Hardy, K. V. (2016). Toward a development of a multicultural relational perspective in training and supervision. In K. V. Hardy & T. Bobes (Eds.), *Culturally sensitive supervision and training: Diverse perspectives and practical application* (pp. 3–10). Routledge.

Hardy, K. V. (Ed.). (2022). *The enduring, invisible, and ubiquitous centrality of whiteness.* W. W. Norton.

REFERENCES

Hardy, K. V. (2023). *Racial trauma: Clinical strategies and techniques for healing invisible wounds.* W. W. Norton.

Hardy, K. V., & Bobes, T. (2017). Experiential exercises. In K. V. Hardy & T. Bobes (Eds.), *Promoting cultural sensitivity in supervision: A manual for practitioners* (pp. 99–115). Routledge.

Hardy, K. V., & Laszloffy, T. A. (1995). The cultural genogram: Key to training culturally competent family therapists. *Journal of Marital and Family Therapy, 21*(3), 227–237. https://doi.org/10.1111/j.1752-0606.1995.tb00158.x

Laszloffy, T., & Habekost, J. (2010). Using experiential tasks to enhance cultural sensitivity among MFT trainees. *Journal of Marital and Family Therapy, 36*(3), 333–346. https://doi.org/10.1111/j.1752-0606.2010.00213.x

Winawer, H. (2022). How I was taught "unseeing" to internalize white supremacy: Understanding and undoing, a personal narrative. In K. V. Hardy (Ed.), *The enduring, invisible, and ubiquitous centrality of whiteness* (pp. 405–428). W. W. Norton.

Chapter 2

American Psychiatric Association. (2022). *Diagnostic and statistical manual of mental disorders* (5th ed., text rev.).

DeGruy Leary, J. (2005). *Post traumatic slave syndrome: America's legacy of enduring injury and healing.* Uptone Press.

Fisher, J. (2021). *Transforming the living legacy of trauma: A workbook for survivors and therapists.* PESI Publishing and Media.

Hardy, K. V. (1989). The theoretical myth of sameness: A critical issue in family therapy training and treatment. *Journal of Psychotherapy and the Family, 6*(1–2), 17–33. https://doi.org/10.1300/J287v06n01_02

Hardy, K. V. (2013). Healing the hidden wounds of racial trauma. *Reclaiming Children and Youth, 22*(1), 24–28.

Hardy, K. V. (Ed.). (2022). *The enduring, invisible, and ubiquitous centrality of whiteness.* W. W. Norton.

Hardy, K. V. (2023). *Racial trauma: Clinical strategies and techniques for healing invisible wounds.* W. W. Norton.

Hardy, K. V., & Bobes, T. (2016). Core competencies for executing culturally sensitive supervision and training. In K. V. Hardy & T. Bobes (Eds.), *Culturally sensitive supervision and training: Diverse perspective and practical applications* (pp. 11–15). Routledge.

Herman, J. L. (1997). *Trauma and recovery: The aftermath of violence—from domestic abuse to political terrors.* Basic Books.

Levine, P. A. (2015). *Trauma and memory: Brain and body in a search for the living past.* North Atlantic.

Menakem, R. (2017). *My grandmother's hands: Racialized trauma and the pathway to mending our hearts and bodies.* Central Recovery Press.

van der Kolk, B. A. (2014). *The body keeps the score: Brain, mind, and body in the healing of trauma.* Penguin.

Wise Rowe, S. (2020). *Healing racial trauma: The road to resilience.* InterVarsity Press.

Chapter 3

Alford, K. (2022). The uphill climb of black men: Therapeutic treatment and educational considerations for mental health engagement. In K. V. Hardy (Ed.), *The enduring, invisible, and ubiquitous centrality of whiteness* (pp. 472–492). W. W. Norton.

Hardy, K. V. (Ed.). (2022). *The enduring, invisible, and ubiquitous centrality of whiteness*. W. W. Norton.

Hardy, K. V. (2023). *Racial trauma: Clinical strategies and techniques for healing invisible wounds*. W. W. Norton.

Hardy, K. V., & Bobes, T. (Eds.). (2016). *Culturally sensitive supervision and training: Diverse perspectives and practical applications*. Routledge.

Hardy, K. V., & Laszloffy, T. A. (1995). The cultural genogram: Key to training culturally competent family therapists. *Journal of Marital and Family Therapy, 21*(3), 227–237. https://doi.org/10.1111/j.1752-0606.1995.tb00158.x

Hardy, K. V., & Laszloffy, T. A. (2008). The dynamics of a pro-racist ideology: Implications for family therapists. In M. McGoldrick & K. V. Hardy (Eds.), *Re-visioning family therapy: Race, culture, and gender in clinical practice* (2nd ed., pp. 225–237). Guilford.

Laszloffy, T., & Habekost, J. (2010). Using experiential tasks to enhance cultural sensitivity among MFT trainees. *Journal of Marital and Family Therapy, 36*(3), 333–346. https://doi.org/10.1111/j.1752-0606.2010.00213.x

Sung, I. I. H. (2022). Silenced by whiteness: A personal account. In K. V. Hardy (Ed.), *The enduring, invisible, and ubiquitous centrality of whiteness* (pp. 210–222). W. W. Norton.

Chapter 4

Baldwin, J. (1962, January 14). As much truth as one can bear. *New York Times*, Section T.

Brown, A. M. (2020). *We will not cancel us: And other dreams of transformative justice*. AK Press.

Hardy, K. V. (2016). Antiracist approaches for shaping theoretical and practice paradigms. In A. J. Carten, A. B. Siskind, & M. Pender Greene (Eds.), *Strategies for deconstructing racism in the health and human services* (pp. 125–139). Oxford University Press.

Hardy, K. V. (2018a). *Characteristics of an emerging anti-racist organization* [Handout]. Eikenberg Institute for Relationships. https://irp-cdn.multiscreensite.com/226e693c/files/uploaded/Anti-Racism_2018-PDF.pdf

Hardy, K. V. (2018b). The self of the therapist in epistemological context: A multicultural relational perspective. *Journal of Family Psychotherapy, 29*(1), 17–29.

Hardy, K. V. (Ed.). (2022). *The enduring, invisible, and ubiquitous centrality of whiteness*. W. W. Norton.

Hardy, K. V. (2023). *Racial trauma: Clinical strategies and techniques for healing invisible wounds*. W. W. Norton.

Hardy, K. V., & Bobes, T. (Eds.). (2016). *Culturally sensitive supervision and training: Diverse perspectives and practical applications*. Routledge.

Johnson, S. M. (2019). *Attachment theory in practice: Emotionally focused therapy (EFT) with individuals, couples, and families*. Guilford.

Okun, T. (2022). *What is white supremacy culture?* White Supremacy Culture. https://www.whitesupremacyculture.info/what-is-it.html

Washington, H. A. (2007). *Medical apartheid: The dark history of medical experimentation on black Americans from colonial times to the present.* Penguin Random House.

Watts-Jones, T. D. (2010). Location of self: Opening the door to dialogue on intersectionality in the therapy process. *Family Process, 49*(3), 405–420. https://doi.org/10.1111/j.1545-5300.2010.01330.x

Chapter 5

Cassell, E. J. (2004). *The nature of suffering and the goals of medicine* (2nd ed.). Oxford University Press.

Duffy, T. (Ed.). (2007). *Creative interventions in grief and loss therapy: When the music stops, a dream dies.* Haworth Press.

Hardy, K. V. (2023). *Racial trauma: Clinical strategies and techniques for healing invisible wounds.* W. W. Norton.

Hardy, K. V., & Laszloffy, T. A. (1995). The cultural genogram: Key to training culturally competent family therapists. *Journal of Marital and Family Therapy, 21*(3), 227–237. https://doi.org/10.1111/j.1752-0606.1995.tb00158.x

Hardy, K. V., & Laszloffy, T. A. (2006). *Teens who hurt: Clinical interventions to break the cycle of adolescent violence.* Guilford.

Raheim, S. (2019). The power of song to promote healing, hope, and justice: Lessons from the African American experience. In M. McGoldrick & K. V. Hardy (Eds.), *Re-visioning family therapy: Addressing diversity in clinical practice* (3rd ed., pp. 449–463). Guilford.

Rosen, S. (Ed.). (1991). *My voice will go with you: The teaching tales of Milton H. Erickson* (Reprint ed.). W. W. Norton.

White, M., & Epston, D. (1990). *Narrative means to therapeutic ends.* W. W. Norton.

Chapter 6

Baudrillard, J. (1986). *America.* Verso.

Diamond, A. (2020, May 19). The 1924 law that slammed the door on immigrants and the politicians who pushed it back open. *Smithsonian Magazine.* https://www.smithsonianmag.com/history/1924-law-slammed-door-immigrants-and-politicians-who-pushed-it-back-open-180974910/

Hahami, E. (2022, August 5). *Charles Coughlin's mass circulation of antisemitic propaganda.* Medium. https://medium.com/the-social-justice-tribune/charles-coughlins-mass-circulation-of-antisemitic-propaganda-5ebee5aed2fb

The International Jew. (2024, February 13). In Wikipedia. https://en.wikipedia.org/wiki/The_International_Jew

Katz, J. K. (n.d.a). *A tool for transcending Jewish trauma.* Transcending Jewish Trauma. https://www.transcendingjewishtrauma.com/

Katz, J. K. (n.d.b). *Map.* Transcending Jewish Trauma. https://www.transcendingjewishtrauma.com/map

Lerner, M. (2023, March 3). A revised Jewish understanding of the state of Israel. *Tikkun.* https://www.tikkun.org/a-jewish-renewal-understanding/

Margaritoff, M. (2020, September 16). *How Charles Lindbergh wrecked his legacy push-*

ing anti-Semitism and neutrality toward the Nazis. ATI. https://allthatsinteresting.com/charles-lindbergh-antisemitism

Messianic Jewish Family Bible Society. (2014). *Exodus 23*. Bible, Tree of Life Version. YouVersion. https://www.bible.com/bible/314/EXO.23.TLV

Number of Jews at Exodus. (n.d.). Aish. https://aish.com/number_of_Jews_at_Exodus/

Paradise, A. M. (n.d.). *A collective for collective liberation*. AMP. https://ameliaparadise.com/justice/jewish-bridge-project/

Ward, E. K. (2017, June 29). *Skin in the game: How antisemitism animates white nationalism*. Political Research Associates. https://politicalresearch.org/2017/06/29/skin-in-the-game-how-antisemitism-animates-white-nationalism

Chapter 7

Baker, B. (2022, March 29). *What Southern black women can teach us (and the country) about ourselves*. Refinery29. https://www.refinery29.com/en-us/2022/03/10921290/southern-black-women-feminism-imani-perry

Berry, D. R., & Gross, K. N. (2020). *A black women's history of the United States*. Beacon.

Closson, T. (2023, June 2). Stuyvesant High School admitted 762 new students. Only 7 are black. *New York Times*. https://www.nytimes.com/2023/06/02/nyregion/stuyvesant-high-school-black-students.html

Collins, P. H. (2020). *Black feminist thought: Knowledge, consciousness and the politics of empowerment*. Routledge.

Del Cerro, X. (2023, January 11). Utility outages at NYCHA complexes increased last year, leaving thousands without heat, hot water. *Brooklyn Paper*. https://www.brooklynpaper.com/heat-hot-water-outages-increased-nycha-2022/

Hamad, R. (2020). *White tears/brown scars: How white feminism betrays women of color*. Catapult.

Hardy, K. V. (2013). Healing the hidden wounds of racial trauma. *Reclaiming Children and Youth, 22*(1), 24–28.

Hardy, K. V. (2016). Antiracist approaches for shaping theoretical and practice paradigms. In A. J. Carten, A. B. Siskind, & M. Pender Greene (Eds.), *Strategies for deconstructing racism in the health and human services* (pp. 125–139). Oxford University Press.

Hardy, K. V. (2023). *Racial trauma: Clinical strategies and techniques for healing invisible wounds*. W. W. Norton.

hooks, b. (2015). *Sisters of the yam: Black women and self-recovery* (2nd ed.). Routledge.

Nadal, K. L. (2017). "Let's get in formation": On becoming a psychologist-activist in the 21st century. *American Psychologist, 72*(9), 935–946. https://doi.org/10.1037/amp0000212

National Museum of African American History and Culture. (n.d.). *Popular and pervasive stereotypes of African Americans*. https://nmaahc.si.edu/explore/stories/popular-and-pervasive-stereotypes-african-americans

New York Times. (1990, January 3). The mosaic thing. https://www.nytimes.com/1990/01/03/opinion/the-mosaic-thing.html

NYCHA. (n.d.). *Developments*. New York City Housing Authority. https://www.nyc.gov/site/nycha/about/developments.page

NYCHA. (2023). *NYCHA 2023 fact sheet*. New York City Housing Authority. https://www.nyc.gov/assets/nycha/downloads/pdf/NYCHA-Fact-Sheet-2023.pdf

Perry, I. (2022). *South to America: A journey below the Mason-Dixon to understand the soul of a nation.* HarperCollins.

Russ, G., Vasan, A., & Aggarwala, R. (2022, September 9). *Water testing at Riis houses.* [Memorandum]. New York City Housing Authority. https://www.nyc.gov/site/nycha/residents/riis-houses-water.page

Shapiro, E., & Lai, K. K. R. (2019, June 3). How New York's elite public schools lost their black and Hispanic students. *New York Times.* https://www.nytimes.com/interactive/2019/06/03/nyregion/nyc-public-schools-black-hispanic-students.html

Smith, G. B. (2022, September 6). *No more arsenic found in NYCHA water but frustrations, testing continue.* NBC New York. https://www.nbcnewyork.com/news/local/no-more-arsenic-found-in-the-nycha-building-water-but-frustrations-testing-continue/3851650/

Tatum, B. D. (2021). *Why are all the black kids sitting together in the cafeteria? And other conversations about race.* Penguin.

Watts-Jones, T. D. (2010). Location of self: Opening the door to dialogue on intersectionality in the therapy process. *Family Process, 49*(3), 405–420. https://doi.org/10.1111/j.1545-5300.2010.01330.x

Chapter 8

Blades, R. (1979). Plastico [Song]. On *Siembra* [Album]. Fania.

Cambridge Dictionary. (n.d.). Mestizo. https://dictionary.cambridge.org/us/dictionary/english/mestizo?q=mestiza

Escobar, J. I. B. (2016). Afro-Colombian integration in mestizo cities: The case of Bogotá. *Analysis of Urban Change, Theory, Action, 20*(1), 130–141. https://doi.org/10.1080/13604813.2015.1096053

Lobo, G. J., & Morgan, N. (2004). ¿Lo decimos con cariño? Articulating blackness in Colombia: Affection, difference or inequality? *Journal of Iberian and Latin American Research, 10*(1), 83–97. https://doi.org/10.1080/13260219.2004.10429982

Ortiz Cassiani, J. (2019). *El incómodo color de la memoria: Columnas y crónicas de la historia negra.* Libros Malpensante.

Sanchez Castaneda, P. A. (2018). *Mending identity: The revitalization process of the Muisca of Suba* [Master's thesis]. Florida International University. https://doi.org/10.25148/etd.FIDC006539

Telles, E. E. (2014). *Pigmentocracies: Ethnicity, race and color in Latin America.* University of North Carolina Press.

Vásquez-Padilla, D. H., & Hernández-Reyes, C. E. (2020). Interrogando la gramática racial de la blanquitud: Hacia una analítica del blanqueamiento en el orden racial colombiano. *Latin American Research Review, 55*(1), 64–80. https://doi.org/10.25222/larr.170

Woods, J. (2019, October 3). *A word about the word campesino.* Heifer International. https://www.heifer.org/blog/a-word-about-the-word-campesino.html

Zamora, S. (2022). *Racial baggage: Mexican immigrants and race across the border.* Stanford University Press.

Chapter 9

Hardy, K. V. (2015). *How to talk effectively about racism* [Handout]. https://traumatransformed.org/documents/Effectively-Talk-About-Race-Dr.-Ken-Hardy-11x17.pdf

Hardy, K. V. (2018). The self of the therapist in epistemological context: A multicultural relational perspective. *Journal of Family Psychotherapy, 29*(1), 17–29. https://doi.org/10.1080/08975353.2018.1416211

Hardy, K. V. (2023). *Racial trauma: Clinical strategies and techniques for healing invisible wounds.* W. W. Norton.

King, M. L., Jr. (2018). *Letter from Birmingham jail.* Penguin Classics.

Okun, T. (2022). *What is white supremacy culture?* White Supremacy Culture. https://www.whitesupremacyculture.info/what-is-it.html

Semuels, A. (2016, July 22). The racist history of Portland, the whitest city in America. *Atlantic.* https://www.theatlantic.com/business/archive/2016/07/racist-history-portland/492035/

Takaki, R. (1989). *Strangers from a different shore: A history of Asian Americans.* Little, Brown.

Chapter 10

Anti-Defamation League. (n.d.). *Antisemitism in American history.* ADL. https://antisemitism.adl.org/antisemitism-in-american-history/

Biography.com Editors. (2021, March 26). *Lena Horne.* Biography. https://www.biography.com/musicians/lena-horne

Boyd-Franklin, N. (2003). *Black families in therapy: Understanding the African American experience* (2nd ed.). Guilford.

Bradley Braves. (2023, July 2). In *Wikipedia.* https://en.wikipedia.org/w/index.php?title=Bradley_Braves&oldid=1162976163

Don-El. (2020, December 29). *Sterling K Brown—Running with a mask* [Video]. YouTube. https://www.youtube.com/watch?v=jhNeAEdxSsc

Editors of Encyclopaedia Britannica. (2024). Deutschlandlied: German national anthem. In *Britannica.* https://www.britannica.com/topic/Deutschlandlied

Hare-Mustin, R. T. (1987). The problem of gender in family therapy theory. *Family Process, 26*(1), 15–27.

Johnson, S. (2008). *Hold me tight: Sevens conversations for a lifetime of love.* Little, Brown.

Johnson, S. M. (2019). *Attachment theory in practice: Emotionally focused therapy (EFT) with individuals, couples, and families.* Guilford.

Kodé, A. (2023, April 4). How a TikToker brought hundreds of transplants to a midwestern city. *New York Times.* https://www.nytimes.com/2023/03/29/realestate/tiktok-peoria-illinois.html

Leichtag Foundation. (n.d.). *Population of Jews of color is increasing in U.S., despite undercounting in population studies.* https://leichtag.org/press-release-population-of-jews-of-color-is-increasing-in-u-s-despite-undercounting-in-population-studies/

Mazzig, H. (2019, May 20). Op-ed: No, Israel isn't a country of privileged and powerful white Europeans. *Los Angeles Times.* https://www.latimes.com/opinion/op-ed/la-oe-mazzig-mizrahi-jews-israel-20190520-story.html

McHugh, J. (2022, April 3). The Jewish travel guide that inspired the Green Book. *Washington Post.* https://www.washingtonpost.com/history/2022/04/03/jewish-vacation-guide-green-book/

Tarter, S. (2018, October 8). Peoria home to 12,000 Caterpillar workers. *State Journal-Register.* https://www.sj-r.com/story/news/2018/10/08/peoria-home-to-12-000/9616322007/

Chapter 11

Hardy, K. V. (2008). On becoming a GEMM therapist: Work harder, be smarter, and never discuss race. In M. McGoldrick & K. V. Hardy (Eds.), *Re-visioning family therapy: Addressing diversity in clinical practice* (3rd ed.). Guilford.

Hardy, K. V. (2013). Healing the hidden wounds of racial trauma. *Reclaiming Children and Youth, 22*(1), 24–28.

Hardy, K. V. (2023). *Racial trauma: Clinical strategies and techniques for healing invisible wounds.* W. W. Norton.

Menakem, R. (2017). *My grandmother's hands: Racialized trauma and the pathway to mending our hearts and bodies.* Central Recovery Press.

Chapter 12

Adil, Z. S. (2021, June 10). Name mispronunciations leave lasting impact on individuals. *Standard.* https://standard.asl.org/18485/features/name-pronunciations-leave-lasting-impact-on-individuals/

Appleton, D. B. (2023, May 16). *Period Arabic names and naming practices.* Society for Creative Anachronism, Inc. https://heraldry.sca.org/names/arabic-naming2.htm

Chao, M. (2021, May 27). *What's in a name? For Asian immigrants, a chance to "assimilate or vanish."* NorthJersey. https://www.northjersey.com/story/news/2021/05/27/hidden-history-behind-asian-americans-anglicized-names/4892915001/

Evason, N. (2021). *Naming.* Cultural Atlas. https://culturalatlas.sbs.com.au/american-culture/american-culture-naming

Flückiger, C., Del Re, A. C., Wampold, B. E., & Horvath, A. O. (2018). The alliance in adult psychotherapy: A meta-analytic synthesis. *Psychotherapy, 55*(4), 316–340. https://doi.org/10.1037/pst0000172

Golestani, N., & Zatorre, R. J. (2009). Individual differences in the acquisition of second language phonology. *Brain and Language, 109*(2–3), 55–67. https://doi.org/10.1016/j.bandl.2008.01.005

Hardy, K. V. (Ed.). (2022). *The enduring, invisible, and ubiquitous centrality of whiteness.* W. W. Norton.

Hardy, K. V. (2023). *Racial trauma: Clinical strategies and techniques for healing invisible wounds.* W. W. Norton.

Horowitz, J. M., Brown, A., & Cox, K. (2019, April 9). *Race in America 2019.* Pew Research Center. https://www.pewresearch.org/social-trends/wp-content/uploads/sites/3/2019/04/Race-report_updated-4.29.19.pdf

Hwang, W.-C. (2016). *Culturally adapting psychotherapy for Asian heritage populations: An evidence-based approach.* Academic Press.

Johnson, A. (2003). *Families of the forest: The Matsigenka Indians of the Peruvian Amazon.* University of California Press.

Kang, S. K., DeCelles, K. A., Tilcsik, A., & Jun, S. (2016). Whitened résumés: Race and self-presentation in the labor market. *Administrative Science Quarterly, 61*(3), 469–502. https://doi.org/10.1177/0001839216639577

Kohli, R., & Solórzano, D. G. (2012). Teachers, please learn our names! Racial microaggressions and the K–12 classroom. *Race Ethnicity and Education, 15*(4), 441–462. https://doi.org/10.1080/13613324.2012.674026

Nguyen, B. (2021, April 1). America ruined my name for me: So I chose a new one.

New Yorker. https://www.newyorker.com/culture/personal-history/america-ruined-my-name-for-me

Notzon, B., & Nesom, G. (2005). The Arabic naming system. *Science Editors, 28*(1), 20–21.

Roberts, S. O., Bareket-Shavit, C., Dollins, F. A., Goldie, P. D., & Mortenson, E. (2020). Racial inequality in psychological research: Trends of the past and recommendations for the future. *Perspectives on Psychological Science, 15*(6), 1295–1309. https://doi.org/10.1177/1745691620927709

Roberts, S. O., & Mortenson, E. (2022). Challenging the white = neutral framework in psychology. *Perspectives on Psychological Science, 18*(3), 597–606. https://doi.org/10.1177/17456916221077117

United Nations. (n.d.). *Slave trade.* https://www.un.org/en/observances/decade-people-african-descent/slave-trade

United States Census Bureau. (2023). *Population estimates, July 1, 2023* (V2023) [Data set]. https://www.census.gov/quickfacts/fact/table/US

Waxman, O. B. (2022, May 17). The history of Native American boarding schools is even more complicated than a new report reveals. *Time.* https://time.com/6177069/american-indian-boarding-schools-history/

Zhao, X., & Biernat, M. (2018). "I have two names, Xian and Alex": Psychological correlates of adopting Anglo names. *Journal of Cross-Cultural Psychology, 49*(4), 587–601. https://doi.org/10.1177/0022022118763111

Chapter 13

Armstrong, L. (1967). What a wonderful world [Song]. On *What a Wonderful World* [Album]. ABC.

Arye, L. (n.d.). *What is unintentional music?* http://processworklane.com/unintentional-music/

Campbell-Stephens, R. M. (2021). *Educational leadership and the global majority: Decolonising narratives.* Springer.

Choudhury, S. (2015). *Deep diversity: Overcoming us vs. them.* Between the Lines.

Coates, T. (2015). *Between the world and me.* Random House.

Fisher, J. (2017). *Healing the fragmented selves of trauma survivors: Overcoming internal self-alienation.* Routledge.

Hall, J. W. (Ed.). (2004). *Conversations with Audre Lorde.* University Press of Mississippi.

Hardy, K. V. (2016). Antiracist approaches for shaping theoretical and practice paradigms. In A. J. Carten, A. B. Siskind, & M. Pender Greene (Eds.), *Strategies for deconstructing racism in the health and human services* (pp. 125–139). Oxford University Press.

Hardy, K. V. (2023). *Racial trauma: Clinical strategies and techniques for healing invisible wounds.* W. W. Norton.

IAPOP. (n.d.). Worldwork seminars. International Association of Process Oriented Psychology. http://worldwork.org/about/worldwork-seminars/

Kinouani, G. (2021). *Living while black: The essential guide to overcoming racial trauma.* Ebury Press.

Lorde, A. (2007). Age, race, class, and sex: Women redefining difference. In *Sister outsider: Essays and speeches by Audre Lorde* (Revised ed., pp. 114–123). Crossing Press.

Mindell, A. (1995). *Sitting in the fire: Large group transformation using conflict and diversity.* Lao Tse Press.

Moraga, C., & Anzaldúa, G. (Eds.). (1981). *This bridge called my back: Writings by radical women of color.* Persephone Press.

Nieto, L., Boyer, M. F., Goodwin, L., Johnson, G. R., & Smith, L. C. (2014). *Beyond inclusion, beyond empowerment: A developmental strategy to liberate everyone* (Revised ed.). Cuetzpalin.

Okun, T. (2019, June 20). *White dominant culture and something different: A worksheet.* SoCal Grantmakers. https://socalgrantmakers.org/resources/white-dominant-culture-something-different

Seppälä, E. (2016, March 31). *A loving-kindness meditation to boost compassion.* Mindful. https://www.mindful.org/a-loving-kindness-meditation-to-boost-compassion/

Simone, N. (1967). I wish I knew how it would feel to be free [Song]. On *Silk and Soul* [Album]. RCA.

Tutu, D., & Tutu, M. (2014). *The book of forgiving: The fourfold path for healing ourselves and our world.* HarperOne.

Chapter 14

American Psychiatric Association. (2022). *Diagnostic and statistical manual of mental disorders* (5th ed., text rev.).

Anderson, C. (2016). *White rage: The unspoken truth of our racial divide.* Bloomsbury USA.

Anen, S. J. (2022). Narcissistic states of white privilege and the constructive potential of shame. *Psychoanalytic Dialogues, 32*(6), 621–683. https://doi.org/10.1080/10481885.2022.2128677

Ani, M. (1994). *Yurugu: An African-centered critique of European cultural thought and behavior.* Africa World Press.

Carter, R. T. (Ed.). (2004). *Handbook of racial-cultural psychology and counseling: Training and practice* (2nd ed.). John Wiley and Sons.

DiAngelo, R. (2016). *What does it mean to be white? Developing white racial literacy* (Revised ed.). Peter Lang.

Drustrup, D. (2020). White therapists addressing racism in psychotherapy: An ethical and clinical model for practice. *Ethics and Behavior, 30*(3), 181–196. https://doi.org/10.1080/10508422.2019.1588732

Drustrup, D. (2021). Talking with white clients about race. *Journal of Health Service Psychology, 47*(2), 63–72. https://doi.org/10.1007/s42843-021-00037-2

Du Bois, W. E. B. (1935). *Black reconstruction in America 1860–1880.* Hartcourt Brace and Howe.

Hardy, K. V. (2023). *Racial trauma: Clinical strategies and techniques for healing invisible wounds.* W. W. Norton.

Helms, J. E. (2008). *A race is a nice thing to have: A guide to being a white person or understanding the white persons in your life* (2nd ed). Microtraining Associates.

Helms, J. E. (2017). The challenge of making whiteness visible: Reactions to four whiteness articles. *Counseling Psychologist, 45*(5), 717–726. https://doi.org/10.1177/0011000017718943

Helms, J. E., & Cook, D. A. (1999). *Using race and culture in counseling and psychotherapy: Theory and process.* Allyn and Bacon.

Jacobs, L. M. (2014). Learning to love white shame and guilt: Skills for working as a white therapist in a racially divided country. *International Journal of Psy-*

choanalytic Self Psychology, 9(4), 297–312. https://doi.org/10.1080/15551024.2014.948365

Kalibatseva, Z., & Leong, F. T. L. (2014). A critical review of culturally sensitive treatments for depression: Recommendations for intervention and research. *Psychological Services, 11*(4), 433–450. https://doi.org/10.1037/a0036047

Kendi, I. X. (2017). *Stamped from the beginning: The definitive history of racist ideas in America*. Bold Type Books.

Lateiner, A. (2016, March 7). Grieving the white void. Medium. https://abelateiner.medium.com/grieving-the-white-void-48c410fdd7f3

Malamed, C. R. (2021). A white person problem: Conducting white/white treatment with a social justice lens. *Psychoanalytic Social Work, 28*(2), 149–172. https://doi.org/10.1080/15228878.2021.1877752

McIntosh, P. (1988). *White privilege and male privilege: A personal account of coming to see correspondences through work in women's studies*. Wellesley College, Center for Research on Women.

Menakem, R. (2017). *My grandmother's hands: Racialized trauma and the pathway to mending our hearts and bodies*. Central Recovery Press.

Miller, A. (1979). *The drama of the gifted child: The search for the true self*. HarperCollins.

Miller, A. E., & Josephs, L. (2009). Whiteness as pathological narcissism. *Contemporary Psychoanalysis, 45*(1), 93–119. https://doi.org/10.1080/00107530.2009.10745989

Myers, L. J. (1993). *Understanding an Afrocentric world view: Introduction to optical psychology* (2nd ed.). Kendall/Hunt.

Okun, T. (2023, August). *What is white supremacy culture?* White Supremacy Culture. https://www.whitesupremacyculture.info/what-is-it.html

Parker, R. N. (2019). Slavery in the white psyche. *Psychoanalytic Social Work, 26*(1), 84–103. https://doi.org/10.1080/15228878.2019.1604240

Smith, L. (1994). *Killers of the dream* (Reissue ed.). W. W. Norton.

Stovall, N. (2019, August 12). *Whiteness on the couch*. Longreads. https://longreads.com/2019/08/12/whiteness-on-the-couch/

Sue, S. (1998). In search of cultural competence in psychotherapy and counseling. *American Psychologist, 53*(4), 440–448. https://doi.org/10.1037/0003-066X.53.4.440

Suyemoto, K. L., Trimble, J. E., Cokley, K. O., Neville, H. A., Mattar, S., & Speight, S. L. (2019). *APA guidelines on race and ethnicity in psychology: Promoting responsiveness and equity*. American Psychological Association.

Tatum, B. D. (1997). *Why are all the black kids sitting together in the cafeteria?* Basic Books.

Thandeka. (2001). *Learning to be white: Money, race and God in America*. Continuum.

Thandeka. (2018). Whites: Made in America: Advancing American philosophers' discourse on race. *The Pluralist, 13*(1), 26–50. https://doi.org/10.5406/pluralist.13.1.0026

Wilcox, M. M. (2023). Oppression is not "culture": The need to center systemic and structural determinants to address anti-black racism and racial trauma in psychotherapy. *Psychotherapy, 60*(1), 76–85. https://doi.org/10.1037/pst0000446

Wright, B. E. (1984). *The psychopathic racial personality and other essays*. Third World Press.

Yancy, G. (2012). *Look, a white! Philosophical essays on whiteness*. Temple University Press.

Chapter 15

Akbar, M., & Parker, T. L. (2021). *Equity, diversity, and inclusion framework.* American Psychological Association. https://www.apa.org/about/apa/equity-diversity-inclusion/framework

Akbar, M., Parker, T., Hintz, V., & Dawood, N. (2022). *Psychology's role in dismantling systemic racism: Racial equity action plan.* American Psychological Association. https://www.apa.org/about/apa/addressing-racism/racial-equity-action-plan.pdf

Almeida, R. V. (2019). *Liberation based healing practices.* Institute for Family Services.

American Association for Marriage and Family Therapy. (2020, June 1). AAMFT statement on MFT responsibility to counter racism. *The AAMFT Blog.* https://blog.aamft.org/2020/06/aamft-statement-on-mft-responsibility-to-counter-racism.html

American Psychological Association. (2021, October 29). *Apology to people of color for APA's role in promoting, perpetuating, and failing to challenge racism, racial discrimination, and human hierarchy in U.S.* https://www.apa.org/about/policy/racism-apology

Bawa, H., Gooden, S., Maleque, F., Naseem, S., Naz, S., Oriaku, E. Z. O., Thomas, R. S., Vipulananthan, V., Bains, M., & Shiel, L. (2019). The journey of BME aspiring psychologists into clinical psychology training: Barriers and ideas for inclusive change. *Clinical Psychology Forum, 323*(3), 3–7. https://doi.org/10.53841/bpscpf.2019.1.323.3

Bhatia, S. (2018). *Decolonizing psychology: Globalization, social justice, and Indian youth identities.* Oxford University Press.

Billings, D. (2016). Deconstructing white supremacy. In A. Carten, A. Siskind, & M. Pender Greene (Eds.), *Strategies for deconstructing racism in the health and human services* (pp. 91–100). Oxford University Press.

BlackDeer, A. A., & Ocampo, M. G. (2022). #Socialworksowhite: A critical perspective on settler colonialism, white supremacy, and social justice in social work. *Advances in Social Work, 22*(2), 720–740. https://doi.org/10.18060/24986

Carten, A., Siskind, A., & Pender Greene, M. (Eds.). *Strategies for deconstructing racism in the health and human services.* Oxford University Press.

Castañeda-Sound, C. L., Rowe, D. M., Binazair, N., & Cabrera, M. L. (2020). Liberation, inspiration, and critical consciousness: Preparing the next generation of practitioners. In L. Comas-Díaz & E. T. Rivera (Eds.), *Liberation psychology: Theory, method, practice, and social justice* (pp. 265–282). American Psychological Association.

Comas-Díaz, L. (2020). Liberation psychotherapy. In L. Comas-Díaz & E. T. Rivera (Eds.), *Liberation psychology: Theory, method, practice, and social justice* (pp. 169–185). American Psychological Association.

DiAngelo, R. J. (2006). My class didn't trump my race: Using oppression to face privilege. *Multicultural Perspectives, 8*(1), 51–56. https://doi.org/10.1207/s15327892mcp0801_9

DiAngelo, R. (2018). *White fragility: Why it's so hard for white people to talk about racism.* Beacon.

DiAngelo, R. (2021). *Nice racism: How progressive white people perpetuate racial harm.* Beacon.

Dimuro, G. (2018, April 4). *Southerners actually thought slaves escaping was a sign of mental illness.* ATI. https://allthatsinteresting.com/drapetomania

Duran, E. (2019). *Healing the soul wound: Trauma-informed counseling for indigenous communities* (2nd ed.). Teachers College Press.

Hardy, K. V. (2008). On becoming a GEMM therapist: Work harder, be smarter, and *never* discuss race. In M. McGoldrick & K. V. Hardy (Eds.), *Re-visioning family therapy: Race, culture, and gender in clinical practice* (2nd ed., pp. 461–468). Guilford.

Hardy, K. V. (2013). Healing the hidden wounds of racial trauma. *Reclaiming Children and Youth, 22*(1), 24–28.

Hardy, K. V. (2020). *Critical relational factors for promoting and sustaining difficult conversations* [Handout]. Eikenberg Institute for Relationships. https://www.mentoring.org/wp-content/uploads/2022/02/Critical-Relational-Factors.pdf

Hardy, K. V. (2022). On being black in white places: A therapist's journey from margin to center. In K. V. Hardy (Ed.), *The enduring, invisible, and ubiquitous centrality of whiteness* (pp. 447–471). W. W. Norton.

Hardy, K. V. (2023). *Racial trauma: Clinical strategies and techniques for healing invisible wounds.* W. W. Norton.

Hardy, K. V., & Laszloffy, T. A. (2005). *Teens who hurt: Clinical interventions to break the cycle of adolescent violence.* Guilford.

Hardy, K. V., & McGoldrick, M. (2008). Re-visioning training. In M. McGoldrick & K. V. Hardy (Eds.), *Re-visioning family therapy: Race, culture, and gender in clinical practice* (2nd ed., pp. 442–460). Guilford.

Holmes, D. E. (2016). Culturally imposed trauma: The sleeping dog has awakened. Will psychoanalysis take heed? *Psychoanalytic Dialogues, 26*(6), 641–654. https://doi.org/10.1080/10481885.2016.1235454

Holmes, D. E. (2017, Winter/Spring). The fierce urgency of now: An appeal to organized psychoanalysis to take a strong stand on race. *American Psychoanalyst, 51*(1), 1, 8–9.

Huff, C. (2021, October 1). Psychology's diversity problem. *Monitor on Psychology.* https://www.apa.org/monitor/2021/10/feature-diversity-problem

Leonardo, Z. (2004). The color of supremacy: Beyond the discourse of "white privilege." *Educational Philosophy and Theory, 36*(2), 137–152. https://doi.org/10.1111/j.1469-5812.2004.00057.x

Mackey, C., Hernandez, N., Lechuga-Peña, S., & Mitchell, F. (2022). Disrupting white supremacy: Testimonios to reveal the experiences of women of color in social work doctoral education. *Advances in Social Work, 22*(2), 647–679. https://doi.org/10.18060/24776

McIntosh, P. (2002). White privilege: Unpacking the invisible knapsack. In P. S. Rothenberg (Ed.), *White privilege: Essential readings on the other side of racism* (pp. 97–101). Worth.

National Association of Social Workers. (n.d.). *Justice, equity, diversity, inclusion and the social work profession.* https://www.socialworkers.org/About/Ethics/Ethics-Education-and-Resources/Ethics-Resources-for-Racial-Equity/A-Message-About-Racism

National Association of Social Workers. (2020, August 21). *Social workers must help dismantle systems of oppression and fight racism within social work profession.* https://www.socialworkers.org/News/News-Releases/ID/2219/Social-Workers-Must-Help-Dismantle-Systems-of-Oppression-and-Fight-Racism-Within-Social-Work-Profession

Rivera, E. T., & Comas-Díaz, L. (2020). Introduction. In L. Comas-Díaz & E. T. Rivera (Eds.), *Liberation psychology: Theory, method, practice, and social justice* (pp. 3–13). American Psychological Association.

REFERENCES

Rothenberg, P. S. (2016). *White privilege: Essential readings on the other side of racism* (5th ed.). Worth.

Stoute, B. J. (2023). Racism and health equity: A challenge for the therapeutic dyad. In B. J. Stoute & M. Slevin (Eds.), *The trauma of racism: Lessons from the therapeutic encounter* (pp. 8–12). Routledge.

Watts-Jones, T. D. (2010). Location of self: Opening the door to dialogue on intersectionality in the therapy process. *Family Process, 49*(3), 405–420. https://doi.org/10.1111/j.1545-5300.2010.01330.x

Wise, T. (2016). Membership has its privileges: Thoughts on acknowledging and challenging whiteness. In P. S. Rothenberg (Ed.), *White privilege: Essential readings on the other side of racism* (5th ed., pp. 163–166). Worth.

Index

AAMFT. *see* American Association for Marriage and Family Therapy (AAMFT)
"ABD" (completed all but dissertation), 252
accountability
　racial. *see* racial accountability
acknowledgment
　racial, 50–53
　in soul work, 176–77
"Adjustment Reactions:, xxiv
Almeida, R. V., 254
"A Map of Internalized Anti-Semitism for White Ashkenazi Jews in the U.S."
　described, 109–10
America, 99
"American"
　whiteness in being, xxi
American Association for Marriage and Family Therapy (AAMFT)
　on racism, 248
American Psychological Association (APA)
　Center for Workforce Studies of, 255
　on promoting/perpetuating racism and racial discrimination, 247–49
　Racial Equity Action Plan of, 249
Anen, S. J., 232
Anglicizing
　of names, 187–88
Ani, M., 232
anti-Blackness bias
　ramifications of, 137–40

as threat to racially informed clinical work, 137–40
APA. *see* American Psychological Association (APA)
Arabic names, 186
"A Revised Jewish Understanding of the State of Israel," 110
Armstrong, L., 219
Arye, L., 198–225
assaulted sense of self
　defined, 183
attitude(s)
　racial, 135–42
authentic curiosity-based inquiry
　engaging through, 32–34
authenticity
　defined, 25
awareness
　racial. *see* racial awareness
Ayre, L., xv

Baker, B., 128
Baldwin, J., 73
Baudrillard, J., 99
becoming
　process of, 3–73. *see also* becoming process
　of racially sensitive therapist, 59
becoming process, 3–73
　addressing racial microaggressions in, 30–36
　broker of permission in, 25–27

INDEX

challenging theoretical myth of sameness in, 22–23
developing racial lens in, 24
developing racially sensitive trauma-informed lens in, 36–38
developing racial sense of self in, 23–24
developing relational muscles in, 25
principles, preparation, and practice in, 21–38
repairing race-related ruptures/missteps in, 27–30
being
  described, 9–10
  in seeing, being, and doing process, 9–10
belief(s)
  racial, 135–42
belongingness
  promoting, 261
Bhatia, S., 263
bias(es)
  anti-Blackness. see anti-Blackness bias
Biernat, M., 188
Billings, D., Rev., 253
Bing, V. M., xv–xvi, 113–33, 246–64
BlackDeer, A. A., 252, 253
Black Families in Therapy, 166
Black Lives Matter movement, 241
Black people. *see also under* People of Color (POC)
  lack of humanness in treatment of, xxi–xxii
  marginalization of, xxi–xxii
  rules of human compassion/engagement for, xxii
  soul work for, 171–81. *see also under* soul work
Black therapist
  whitened. *see* whitened Black therapist
Blades, R., 144
blanqueamiento, 137
Bobes, T., xvi, 39–57
Boyd-Franklin, N., xxiii
broker of permission
  in becoming process, 25–27
  being, 48–49
  case example, 26–27
Brown people. *see also under* People of Color (POC)
  lack of humanness in treatment of, xxi–xxii
  marginalization of, xxi–xxii
  soul work for, 171–81. *see also under* soul work
Brown, S. K., 165

Cassell, E. J., 86
Cassiani, J. O., 137
Center for Workforce Studies of APA, 255
Child Protective Services, 124–25
Choudhury, S., 212
class conscious
  yet oblivious to white supremacy, 143–46
Clients of Color. *see also* Communities of Color
  attention paid to, 171–72
  clinical treatment as on-the-job training, 6
  serving of, 226
  working effectively with, xxiv–xxv
clinical competencies
  seeing, being, doing process and, 17–19
  SOT work and, 17–19
clinical training/supervision
  cultural storytelling in, 93–97
  need for racial reckoning in, 246–64. *see also under* racial reckoning
Coates, T., 222
Collins, P. H., 122–23
Colombia
  racial baggage I brought from, 134–46
colonial racial mentality
  as threat to racially informed clinical work, 141–42
color
  clients of. *see* Clients of Color
  communities of. *see* Communities of Color
  families of. *see* Families of Color
  people of. *see* People of Color (POC)
color blindness
  myth of, xxiv–xxv
Comas-Díaz, L., 263
Communities of Color. *see also* Clients of Color
  healing in, 171–81. *see also under* healing; soul work
  soul work for, 171–81
community
  lessons from my mother related to, 124–25
compassion
  lessons from my mother related to, 124–25

INDEX

competency(ies)
  clinical. *see* clinical competencies
complexity
  defined, 25
congruency
  defined, 25
conscious
  class. *see* class conscious
consultation
  organizational. *see* organizational consultation
"controlling images," 122–23
conversation(s)
  racial, 177–78, 239–40
Cook, D. A., 238
core competency tasks
  supervisory, 41–49. *see also under* supervisory core competency tasks
Coughlin, Father, 103
countertransference reactions
  race and, 234–35
  whiteness and, 234–35
COVID-19
  racial reckoning and, 246–47
Cultural Genogram, 13–14
cultural sensitivity
  described, 40
cultural storytelling
  in clinical training/supervision, 93–97
  described, 78–79
  as therapeutic tool, 80–83
  as tool for promoting racial sensitivity, 77–98. *see also under* racial and cultural storytelling
culture(s)
  group. *see* group culture
  stories/storytelling impact on, 77–98
  white. *see* white culture
  white supremacist. *see under* white supremacist culture
curiosity-based inquiry
  authentic, 32–34
Cushing, B. B., xvi–xvii, 99–112

DARVO (deny, attack, and reverse victim and offender), 232
decolonizing psychology
  adopting, 263–64
DeGruy Leary, J., xxiii, 35
DEIB (diversity, equity, inclusion, and belonging) training

for faculty/students, 262–63
Del Cerro, X., 114
democratic sanity, 228
Denial of the Existence of the Oppression, 110
Desire to Control, 110
devaluation
  defined, 251
  internalized, 123–24
development
  white child. *see* white child development
  white racial identity, 238
Diagnostic and Statistical Manual of Mental Disorders (DSM)
  on racial trauma, 35–36
Dinkins, D., Mayor, 116
disclosure(s)
  racial, 50–53
discrimination
  racial. *see* racial discrimination
discussion(s)
  racial, 50–53
"Does Jewish Identity Cloud or Clarify an Understanding of Race?"
  diary notes, 158–68. *see also under* Jewish identity
doing
  described, 10–11
  in seeing, being, and doing process, 10–11
domestic(s)
  early life as, 117–18
  life of, 113–33. *see also under* "My Mother/your mammy and the Making of a Racially Sensitive Therapist"
  shame of, 118–19
"Don't Think I'm a Racist, But . . ."
  case example, 241–42
Drive for Acceptance by Way of Perfection, 109–10
Drive for Security, 109
Drustrup, D., 234
DSM. *see Diagnostic and Statistical Manual of Mental Disorders* (DSM)
Duffy, T., 81
Duran, E., 263

educational training
  need for racial reckoning in, 246–64. *see also under* racial reckoning

INDEX

EFT. *see* emotionally focused therapy (EFT)
El Incómodo Color de la Memoria, 137
emotionally focused therapy (EFT)
   described, 60
Epston, D., 80–81, 85
equity-focused training
   racially sensitive, 58–73. *see also under* racially sensitive, equity-focused training
Erickson, M., 80
ethic(s)
   work-related. *see* work ethic
Even the Rat was White, xxiii
experiential group-based SOT approaches, 12–13

Families of Color
   attention paid to, 171–72
Fisher, J., 221
Floor is Not the Floor, 211
Floyd, G., 61, 149, 158, 232, 241, 246–47
Ford, H., 103
fortitude
   lessons from my mother related to, 125
friendship(s)
   yielding to shame, 121–23
funding
   racially informed. *see under* racially informed research/funding

GEMM (good, effective, mainstream, minority) process, 173, 174
GEMM (good, effective, mainstream, minority) therapist, 256–57
genogram(s)
   in SOT work, 13–14
graduate Students of Color
   increasing funding to support, 262
Grossinger's Hotel, 163–64
group-based SOT approaches
   experiential, 12–13
group culture
   training, 65–67
Guthrie, E. V., xxiii

Habekost, J., 13
Hamad, R., 119
Hardy, K. V., xvii, xxiii, 5–59, 77–98, 122–24, 127, 129, 132, 171–83, 210, 214, 216, 221, 224, 234, 251, 256–57, 259
Hare-Mustin, R. T., 164–65

harm
   racial. *see* racial harm in helping relationships
healing
   beyond therapy room, 180–81
   in Communities of Color, 171–81. *see also under* soul work
   hope for, 109–10
   soul work in, 171–81. *see also under* soul work
healing process
   defined/altered by realities of race, 173
healing strategies
   racially relevant, 179–80
Helms, J. E., 232, 238, 242
helping professions
   response to racial reckoning, 247–49
homelessness
   psychological, 183
hooks, b, 126
hope for healing, 109–10
Horne, L., 161
Huff, C., 255

identity(ies)
   forming of, 230–31
   Jewish. *see* Jewish identity
   personal. *see* personal identity
   social. *see* social identity
   white. *see* white identity
ideology
   racist. *see* racist ideology
   white supremacist. *see* white supremacist ideology
"I Didn't Wanna Talk About This," 54–56
image(s)
   "controlling," 122–23
immigration
   policies/practices regarding, xxi
"ink spots" in the room, 120
intelligence
   whiteness and, 115–17
intensity
   defined, 25
intensive dyadic SOT work, 11–12
intensive racial sensitivity groups, 14–17
   questions for, 15–16
internalized devaluation
   defined, 123–24
   described, 123–24
"Intersection of Whiteness, Trauma, and Relationship," 147–57

intimacy
  defined, 25
invisible racial baggage, 134–46
invisible wounds
  of racial trauma, 178–79
"I Wish I Knew How It Would Feel to Be Free," 219

Jacobs, L. M., 228
Jewish
  to core, 102–3
  in United States, 99–112. *see also under* "On Being White and Jewish in the United States"
  white and, 99–112. *see also under* "On Being White and Jewish in the United States"
Jewish Bridge Project, 109
Jewish identity
  diary notes, 158–68
  understanding race related to, 158–68
"Jewish Justice Circle: Awakening to Whiteness" workshop, 109
Jews in Israel, 159
Jews of Color, 159
Johnson-Reed Act, 103
Johnson, S., 166
Join the Reckoning (JTR), 252
Josephs, L., 232–34
JTR. *see* Join the Reckoning (JTR)
Judaism
  Love, 110
  Settler-, 110

Katz, E., xvii, 158–68
Katz, J. K., 109
King, M. L., Jr., 149
Kinouani, G., 207
Kohli, R., 188–89
Kumar, N., xviii, 182–97

Laszloffy, T., 13, 78, 81–82, 94
leadership
  training-related, 62–65
Lee, S. R. C., xviii, 58–73, 147–57
Leonardo, Z., 254
Lerner, M., Rabbi, 110
liberated
  described, 110–12
liberatory
  described, 110–12
life lessons
  from my mother, 124–28. *see also under* life lessons from my mother

life lessons from my mother, 124–28
  community- and compassion-related, 124–25
  cultivating tools to withstand white supremacist ideology, 127
  patience-related, 126
  reflections on, 127–28
  strength- and fortitude-related, 125
  work ethic–related, 126
Lindbergh, C., 103
Lit on Fire Books, 167
Lopez-Henriquez, G., xviii, 134–46
Lorde, A., 212
loss of voice
  systemic racism resulting in, 122
Love Judaism, 110

Mackey, C., 252
Malamed, C. R., 233
Martin, A., 167
McGoldrick, M., xxiii
McHugh, J., 163–64
meaning
  pursuit of, 31
Menakem, R., xxiii, 35, 229, 231
mental health care
  integrating alternative approaches to, 262
Mestizo privilege
  as threat to racially informed clinical work, 136–37
method
  pursuit of, 31, 33–34
microaggression(s)
  racial. *see* racial microaggressions
microaggression mini-model, 31–34
  case example, 32–33
Miller, A. E., 231–34
Mindell, A., 201
mispronunciation of names
  racial trauma triggers associated with, 188–91
Mizrachi Jews, 159
mocking of names
  racial trauma triggers associated with, 191–92
motivation
  pursuit of, 31
movie(s)
  as stories, 82–83
MRP. *see* Multicultural Relational Perspective (MRP)
Multicultural Relational Perspective (MRP)
  described, 12

muscle(s)
　relational, 25
Myers, L. J., 228
My Grandmother's Hands, 243
"My Mother/your mammy and the Making of a Racially Sensitive Therapist," 113–33. *see also* domestic(s)
　described, 128–32
　early life as domestic, 117–18
　entering predominantly white spaces and internalizing racism, 120–21
　humble beginnings, 114–15
　intelligence and whiteness, 115–17
　internalized devaluation, 123–24
　introduction, 113
　lessons of white supremacy, 121–23
　life lessons from my mother, 124–28. *see also under* life lessons from my mother
　shame of domestics, 118–19. *see also* domestic(s)

name(s), 182–97
　addressing in therapy, 192–97
　Anglicizing of, 187–88
　Arabic, 186
　cultural–racial significance of, 14
　in enhancing therapeutic alliance/ addressing racial trauma, 182–97
　experiences related to, 195–96
　"how do I pronounce it?," 193–94
　"how do you feel about discussing this with me?," 196–97
　information encoded in, 185–86
　mispronunciation of, 188–91
　mocking of, 191–92
　nicknaming, 187–88
　in personal identity, 183–85
　racial trauma triggers associated with, 187–92
　renaming, 187–88
　significance of, 183–86
　in social identity, 185
　"tell me about your," 194
　"what does it mean to you?," 194–95
　"what would you like me to call you?," 192–93
　"whitening" of, 188
　white supremacist ideology and, 188–91
　why they matter, 183–86
narration
　as means to stories, 80–81
Narrative Means to Therapeutic Ends, 80–81

NASW. *see* National Association of Social Workers (NASW)
National Association of Social Workers (NASW)
　on racist ideology and practices, 247
Nealy, E. C., xxiii
New York City Housing Authority (NYCHA)
　described, 114–15
Nguyen, B., 191
nicknaming
　racial trauma triggers associated with, 187–88
Nieto, L., 211
Nightingale, M., 166
NYCHA. *see* New York City Housing Authority (NYCHA)

Ocampo, M. G., 252, 253
Okun, T., 228
"On Being White and Jewish in the United States," 99–112
　hope for healing, 109–10
　indoctrination into whiteness, 103–5
　Jewish to the core, 102–3
　liberated and liberatory, 110–12
　precariously white, 106–7
　prologue, 99–101
　saturated in whiteness, 105–6
　singled out among whites, 107–8
　TJT in, 109
"oppositional and defiant"
　Youth of Color as, xxiv
organizational consultation
　in racially sensitive, equity-focused training, 71–73

Parker, R. N., 231, 232
PAST model, 132
patience
　lessons from my mother related to, 126
People of Color (POC). *see also under* Black people; Brown people
　clinical/educational training and, 246–64. *see also under* racial reckoning
　lack of humanness in treatment of, xxi–xxii
　marginalization of, xxi–xxii
　on parameters of whiteness, xxiv
　rules of human compassion/engagement for, xxii
　soul work for, 171–81
　whiteness traumatizing, 182
People of the Global Majority, 199, 201, 211, 214, 217, 220, 224–25

People's Institute for Survival and Beyond (PISAB), 253
   Undoing Racism Workshop with, 241–42
Peoria Guild of Black Artists, 167
PERLA. see Project on Ethnicity and Race in Latin America (PERLA)
permission
   broker of, 48–49
Perry, I., 128
personal identity
   names in, 183–85
personal philosophy and model of supervision (PPMOS)
   articulation of, 41–42
PISAB. see People's Institute for Survival and Beyond (PISAB)
"Plastico," 144
POC. see People of Color (POC)
power
   core principles of, 43–44
   developing understanding of phenomenology of, 42–44
PPMOS. see personal philosophy and model of supervision (PPMOS)
"Prayer Before the Prayer," 223
pride
   shame to, 113–33. see also under "My Mother/your mammy and the Making of a Racially Sensitive Therapist"
privilege
   core principles of, 43–44
   developing understanding of phenomenology of, 42–44
   Mestizo, 136–37
Process Work Institute, 199
Project on Ethnicity and Race in Latin America (PERLA), 144
psychological homelessness
   defined, 183
psychology
   decolonizing, 263–64
public housing projects
   life in, 114–15
pursuit of meaning, 31
pursuit of method, 31
   case example, 33–34
pursuit of motivation, 31

race. see also under racial
   as artery vs. appendage, 44–45
   countertransference reactions related to, 234–35
   defined, 227
   developing understanding of phenomenology of, 42–44
   idiosyncratic acknowledgments, discussions, and disclosures about, 50–53
   inattention in clinical education, training, and practice, 6–7
   Jewish identity clouding vs. clarifying, 158–68
   need for racial reckoning in clinical/educational training and, 246–64. see also under racial reckoning
   ruptures/missteps related to, 27–30
   therapy and, 5–20
   whiteness and, 234–35
   white therapists working with white clients around, 226–45. see also under white therapists working with white clients around race
race-related ruptures/missteps
   repairing of, 27–30
race talk
   leaning into, 239–40
   in soul work, 177–78
racial accountability
   case example, 54–56
   executing acts of, 53–56
racial acknowledgment, 50–53
racial and cultural storytelling, 13, 77–98. see also cultural storytelling; racial storytelling
   as clinical tool for promoting racial sensitivity, 77–98
   impact of, 77–79
   impediments to integrating in therapy, 83–85
   stories of struggle, 88–90
   stories of suffering, 86–88
   stories of survival, 90–93
racial attitudes
   preestablished, 135–42
racial awareness
   in racially sensitive supervision, 39–40
Racial Awareness Sensitivity Exercise (RAASE), 13
racial baggage
   anti-Blackness bias, 137–40
   class conscious yet oblivious to white supremacy, 143–46
   colonial racial mentality, 141–42
   described, 134–35
   invisible, 134–46

INDEX

Mestizo privilege, 136–37
  preestablished racial beliefs and attitudes in, 135–42
  unpacking, 134–46
racial beliefs
  preestablished, 135–42
racial conversations
  promoting, 261
racial disclosure(s), 50–53
racial discrimination
  APA on, 247–49
racial discussion(s), 50–53
Racial Equity Action Plan
  of APA, 249
Racial Genogram, 13–14
racial harm
  in helping relationships, 198–225. *see also under* racial harm in helping relationships
racial harm in helping relationships, 198–225
  attempted repair, 208
  contours of complexity, 218–21
  histories, 202–11
  how we met, 199–200
  inner work, 210–11
  introduction, 198–99
  larger field, 200–2
  memory/accountability, 215–17
  reflections/offers, 222–24
  request/questions, 211–15
  ruptures, 202–8
  surviving/withdrawing, 209–10
  three years later, 211–17
  what writing together taught, 218–21
racial history
  asking about at intake, 244
racial issues. *see also under* race
  in therapy, 5–20
racial lens
  developing of, 8–9, 24
racially informed research/funding
  increasing access to, 261–62
racially sensitive, equity-focused training, 58–73
  background, 60–62
  moving toward, 58–73
  organizational consultation in, 71–73
  systemic issues in, 71–73
  training content in, 70–71
  training group culture in, 65–67
  training leadership in, 62–65
  training method in, 67–70

racially sensitive supervision, 39–57
  disclosing location of self in, 49–50
  executing acts of racial accountability in, 53–56
  idiosyncratic acknowledgments, discussions, and disclosures about race in, 50–53
  practical guide for supervisors, 39–57
  racial awareness in, 39–40
  racial sensitivity in, 40–41
  supervisory core competency tasks in, 41–49
racially sensitive therapist
  becoming, 3–73. *see also under* becoming process
racially sensitive trauma-informed lens
  developing of, 36–38
racial mentality
  colonial, 141–42
racial microaggressions
  addressing, 30–36
  case examples, 32–34
racial realities
  healing process defined/altered by, 173
racial reckoning, 246–64
  adopting decolonizing psychology/clinical fields of study as paradigm shift in, 263–64
  being intentional about promoting belongingness in, 261
  in clinical/educational training, 246–64
  in COVID years, 246–47
  Eurocentric models, 249–51
  helping professions' response in, 247–49
  hiring diverse faculty in, 261
  implementing DEIB training for faculty/students in, 262–63
  increasing access to racially informed research/funding in, 261–62
  increasing funding to support graduate Students of Color in training in, 262
  integrating alternative approaches to mental health care in, 262
  mandating racially focused SOT work in, 261
  need for, 246–64
  persistence of white-centered teaching/training in, 255–57
  personal reflections, 257–59
  promoting racial conversations in, 261
  reclaiming my soul in, 259–60

racial reckoning (*continued*)
  recommendations, 260–64
  struggle for Students of Color in academia in, 251–53
  white-centered scholarship in, 253–55
racial resilience, 224
racial self-interrogation
  developing skills to engage in, 45–48
racial sense of self
  developing of, 8–9, 23–24
racial sensitivity
  defined, 40
  described, 40–41
  intensive groups, 14–17
  racial and cultural storytelling as tool for promoting, 77–98
  in racially sensitive supervision, 40–41
racial socialization
  defined, 229
  described, 229–31
  white child development and, 229–31
racial stories, 75–168
racial storytelling
  described, 79
  as therapeutic tool, 80–83
racial trauma
  addressing invisible wounds of, 178–79
  DSM on, 35–36
  names in addressing, 182–97. see also under name(s)
  names triggering, 187–92. see also under name(s)
racism
  AAMFT on, 248
  APA on, 247–49
  internalizing of, 120–21
  systemic. see systemic racism
racist ideology
  NASW on, 247
racist practices
  NASW on, 247
Raheim, S., 81
rank
  defined, 201
RASE. see Racial Awareness Sensitivity Exercise (RASE)
relational muscles
  developing of, 25
  types of, 25
relational repair
  in becoming process, 27–30
relationship(s)
  racial harm in helping, 198–225. see

  also under racial harm in helping relationships
  trauma, whiteness and, 147–57
renaming
  racial trauma triggers associated with, 187–88
research
  racially informed, 261–62
resilience
  racial, 224
Rivera, E.T., 263
Rubidge, Y., xviii–xix, 198–225

sameness
  theoretical myth of, 22–23
sanity
  democratic, 228
scholarship
  white-centered, 253–55
seeing
  described, 8
  in racial lens development, 8–9
  in racial sense of self development, 8–9
  in seeing, being, and doing process, 8–9
seeing, being, doing process, 7–11
  being in, 9–10
  clinical competencies and, 17–19
  described, 7
  doing in, 10–11
  seeing in, 8–9
  SOT strategies in, 11–17. see also *specific strategies and* Self of the Therapist (SOT) strategies
  what it is not, 7
Seewaldt, V., xix, 226–45
self
  assaulted sense of, 183
  disclosing location of, 49–50
  racial sense of, 8–9, 23–24
  of therapist, 75–168
self-disclosure
  commitment to effective use of, 32–34
self-examination
  white therapists working with white clients around race–related, 240–41
Self-Hatred, 110
self-interrogation
  racial. see racial self-interrogation
Self of the Therapist (SOT) strategies
  clinical competencies, 17–19
  experiential group-based, 12–13
  exploring cultural–racial significance of names, 14

INDEX

genograms, 13–14
intensive dyadic SOT work, 11–12
intensive racial sensitivity groups, 14–17
MRP in, 12
seeing, being, doing process and, 11–17
Self of the Therapist (SOT) work, 7
intensive dyadic, 11–12
mandating racially focused, 261
Sense of Powerlessness and of Not Belonging, 110
sense of self
assaulted, 183
racial, 8–9, 23–24
sense of voicelessness, 122, 257
sensitivity
cultural. *see* cultural sensitivity
racial. *see* racial sensitivity
Settler-Judaism, 110
shame
of domestics, 118–19
friendships yielding to, 121–23
to pride, 113–33. *see also under* "My Mother/your mammy and the Making of a Racially Sensitive Therapist"
Sharpe, R., 246
shonda, 102
Simone, N., 219
Sisters of the Yam, 126
Skin in the Game: How Antisemitism Animates White Nationalism, 107
social identity
names in, 185
socialization
racial. *see* racial socialization
into whiteness, 229–31. *see also* racial socialization
Solórzano, D. G., 188–89
song(s)
as stories, 81–82
SOT. *see under* Self of the Therapist (SOT)
soul work, 171–81. *see also under* healing
acknowledgment in, 176–77
addressing invisible wounds of racial trauma in, 178–79
case example, 174–75
for Clients of Color, 171–81
for Communities of Color, 171–81
embracing/employing racially relevant healing strategies in, 179–80
for Families of Color, 171–81
healing beyond therapy room in, 180–81

as healing work, 171–81. *see also under* healing
as pathway in helping Communities of Color to heal, 176–80
for People of Color, 171–81
race talk in, 177–78
validation in, 176–77
"Sounds Like White Supremacist Culture" case example, 242–43
South to America: A Journey Below the Mason-Dixon to Understand the Soul of a Nation, 128
Specialized High School Admissions Test, 120
story(ies). *see also* racial and cultural storytelling; storytelling
as clinical tool for promoting racial sensitivity, 77–79
movies/video clips as, 82–83
narrative means to, 80–81
racial, 75–168
songs as, 81–82
of struggle, 88–90
of suffering, 86–88
of survival, 90–93
storytelling
cultural, 13, 77–98. *see also* cultural storytelling; racial and cultural storytelling
impact of, 77–79
in promoting racial sensitivity, 77–79
racial, 13, 77–98. *see also under* racial and cultural storytelling; story(ies)
as therapeutic tool, 80–83
Stoute, B. J., 250–51
Stovall, N., 227
strength
lessons from my mother related to, 125
struggle
stories of, 88–90
Students of Color
graduate. *see* graduate Students of Color
struggles of, 251–53
Stuyvesant High School
experiences at, 120–21
suffering
stories of, 86–88
supervision
cultural storytelling in, 93–97
racially sensitive, 39–57. *see also under* racially sensitive supervision

supervisory core competency tasks, 41–49
  articulating PPMOS, 42
  be broker of permission, 48–49
  described, 41
  developing skills to engage in ongoing racial self-interrogation, 45–48
  developing understanding of phenomenology of race, power, and privilege, 42–44
  embracing/promoting race as artery vs. appendage, 44–45
supremacy
  white. *see* white supremacy
survival
  stories of, 90–93
systemic racism
  loss of voice as consequence of, 122

talk
  race, 177–78, 239–40
Taylor, B., 241
teaching
  white-centered. *see* white-centered teaching/training
Telles, E. E., 144
Terror and Sense of Otherness, 109
Thandeka, 229, 231
"the *goldene medina,*" 160
The International Jew, 103
theoretical myth of sameness
  challenging of, 22–23
"the pain is the path," 157
therapeutic alliance
  names in enhancing, 182–97. *see also under* name(s)
therapeutic issues/approaches, 169–264
therapist(s)
  GEMM, 256–57
  hiring of diverse, 261
  self of, 75–168
  white. *see under* white therapists
  whitened Black, 172–75
Therapists of Color
  becoming white-like, xxiv
therapy. *see also under specific components*
  addressing names in, 192–97
  emotionally focused. *see* emotionally focused therapy (EFT)
  racial issues in, 5–20
  seeing, being, doing process in, 5–20. *see also under* seeing, being, doing process

systemic neglect of attention to race within, 5–6
  white identity development and, 231–34
"The Theoretical Myth of Sameness: A Critical Issue in Family Therapy Training and Treatment," xxiii
tikkun olam, 102
TJT. *see* Transcending Jewish Trauma (TJT)
training
  clinical. *see* clinical training/supervision
  cultural storytelling in, 93–97
  DEIB, 262–63
  educational, 246–64
  increasing funding to support graduate Students of Color in, 262
  racially sensitive, equity-focused, 58–73. *see also under* racially sensitive, equity-focused training
  white-centered, 255–57
training content
  in racially sensitive, equity-focused training, 70–71
training group culture
  in racially sensitive, equity-focused training, 65–67
training leadership
  in racially sensitive, equity-focused training, 62–65
training method
  in racially sensitive, equity-focused training, 67–70
Transcending Jewish Trauma (TJT)
  described, 109
transparency
  defined, 25
trauma
  racial. *see* racial trauma
  whiteness, relationship and, 147–57
trauma-informed lens
  racially sensitive, 36–38
Tutu, D., 223
Tutu, M., 223

Undoing Racism Workshop
  with PISAB, 241–42
"Unpacking My Invisible Racial Luggage," 134–46. *see also under* invisible racial baggage
"unseeing"
  described, 8

INDEX

validation
  in soul work, 176–77
video clips
  as stories, 82–83
voice
  loss of. *see* loss of voice; voicelessness
voicelessness
  described, 122
  sense of, 257

Ward, E. K., 107
Watts-Jones, T. D., 130, 261
"What a Wonderful World," 219
white(s)
  Jewish and, 99–112. *see also under* "On Being White and Jewish in the United States"
  precariously, 106–7
  singled out among, 107–8
white affinity
  asking about, 244
white-centered scholarship, 253–55
white-centered teaching/training
  impact/unintended consequences of, 255–57
  persistence of, 255–57
white child development
  racial socialization and, 229–31
white clients
  white therapists working with, 226–45. *see also under* white therapists working with white clients around race
white culture
  described, 227–29
white identity, 230–31
white identity development
  therapy and, 231–34
white-like
  Therapists of Color becoming, xxiv
White, M., 80–81, 85
"white mutual admiration societies," 233
whitened Black therapist
  becoming, 172–75
whiteness. *see also under* "On Being White and Jewish in the United States"
  in being "American," xxi–xxvii
  centrality of, xxi–xxvii
  countertransference reactions related to, 234–35
  in defining what, how, and who is considered human, xxi
  described, 227–28
  intelligence and, 115–17
  pervasive influences of, xxiii
  POC on parameters of, xxiv
  POC traumatized by, 182
  race and, 234–35
  saturated in, 105–6
  socialization into, 229–31
  tenets associated with, xxi
  trauma, relationship and, 147–57
  in United States, 99–112. *see also under* "On Being White and Jewish in the United States"
  white supremacist culture and, 227–29
"whitening"
  of names, 188
white racial identity development
  exploring of, 238
white space(s)
  entering predominantly, 120–21
white supremacist culture
  components of, 228
  described, 227–29
  whiteness and, 227–29
white supremacist ideology
  cultivating tools to withstand, 127
  names and, 188–91
  perpetuation of underlying, xxii–xxiii
white supremacy
  lessons of, 121–23
  oblivious to, 143–46
White Tears/Brown Scars, 119
white therapists
  working with white clients around race, 226–45. *see also under* white therapists working with white clients around race
white therapists working with white clients around race, 226–45
  asking about racial history at intake, 244
  being aware of "white vortex," 243–44
  case examples, 241–45
  challenges related to, 235–36
  demonstrating diligence about leaning into race talk, 239–40
  embracing white affinity, 244
  exploring white racial identity development, 238
  helping clients build increased emotional capacity, 236–37
  introduction, 226–27
  pulling back the lens, 237

white therapists working with white clients around race (*continued*)
    race, whiteness, and countertransference reactions, 234–35
    racial socialization/white child development, 229–31
    rethinking the rules, 238–39
    self-examination, 240–41
    "Sounds Like White Supremacist Culture," 242–43
    techniques/strategies of engagement, 236–40
    white identity development and therapy, 231–34
    whiteness/white supremacist culture, 227–29
"white vortex"
    being aware of, 243–44

"Why Are You Not Enraged?"
    case example, 241
Wilcox, M. M., 226
Winawer, H., 8
Wise Rowe, S., 35
work ethic
    lessons from my mother related to, 126
wound(s)
    invisible. *see* invisible wounds
Wright, B.E., 228, 232

Yancy, G., 232
Youth of Color
    as "oppositional and deviant," xxiv

Zamora, S., 134
Zhao, X., 188